ON THE MOVE

ON THE MOVE

Migration Policies in Latin America and the Caribbean

Andrew Selee,
Valerie Lacarte,
Ariel G. Ruiz Soto,
Diego Chaves-González

Stanford University Press
Stanford, California

Stanford University Press
Stanford, California

Library of Congress Cataloging-in-Publication Data
Names: Selee, Andrew D. author | Lacarte, Valerie author | Ruiz Soto, Ariel G. author | Chaves-González, Diego author
Title: On the move : migration policies in Latin America and the Caribbean / Andrew Selee, Valerie Lacarte, Ariel G. Ruiz Soto, Diego Chaves-González.
Description: Stanford, California : Stanford University Press, 2025. | Includes bibliographical references and index.
Identifiers: LCCN 2025008562 (print) | LCCN 2025008563 (ebook) | ISBN 9781503635142 cloth | ISBN 9781503643291 paperback | ISBN 9781503643307 ebook
Subjects: LCSH: Latin America—Emigration and immigration | Caribbean Area—Emigration and immigration | Latin America—Emigration and Immigration—Government policy | Caribbean Area—Emigration and Immigration—Government policy
Classification: LCC JV7398 .S44 2025 (print) | LCC JV7398 (ebook) | DDC 325.7—dc23/eng/20250312
LC record available at https://lccn.loc.gov/2025008562
LC ebook record available at https://lccn.loc.gov/2025008563

Cover design: Jan Šabach

The authorized representative in the EU for product safety and compliance is: Mare Nostrum Group B.V. | Mauritskade 21D | 1091 GC Amsterdam | The Netherlands | Email address: gpsr@mare-nostrum.co.uk | KVK chamber of commerce number: 96249943

Contents

COSTA RICA

PANAMA

TRINIDAD AND
TOBAGO

VENEZUELA

GUYANA

SURINAME

French Guiana (FR.)

COLOMBIA

Galapagos Islands
(ECUADOR)

ECUADOR

B R A Z I L

PERU

BOLIVIA

PARAGUAY

CHILE

ARGENTINA

URUGUAY

Falkland Islands
(U.K.)

0   1000 km

0   1000 mi

INTRODUCTION
Centuries of Migration and a Decade of Rapid Change

WHEN CAROLAY MORALES HEARD Alexander Beja sing for the first time, on the street in Bogotá, Colombia, she was moved to tears. "He was singing like he was in an auditorium, even though he was standing in the entrance to a parking garage on the street," says Morales, a veteran journalist at one of Colombia's leading radio stations, RCN. "He clearly had something to tell." She stopped walking and started filming him on her cell phone.[1]

What happened next was nothing short of a "miracle of destiny," as she later described it in a video report that went viral and won attention throughout Latin America. A few minutes later, Mario Domm, the founder of one of Latin America's most popular musical groups, Camila, happened to stop by too, and he stayed to listen to Beja's powerful voice, completely mesmerized.

Domm, who is Mexican, had just finished a concert tour in Colombia, and he was so taken with Alexander Beja's singing that he hugged him when the song was finished and, on the spot, promised to take him to Mexico to record a song together in his studio. Domm bought Beja a cell phone at a store nearby, so they could keep in touch, and then gave him a hundred dollars as a tip. It all happened within a few minutes, with the two men promising to follow up, and Domm headed off to the airport to catch his flight back home.

This could be just another story about a famous musician discovering new talent, except for one big wrinkle: Alexander Beja was living in Colombia as an undocumented migrant from Venezuela, a country that has fallen into po-

1

litical and economic chaos, with nearly 7.9 million of its citizens—almost a quarter of the population—moving elsewhere in the world, most since 2015.

Over a third of them, 2.8 million, are now living in Colombia, with another 1.5 million in Peru, between 400,000 to 600,000 in Brazil, Chile, and Ecuador, and over 100,000 in Argentina, the Dominican Republic, Mexico, and Panama. In fact, there were Venezuelans in almost every country in Latin America and the Caribbean by 2019, when Domm met Beja.

Alexander Beja, like numerous other desperate Venezuelans, had embarked on a grueling journey to reach Bogotá, walking for nearly a week from Cúcuta, the first border city inside Colombia. Cúcuta, a municipality where temperatures typically soar to 30 degrees Celsius (over 90 degrees Fahrenheit), becomes a stark contrast as migrants swiftly traverse the freezing mountain passes of the Páramo de Santurbán, which ascend to 4,200 meters above sea level, subjecting them to freezing temperatures. It was during this arduous journey that his shoes finally gave out, forcing him to continue barefoot until he reached the city of Pamplona, where a kind soul offered him an old pair of shoes to continue his trek.

He eventually made it to Bogotá where he began singing in the street to earn enough money to survive. "He felt a lot of rejection because he was Venezuelan," Carolay Morales recounts, something common for many recently arrived Venezuelan migrants, whose mass arrival has generated divergent responses in Colombia and other countries in the region. But Beja persisted, surviving by singing on the street and earning what he could from those who heard him and were drawn to his music. "Singing on the street was really hard," admits Beja.[2]

Despite some public skepticism towards many of the new arrivals, the Colombian government has taken a largely welcoming approach to this massive migration by letting Venezuelans stay and work in the country. Through three very different presidential administrations, it has carried out a series of regularization programs for these migrants, eventually giving over 2 million Venezuelans a ten-year temporary residence permit that allows them to stay and work.[3] It has been a massive undertaking for a country that had far less than 1 percent of its population born abroad in 2010, a percentage that is now over 6 percent, mostly Venezuelans who arrived in precarious circumstances.

Colombians have felt alternately proud of their record in welcoming so many Venezuelan migrants at a time of crisis and worried about how it affects their economy and society, a complex mix of emotions that shapes a contradictory public opinion towards the new arrivals, as it does in many other countries in the region.[4] When Carolay Morales released her video of the encounter between Mario Domm and Alexander Beja, it tapped into the welcoming side of these contradictory feelings. Colombians loved the sense of solidarity with a Venezuelan street singer and his shot at worldwide fame. Beja became something of a local celebrity, instantly recognized on the street as he went out to sing. And Carolay Morales even won the prestigious "King of Spain Award" for her reporting on the story, which made her something of a celebrity in Colombia too.

But for Beja, reality soon began to set in. He was one of the hundreds of thousands of recent migrants who had not yet managed to get any paperwork that would allow him to stay in the country legally. That quickly became a problem as he tried to get to Mexico to record a song in Mario Domm's studio. And since Venezuelan passports are too expensive for all but the wealthiest migrants to afford, Beja had never acquired one before fleeing his own country, and he had little possibility of getting one now in Colombia. He soon started to realize that the promise of recording his first song might never materialize because of these very real complications.

The good news story about a talented Venezuelan immigrant headed for stardom was starting to run into real-world problems because of the rules around migration and mobility. There was enough good will to support his journey, but the migration policies that would allow it to happen did not yet exist.

———————

In almost every large city in Latin America and the Caribbean, you can find migrant musicians, like Alexander Beja, trying to earn a little money by singing to audiences in downtown corridors and the areas of town most likely to attract tourists and businesspeople. In South America and much of the Caribbean, Venezuelan musicians often share the streets and public transportation with locals, creating a vibrant blend of sounds. When wandering the streets in South America, you might even stumble upon mixed groups of local and foreign musicians playing melodies that harmonize beautifully, a testament to the cultural connections forged through migration.

In Costa Rica, however, the musicians are more likely to be Nicaraguans, since Nicaraguan migrants make up about a tenth of the Costa Rican population. The most recent arrival of around 300,000 Nicaraguans followed the brutal crackdown on protests in that country in March of 2018 and included college students, journalists, doctors, and members of farmers' organizations, among others.[5]

In Tapachula, Mexico's largest city near Guatemala, the musicians in the central plaza are often from Honduras or Guatemala, where millions have left since 2014, most hoping to make it to the United States. But there are often a few African drummers somewhere in the corner of the plaza, a reminder of the many people from Cameroon, Congo, Angola, and other places on the African continent who are making their way through Central America and Mexico on their way to the United States.[6] And in downtown Tapachula, right next to the main cathedral, is a Haitian market, where the dominant language is Haitian Creole.

On Mexico's northern border you can dance salsa with Cuban instructors in Ciudad Juarez, across from El Paso, Texas, where a large Cuban community has sprung up. In Tijuana, across from San Diego, California, you can get a good meal, a drink, or a haircut in any one of the Haitian-owned establishments along Avenida Negrete, one the city's most prominent downtown streets, a sign of the growing Haitian community that has set down roots in that border city.[7]

And, of course, the Dominican Republic's national musical style, merengue, is itself influenced by Haitian Méringue and Konpa music, a visible impact of the around a half million Haitians who live across the border in the Dominican Republic and the long, rich, but deeply conflicted ties between these two countries that share an island.[8] And Haitian music is also on the streets on Santiago, Chile, and São Paulo, Brazil, these days, as Haitians move to other cities around the Americas.

The Americas are a region on the move. We are used to hearing the stories of Latin American and Caribbean migrants in other countries outside the region—in the United States, Canada, and Europe—and these diasporas abroad, and their relationship to their countries of origin are an important element in the development of migration policies in the Americas. Over 30 million Latin American and Caribbean migrants live in other countries outside the region (see table I.1). The largest numbers are in the United States, especially for Mexican and Central American migrants, but Canada has long been a magnet for Caribbean migrants and Europe for many Caribbean and South American migrants, with historical patterns of colonization and language ties often shaping where migrants prefer to go.

Most countries have sought to develop some form of outreach to their di-

TABLE I.1 Latin American and Caribbean Immigrants Residing in Select Countries in North America, Europe, Asia, Oceania, and Africa, 2020.

Country/Region	Immigrant Population
North America	25,535,633
United States	24,590,255
Canada	943,145
Other Countries	2,233
Europe	5,395,924
Spain	2,819,392
Italy	669,633
United Kingdom	425,137
France	325,015
Netherlands	279,072
Other Countries	877,675
Asia	414,658
Oceania	214,569
Africa	32,524

Source: Authors' tabulations of data from the United Nations' Department of Economic and Social Affairs, Population Division, "International Migrant Stock 2020: Destination and Origin," accessed September 23, 2024, https://www.un.org/development/desa/pd/content/international -migrant-stock.

asporas abroad, since diasporas influence day-to-day life through the transmission of cultural ideas, political opinions, and especially financial transfers. In many countries, policies on outreach to diasporas are often the most developed elements of migration policy, though the degree of sophistication and attention varies from country to country and over time. And increasingly some countries have developed policies to encourage diasporas to invest in their countries of origin or even return home.

We are also used to hearing the story of migrants headed to the U.S. border, and this is also another key part of the migration story in the Americas. Historically, most migrants who crossed the U.S. border came from Mexico and Central America. The Darien Gap, an inhospitable strip of jungle between Colombia and Panama where no roads existed, became a natural barrier that separated South America from Central America.

This sharp dividing line between Central and South America also meant that most migrants from South America, including Venezuelans after the crisis in that country, migrated within South America unless they could qualify for a visa to the United States or Canada. Spain allowed most Latin Americans to enter visa-free, as did Portugal for Brazilians, but that required having contacts in those countries who could host you while finding work.

And for people living in the Caribbean, other Caribbean countries were usually the best options for mobility, unless they could get a visa to another country in North America or Europe. There were, of course, a few periods where migrants from Caribbean countries braved the seas to reach the United States in large numbers, but these were particularly dangerous journeys. Generally speaking, the Caribbean, South America, and Central America and Mexico were three different migration systems, each with its own dynamics, with occasional touch points.[9]

But in the 2010s there started to be a small number of migrants, many from Haiti and a few African and South Asian countries, who began to cross through the Darien Gap, which had long separated South America and Central America.[10] At first these were small numbers, a few thousand a year. But since the easing of the COVID-19 pandemic in 2021, the number of people crossing through the Darien Gap has multiplied—reaching over a half-million in 2023 and around 300,000 in 2024. Since then, an infrastructure has developed that allows larger numbers of people to move through the area. This infrastructure includes food, water, and guides, who allow people to move through the jungle. Still others have avoided the journey through the Darien Gap by taking flights into airports in Central America and Mexico before heading north.

From 2022 to 2023, somewhere around 2 million migrants from all over the world reached the U.S. border through Latin America each year, and in 2023, for the first time, the majority came from countries beyond Central America and Mexico.[11] In 2024 the numbers dropped significantly, as the U.S. labor market cooled, the Mexican government increased enforcement efforts, and the U.S. government made it harder to enter the country between ports of entry. But the numbers still remained high by historical standards (See figure I.1).

It is hard to know the exact numbers of those who have actually entered the United States, since many of those who arrive are deported to their countries of origin while still others cross without detection. What we do know is that millions of people have moved through multiple countries of the hemisphere since 2021, often starting in South America and then through Cen-

FIGURE I.1   Migrant Encounters between Ports of Entry at the U.S.-Mexico Border, by Fiscal Year, 1970–2024.

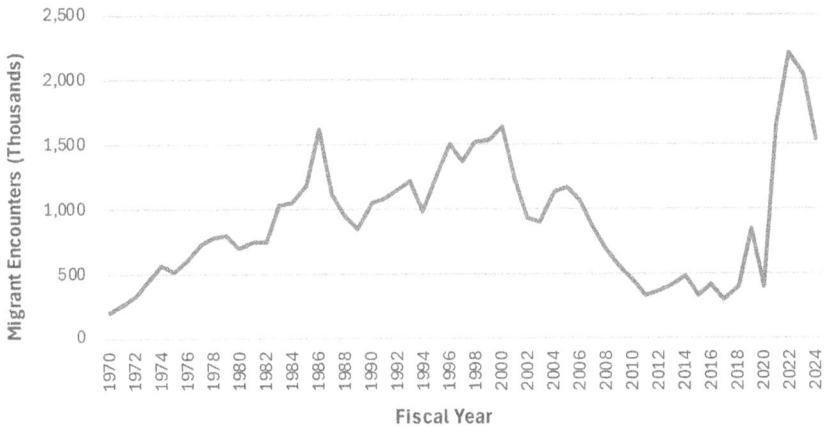

Notes: Migrant encounters by U.S. Border Patrol are recorded events, not of individual people, and in some cases may count multiple attempts by the same person to enter the United States. Encounters include formal apprehensions by U.S. Border Patrol of migrants crossing without authorization plus short-term detentions and returns of migrants to Mexico under a special expulsion authority known as Title 42 that was in effect from March 2020 through May 2023.

Sources: Authors' tabulations of migrant encounter data from U.S. Border Patrol. See U.S. Border Patrol, "Total Encounters by Fiscal Year, FY 1960–2020," accessed January 5, 2025, https://www. cbp.gov/sites/default/files/assets/documents/2021-Aug/US59B8~1.PDF; U.S. Customs and Border Protection, "Southwest Land Border Encounters," updated March 12, 2025, https://www.cbp.gov/ newsroom/stats/southwest-land-border-encounters.

tral America and Mexico, to reach the U.S. border. Countries along this route have had to develop policies on how to respond to transit migration through their countries. Some have tried to stop this forward movement; others to help those passing through; and a few have offered refuge or other forms of legal status to those who want to stay along the way. Many countries have done a mix of all three.

However, much of the migration in the Western Hemisphere today is actually not to the United States but rather within Latin America and the Caribbean. In fact, no region in the world saw a faster rise in immigration in the period from 2010 to 2023, where the number of people living in a country different from the one where they were born more than doubled in the space of just over a decade from 8.3 million in 2010 to 18.2 million in 2023 (table I.2).[12] This is a huge change from only a few years ago when most migrants from

TABLE 1.2 Immigrant Population in Select Latin American and Caribbean Countries, 1990–2023.

	1990	1995	2000	2005	2010	2015	2020	2023
Total	7,135,971	6,661,553	6,539,738	7,184,113	8,326,588	9,441,503	14,794,623	18,151,119
Colombia	104,277	106,943	109,609	106,523	130,309	159,407	1,905,393	2,982,435
Argentina	1,649,919	1,595,069	1,540,219	1,674,163	1,805,957	2,086,301	2,281,728	2,269,383
Peru	56,688	56,732	66,300	77,877	104,706	154,774	1,224,519	1,824,634
Chile	107,501	142,417	177,332	276,360	375,388	639,724	1,645,015	1,654,177
Brazil	798,517	741,557	684,596	638,582	592,640	710,304	1,079,708	1,399,661
Mexico	695,674	458,549	538,051	712,648	969,710	1,013,691	1,197,624	1,240,355
Ecuador	78,663	115,093	151,523	189,893	375,253	387,513	784,787	840,704
Dominican Republic	291,151	323,381	355,611	375,417	395,479	549,289	603,794	693,872
Costa Rica	417,628	364,287	310,946	358,398	405,779	411,697	520,729	521,563
Panama	62,744	70,848	83,410	109,461	157,788	184,710	313,165	251,770
Trinidad & Tobago	50,666	45,994	41,753	44,812	48,226	50,021	78,849	91,066
Bahamas	26,855	31,654	36,454	45,531	54,745	59,241	63,583	63,583
Belize	30,404	33,446	36,488	41,438	46,390	54,615	62,043	62,043
Barbados	24,024	26,224	28,424	30,624	32,825	34,475	34,869	34,869
Guyana	4,095	6,352	8,610	10,868	8,182	8,661	31,169	29,519
All Others	2,737,165	2,543,007	2,370,412	2,491,518	2,823,211	2,937,080	2,967,648	4,191,485

Notes: To illustrate the extent of Venezuelan mobility across Latin America and the Caribbean in recent years, immigrant stock for 2023 combines 2020 population estimates of non-Venezuelan immigrants from the UN Department of Economic and Social Affairs (UNDESA) with 2023 estimates of Venezuelan refugees, migrants, and asylum seekers from the Inter-Agency Coordination Platform for Refugees and Migrants from Venezuela (R4V). While UNDESA methodology relies primarily on population censuses and some representative surveys to produce estimates, R4V estimates are based on a diverse set of government databases and therefore do not necessarily imply individual identification nor registration of each individual. Government sources may undercount immigrants who are in vulnerable conditions or are difficult to survey, like immigrants in irregular status. Because of methodological differences and ongoing improvements across government databases, these estimates are regularly updated and can vary. Sources: Authors' calculations based on population data estimates from UN DESA "International Migrant Stock 2020: Destination and Origin," https://www.un.org/development/desa/pd/content/international-migrant-stock, and R4V, "Refugees and Migrants from Venezuela," updated November 2023, https://www.r4v.info/en/document/r4v-latin-america-and-caribbean-venezuelan-refugees-and-migrants-region-nov-2023.

Latin American and Caribbean countries were almost exclusively looking to get to the United States, Canada, or Europe.

A series of displacement crises in the Americas, most notably the collapse of the Venezuelan economy in the midst of political turmoil and persecution, have accounted for a significant part of this shift. Nicaragua has gone through a similar political and economic crisis, while Haiti has faced a descent into chaos since a massive earthquake in 2010, with the rise of control by gangs across the country.[13] In fact, these three crises alone account for about 75 percent of the increase in immigrants living in the Americas between 2010 and 2020.[14]

This is somewhat unusual around the world, where displacement crises generally only account for around 7 to 12 percent of global migration movements across borders.[15] However, it indicates how much this series of displacement crises from Haiti, Nicaragua, and Venezuela changed patterns of mobility in the region. At least some of those fleeing other countries, including Colombia, Cuba, Ecuador, El Salvador, Guatemala, Honduras, and Mexico, are likely displaced by direct threats from organized crime groups, local gangs, and political officials too, so the actual proportion of displaced migrants is probably even higher.

In addition to this, shifting climate patterns have likely intensified both internal and international migration, as some areas in the Caribbean and Central America become increasingly less sustainable.[16] And natural disasters, especially hurricanes and flooding, serve as particularly visible detonators of migration for many each year, with these incidents increasing in frequency and intensity over time.[17]

However, not all migrants in Latin America and the Caribbean are fleeing from something. As elsewhere in the world, people move for a variety of reasons, including opportunities for work and study, family connections, and adventure.[18] There were also a series of decisions made by policymakers in the Americas over the past two decades that opened up legal opportunities for mobility among neighboring countries and within specific subregions, which further allowed people to seek opportunities across borders within the Americas. Displacement crises were a big part of the story but certainly not the only part.

And for those heading north to the United States, there is growing evidence that labor market openings in the United States are the strongest predictor of the number of migrants arriving at the U.S. border with Mexico, rather than conditions in the region, even if both play a role.[19] Although public debates on migration often focus on why people leave, the demand for workers in countries where migrants go may often explain migration patterns better than conditions in countries of origin, especially for migration from lower to higher income countries.[20]

The interplay between people's aspirations to move and their capabilities to do so generally explain why people move and where they move to, as migration scholar Hein de Haas has outlined in a compelling theoretical framework.[21] Aspirations to migrate increase as people know more about opportunities in other countries that may help improve their circumstances, but these aspirations to move may actually diminish over time as countries grow economically and become more politically stable.[22] Meanwhile, capabilities are shaped by the ability to afford moving to a particular destination, whether by getting a visa or paying for smugglers and associated costs, and by whether a prospective migrant has someone to host them when they arrive and help them navigate the new environment; how they perceive the chances of success in getting to where they want to go; and whether they believe they can get employment and improve their circumstances over time.[23]

Of course, the more migration from one country to another takes place, the easier it becomes for others to follow the same pathway because the social connections make it possible for others to conceive of the same journey and be able to find initial housing and work through those connections in the destination country.[24] And in today's social media environment, where information on migration circulates in real time, including from friends and relatives who have already migrated, this process has accelerated considerably, allowing new migration patterns to develop more quickly than in the past.[25]

While shifting labor market demand may be particularly important in explaining migration to the United States and Europe, developed economies where populations are aging quickly and labor markets increasingly need workers from abroad to meet workforce gaps, many upper middle-income countries in Latin America and the Caribbean, such as Bahamas, Barbados, Chile, Mexico, and Uruguay are also aging quickly and have labor market needs.[26] So these labor market needs—and the different income opportunities across countries—may explain at least some of the increasing international mobility within the region, in addition to the "push" factors that lead people to decide to move.[27]

In practice, it is often hard to tell the difference between someone who moves for opportunity and someone who does so out of necessity, and these are often part of a continuum rather than stark differences.[28] Since some migrants are fleeing a combination of economic distress, poor governance, violence, political conflict, natural disasters, and climate shifts, while also choosing where to go based on economic opportunities or social ties, it can be difficult in these cases to distinguish who is a refugee, a forced migrant, or simply someone seeking a better life. In many cases, these motivations are mixed.[29] Movement within Latin America and the Caribbean today, as well as to other parts of the world, is a kaleidoscope of motivations, with gradations that are often hard to discern.

But whatever the reasons people move, we know that mobility outward to other parts of the world and mobility among countries in the Americas have both increased dramatically in recent years, which has brought to the fore a new set of discussions around public policy to address migration. In fact, for the first time in history, migration policies have become a central issue for governments across the Americas.

This book looks at how countries in the Americas have been building the foundations of migration policies at a time of considerable human mobility in the region and what impacts this has on both migrants and societies in the countries where they move A great deal has been written about U.S. policy on immigration, but much less on the immigration policies of countries in Latin America and the Caribbean. With the dramatic rise in the number of migrants staying in other countries in the hemisphere, this book tries to fill that gap.

Compared to many other parts of the world, Latin American and Caribbean countries have taken a generally open approach to receiving and welcoming migrants, at least when compared to the countries in North America and Europe where most Latin American and Caribbean migrants once settled. There are at least five regional mobility agreements in the Americas—two in the Caribbean, two in South America, and one in Central America—that seek to facilitate movement and often periods of residency among defined subregions, as well as several bilateral agreements among neighbors.[30] And most countries in the Americas have provided legal pathways and access to labor markets, education, and sometimes even healthcare for displaced migrants and refugees who have arrived in their countries.[31]

To be sure, there is often a disjuncture between the stated intentions of policies and their implementation, as we explore in this book, and the general trends often obscure considerable differences from country to country and over time. But there still appears to be a different set of foundations being built for migration policies in the Americas as countries are focusing on this issue for the first time in many years.[32]

At the same time, countries have grown increasingly intent on controlling borders and determining who can enter, even if they often lack the capacity to enforce this fully. This is similar to trends elsewhere in the world, where governments want to know who comes in and to be able to determine priorities on entry. At the same time, this movement towards control is tempered by significant efforts to provide pathways for easy entry to certain groups, usually from within the same subregion, and a general approach to allowing those who have already entered to stay and integrate into local communities.

The dominant theory in migration studies has been the "liberal paradox," developed by James Hollifield and built on the experience of immigration policies in the countries of Europe and North America, which emphasizes that democratic institutions and markets create the conditions for more open migration policies, while the increased movement across borders that results from this creates a countervailing push for more closure.[33]

This dynamic takes place because these destination countries have a set of stakeholders who believe in or benefit from migration, including business leaders, human rights groups, and migrant-led organizations, as well as legal guarantees built into constitutions and law, which courts often extend to include immigrants. At the same time, the feeling of loss of sovereignty, fears about cultural change, and perceived threats to national and public security resulting from increased migration generate pushback against migration among the general public.[34] In recent years, in the United States and Europe, this diffuse public opinion has been increasingly channeled through far-right political leaders and sometimes new political parties that promise to secure borders and reduce migration.[35] As issues around migration have become more salient,[36] the number of engaged stakeholders has increased, and policies have become more hotly contested.

In Latin American and Caribbean countries, however, the pattern appears to be different, at least so far. In general—and with some exceptions we will explore further—there is neither the strong push from business, immigrant-led, or other ethnic groups towards greater openness, nor massive pushback against immigration from the general public. While there was considerable immigration in earlier periods to these countries, the period since World War II has been one of low immigration in most countries. As a result, immigration policies have been dealt with primarily by executive branch decision-makers and, in a few cases, by interested legislators and civil society groups who have a particular interest in the issue. But it has not yet generated the kind of gener-alized public debate or clear-cut stakeholder groups pushing for openness and closure, as in North America and Europe.

There is, however, one prominent exception to this. In the Dominican Republic, immigration from neighboring Haiti has long been a major public issue. Many scholars argue that Dominicans, who share an island with Haiti, have long defined their own national identity vis-à-vis their neighbors, with a backlash against immigration from the country next door serving as a flashpoint for rallying nationalist sentiments.[37] The then authoritarian leader of the Dominican Republic ordered a massacre of thousands of Haitian im-migrants in 1937. More recently, democratically elected governments have also used campaigns to deport Haitian immigrants as a popular measure to build political support.[38] In 2010, the Dominican Supreme Court ruled that the children of undocumented Haitian immigrants were not entitled to Dominican citizenship, even if born in the country, leaving several tens of thousands of children and grandchildren of Haitian immigrants effectively stateless.[39]

There are profound similarities between Dominican attitudes towards Haitian migrants and those in the United States towards other Latin Amer-ican and Caribbean migrants (including, perhaps ironically, Dominicans), which mix both practical fears that poorer neighbors will migrate en masse if there is insufficient control of migration with racial and ethnic fears that sometimes underlie these fears.[40] The Dominican Republic also has a mixture of groups—business and civil society associations—that push for openness, while other groups and diffuse public opinion push for closure, much as the liberal paradox predicts. There is no reason why this could not become the dominant pattern across other countries in Latin America and the Caribbean in the future, but it does not appear to have happened in most countries as of yet.

To be sure, there are similar elements of ethnic, racial, and cultural fears towards Haitians in other parts of Latin America and the Caribbean, and also towards other immigrant groups in other countries, such as Paraguayans and Bolivians in Argentina, Peruvians in Chile, and Guatemalans in southern Mexico. However, there is no other country in the region where immigration has played such a divisive and prominent role in defining national identity as it has in the Dominican Republic, even if there have been moments of tension, patterns of discrimination, and occasional political pushback on immigrants in some other countries.

However, the Dominican experience also suggests that Latin American and Caribbean countries are not immune to immigration becoming a major defining issue. It simply has yet to happen in most other countries. Historically most countries simply invested little attention in migration policy-making until recently, and they took a slightly more laissez-faire approach to immigration. As immigration has become a more prominent issue in most countries, some of the same tensions and definitions of migrants as the "other" have developed, but not yet at the scale or with the consistency seen yet in the Dominican Republic—or Europe or the United States—so far.

Why then do most Latin American and Caribbean countries seem to have policies that are more open towards migration than in those in Europe and the United States? The simplest answer is that there has been much less intra-regional migration in most countries until recently. As a result, migration has not attained the same visibility and salience as an issue until recently.

And before migration became a major issue, in the early twenty-first century, much of the region went through a period of liberalizing migration laws. In practical terms this meant that several countries passed constitutional changes or specific migration laws that decriminalized irregular migration, allowed migrants to have access to the education system, regardless of legal status, and, in some cases, made it possible for citizens of other nearby countries to enter without passports or visas.[41]

Some of this was inspired by human rights organizations, who pushed for liberal laws as part of the region's re-democratization process, especially in

Central and South America.[42] Sometimes diaspora organizations influenced migration legislation, directly or indirectly.[43] In other cases, government leaders saw more open migration laws as a way of pressuring countries where their diasporas lived to pursue more open policies.[44]

Moreover, governments pursued regional mobility agreements during this period as a way of building solidarity among subregions with particularly close ties and as part of efforts to promote regional trade agreements.[45] Diego Acosta has shown how this process has a long history going back to the early nineteenth century in South America, sometimes but not always including Mexico and Spanish-speaking countries in Central America and the Caribbean.[46] There was a strongly symbolic element that had to do with building unity among countries in the hemisphere that shared a common Ibero-American heritage, part of the region's Bolivarian legacy. But in the 1990s and early 2000s, there was also a practical element. Countries began to form subregional economic alliances as part of a response to globalization and the rise of economic blocs elsewhere in the world, which also led to two subregional mobility agreements in South America and one in Central America.[47]

Meanwhile, in the Caribbean, as countries gained independence in the 1960s, they also began looking for ways to build synergies across a space that had strong historical, social, and economic ties already. By the 1970s, they had formed the Caribbean Community, Caricom, which eventually included a mobility agreement as well. Later seven small Caribbean states in the Eastern Caribbean, which are geographically close together and of similar size, built an overlapping organization, the Organization of Eastern Caribbean States, which also included a quite extensive mobility agreement.[48]

And several countries in the region also agreed on a different approach to displacement crises in 1984 under the Cartagena Declaration on Refugees, which expanded the definition of a refugee from the international standard, based on those facing individual persecution to those suffering "generalized violence" and "the breakdown of order," as well as committing signatory governments to incorporating these commitments in their national legislation.[49] The incorporation of these norms into national legislation among the seventeen countries that now acknowledge the Declaration has been uneven and implementation even more so, but it served as an important antecedent for policies to come in the period after 2010.[50]

This early architecture, developed largely before 2010, helped set the stage for the more recent responses to migration since then, as the numbers of those moving increased dramatically. These institutions, agreements, and norms helped shape the decisions that have come afterwards, as countries wrestle with increased migration and major displacement crises.

But the specific set of responses to migration in the Americas requires us to ask a set of key questions. First of all, why have the countries in Latin America and the Caribbean generally exhibited more openness to migration, even at a time of significant mobility across borders? This seems at odds with the liberal paradox and suggests a different trajectory, at least to date, for migration policies in the region than in the more studied destination countries of North America and Europe.[51] At the same time, why have these measures differed among countries, which exhibit quite distinct degrees of openness to migration and have used diverse kinds of measures to address migration?

Secondly, do countries distinguish between policies on entry and permanence? There appears to be a general movement towards greater restrictions on entry in some countries, but this does not always translate into restrictions on those who choose to remain. Is there a difference in how governments respond to migrants who are staying in their countries versus those who are transiting through them? And does it vary depending on where the migrants come? In other words, do they exhibit differential treatment to different migrant groups based on perceived affinity?

Much of the literature on migration describes openness and closure as binary opposites, but there is nothing inherently contradictory in countries pursuing openness with citizens of some countries but not with others or in them pursuing greater control of borders on future entries while maintaining openness to immigrants already living in the country. And there may also be significantly different incentives at play in responding to migrants who choose to stay in a country versus those who are just passing through on their way elsewhere. Indeed, what is apparent in most countries in Latin America and the Caribbean today are differentiated responses to diverse kinds of migration, which creates a mixture of openness and closure at the same time.

To understand why countries have adopted the policies they have, we need to look at the incentives that governments have to implement particular policies.[52] Not all of the migration policies in the Americas pertain to displacement (though many do), but the larger point holds: What incentives do governments have that push them towards openness or closure with regard to particular kinds of migration, and how have they "stretched" their existing policies in new ways—or invented entirely new ones—at a time of significantly increased migration in the region?

In terms of incentives, public opinion clearly matters and is a first variable to consider. While migration was rarely politically salient (with a few notable exceptions) in recent history, it has risen in political visibility in most countries since 2010, so it is likely to be one of the elements that shape migration decision-making. It is true that migration has not become as salient a political issue as in Europe or the United States, but it is far more so than before.

Similarly, geopolitics provides another set of incentives that influence decisions on migration policy and so are a second important variable to consider. In some cases, the desire to build competitive economic zones among neighboring countries has shaped decisions on regional mobility agreements. In other cases, policymakers have decided to grant legal status to displaced populations fleeing from governments they are opposed to as a way of pursuing foreign policy aims. And in still other cases, policymakers have been influenced by pressure from outside powers, including the U.S. government, to implement measures to stop onward migration.

Symbolic politics are a third variable worth considering. Since most countries in the Americas have recent experience with their own citizens migrating abroad, there is a degree of empathy among the general population towards migrants, and governments sometimes use more inclusive migration policies to signal how they want their own citizens to be treated abroad. In addition to this, there is also a sense of regional solidarity in particular subregions, built on historical notions of a shared past,[53] that may make people more sympathetic to receiving nationals from those countries. This has undoubtedly been important both in pursuing regional mobility agreements and in receiving displaced populations.

While there is some debate on whether solidarity and empathy form a durable basis for policy,[54] they may certainly help explain initial decisions (such as entering mobility agreements, changing immigration laws, or implementing measures for the first waves of displaced populations), which then have longer-term consequences for subsequent policy decisions. It is also worth noting, however, that solidarity and empathy may promote inclusion but also exclusion. It depends a great deal on who is considered similar and who is considered different, which may lead to differential forms of treatment for different migrant groups depending on whether people in the destination country see them as part of the same shared history or not.

A fourth and final variable worth examining is institutional capacity. On one hand, governments may choose particular measures because they simply do not have the capacity, resources, or prior experience to do something else, whether it is offering temporary protection instead of refugee status or providing legal pathways instead of implementing border controls. Since migration policy and migration institutions were largely underdeveloped in Latin American and Caribbean countries before 2010, it may well be that decisions after that date followed what policymakers perceived as feasible in the moment that decisions were made. It is key to understand who specifically within government made key decisions at different points in time since distinct parts of government could have markedly different preferences.[55] And, of course, institutional capacity may often explain the divergence between intended policies and actual implementation.

Public opinion, geopolitics, notions of solidarity, and institutional capacities are likely to have shaped the way decisions were made across different countries and across time. In this book, we look separately at the specific policy decisions made in South America, Central America and Mexico, and the Caribbean, and then in the final chapter we try to draw some conclusions on how these four variables explain the policy decisions made across the region in building the foundations of migration policy.

When Alexander Beja arrived in Colombia, a year before he met Mario Domm, he was following a pattern that had been established thousands of years before. After all, the Americas were, from the beginning, a region in motion. The songs Beja was used to singing on the streets of Bogotá—a cappella versions of Boleros, Salsa, and Cumbia—could not have existed without the history of movement from other parts of the world to the Americas, which brought together traditions from Africa, Europe, and the Indigenous peoples of the Americas and blended them into genuinely new musical styles. Many of these styles were then remixed again in the late twentieth century as millions of Latin American and Caribbean migrants, who left their countries in the post–World War II period, met up in New York, Miami, London, Madrid, Paris, and other cities around the world.[56]

Understanding migration policies in the Americas requires knowing the history of mobility in the region, since earlier patterns of mobility helped shape the countries of Latin America and the Caribbean that exist today. And, as it turns out, prior migration patterns explain a great deal about how migrants experience integration in their destination (and new home) countries today.

The region's mobility started with the first arrival of the original inhabitants from Asia, probably more than 15,000 years ago, and then the gradual settlement of North and South America over several centuries.[57] These original inhabitants had managed to reach the south of Chile by at least 12,000 years ago and settled most of the islands in the Caribbean by 6,000 years ago.[58] Most of the original inhabitants were initially hunter-gatherers, fishermen, and farmers, but they also produced several highly complex civilizations with significant territorial extensions, from the earlier Olmec, Toltec, Maya, Zapotec, and Mixtec in Mexico and Central America to the Chavin, Moche, and Nazca in what is now Peru in South America. Even the Caribbean, which was probably populated through at least three different waves of migration from the coasts of what are today Venezuela and Mexico, had relatively large and sophisticated city-states on several islands at the time of first contact with European migrants.[59]

Two later civilizations, the Inca in South America and the Aztec in Mexico, were still very much in their prime when European conquerors first arrived in the hemisphere in the sixteenth and seventeenth centuries, an encounter that set off an entirely new phase in the history of migration in the Americas. This new phase was characterized by the violent collision of three continents: the Indigenous inhabitants of the Americas; European colonists and settlers; and Africans, who were brought against their will to serve as enslaved workers.

Between the first encounter of Europeans and Indigenous peoples in 1492, with Christopher Columbus landing at a small island that is now part of the Bahamas, until the end of colonial rule in most of Latin America in the early 1800s, somewhere between 1.5 to 2 million European colonists and settlers moved to the Americas.[60]

They initially encountered a population of maybe 100 million Indigenous people or more who were native to the region, the largest numbers concentrated in Mexico, Central America, and the Andean region. However, Indigenous peoples were soon decimated by conflict and especially by diseases brought from Europe, with perhaps as few as 5 to 10 million surviving the first century of contact.[61] However, today there are over 45 million people who identify as Indigenous in the Americas, a population that has grown back against the face of often quite difficult odds.[62]

Enslaved Africans were brought forcibly to the Americas in the early seventeenth century, with in over 6.6 million arriving in Latin America and the Caribbean by 1800 and another 3 million in the nineteenth century, for a total of at least 9.3 million (see table I.3).[63] The number of enslaved Africans brought to the Americas far exceeded the number of European colonists (or surviving Indigenous peoples) in many countries, especially in Brazil and in the Caribbean.

In the period from independence to the 1930s several countries in South America, especially Argentina, Brazil, Chile, and Uruguay, and to a lesser extent Cuba, Mexico, and Peru, attracted significant migration from Europe, probably well over 16 million immigrants, mostly drawn from Italy, Spain, Portugal, German-speaking territories, and Eastern Europe.[64] Many of these countries intentionally sought out European immigrants, both for reasons of labor market needs and because of racist beliefs that European immigrants would improve their countries' populations. And many countries had specific prohibitions on Black and Jewish immigration.[65]

And in this period, well over a million people from China, Japan, India, and Indonesia arrived as well,[66] plus perhaps over a half million from the Middle East,[67] bringing new strands to the social and cultural tapestries of the countries in the region. In the case of South and Southeast Asian immigrants, many arrived as indentured workers, and they left an imprint throughout the hemisphere, perhaps most visibly in Guyana, Suriname, and Trinidad and Tobago where their descendants now make up between a third and a half of the population in each country.

There was always some migration within the Americas, especially between neighboring countries and among the islands of the Caribbean.[68] These were generally smaller movements, except for the large-scale migration of hundreds of thousands of inhabitants from the English-speaking Caribbean islands, most of them the descendants of enslaved Africans, to the coastal areas of Venezuela, Colombia, and the countries in Central America in the late nineteenth and early twentieth centuries. Most were brought to mine for gold, construct railways, work in banana plantations, or build the Panama Canal. While some eventually returned to their countries of origin—especially to

TABLE I.3   Arrivals of Different Migrant Populations in the Americas.

	Colonial Period	Post-Colonial Period*
Enslaved Africans	6.2 million	3.1 million
Europeans (including Middle East)	1.6 million	16.8+ million*
Asians	N/A	1.4 million

Note: The division between the "colonial " and "postcolonial " periods is roughly around 1800, which corresponds to the independence period in Spanish-speaking Latin America (but not necessarily in other parts of the region). The number of Europeans in the postcolonial period is only for Latin America and does not include European migrants to the English-, French-, Danish-, and Dutch-speaking Caribbean, although these were much fewer in number.

Sources: Slave Voyages, "The Transatlantic Slave Trade Database" for data on enslaved Africans, https://www.slavevoyages.org/voyage/database#tables; José Moya, "Migration and Historical Formation in Latin America in a Global Perspective," *Sociologias* 20, no. 49 (2018) for data on Europeans and Asians migrating to Latin America; Lomarsh Roopnarine, *The Indian Caribbean: Migration and Identity in the Diaspora* (University of Mississippi Press, 2018), and Rosemarijn Hoefte, *In Place of Slavery: A Social History of British Indian and Javanese Laborers in Suriname* (Gainesville: University Press of Florida, 1998) for Asian migration.

Jamaica and Barbados—most remained, creating robust Afro-Caribbean communities throughout the coastal regions of mainland South and Central America. This migration also helped develop a shared, if constantly evolving, Afro-Caribbean identity that still has implications for today's migration patterns in the Caribbean Basin.[69]

There was also always some movement from Latin America and the Caribbean to the United States and Europe, but this accelerated sharply in the second half of the twentieth century and would become the primary direction of migration after World War II. The largest migration was, of course, that of Mexicans to the United States, which started in the late nineteenth century. This was primarily circular migration, but increasingly as the twentieth century progressed and the new millennium arrived, more and more Mexicans stayed in the United States, until people of Mexican descent made up more than a tenth of the U.S. population, and almost a tenth of Mexicans lived in the United States.[70]

Throughout the twentieth century, there were also migrations from the Caribbean to Europe, the United States, and Canada.[71] From early in the twentieth century and especially after World War II, Cubans, Dominicans, and Haitians headed to the United States, while those from the English, French, and Dutch-speaking Caribbean, including Trinidad and Tobago, Jamaica, and Barbados, headed to Europe, mostly to the United Kingdom, France, and the Netherlands. After the United States and Canada changed their immigration laws in the 1960s, while the United Kingdom almost simultaneously tightened its immigration policies, the number of migrants from the Caribbean increased noticeably in both the United States and Canada, leading to large immigrant communities from almost every Caribbean country and territory in those two countries.[72]

South American migration began in the early 1970s, with the advent of military dictatorships in several countries that drove people to flee to other Latin American countries, especially to Venezuela, or further to Europe, Canada, and the United States. Migration from South America increased significantly in the 1990s, for a mixture of economic and political reasons, with large numbers of Colombians, Ecuadorians, Peruvians, Bolivians, and others heading to Venezuela, which was in the middle of an oil boom, as well as to Spain and the United States. There were also smaller but still significant movements from almost every other country to Europe and North America.[73]

And migrants from some of the less wealthy countries, like Peru, Bolivia, and Paraguay, often found their ways to comparatively better-off neighboring countries like Argentina, Brazil, Chile, and Venezuela.[74] By 1990, Venezuela and Argentina concentrated by far the largest number of migrants in the Americas.[75]

In the 1970s and especially the 1980s, a new migration from Central America to the United States began, which since 2018 has grown even further and competes with Mexican migration as the most important movement towards the United States.[76] Salvadorans were the first national group to settle in large numbers in the United States, but Guatemalans and Hondurans have grown in numbers in recent years as well (see chapter 2).

And while most of these Central American migrants have been headed to the United States, increasing numbers of them have been staying in Mexico[77] or heading to Costa Rica, a country where roughly one in seven residents is now foreign-born.[78] In fact, in the period from January 2019 through November 2023, Mexico received 497,060 asylum applications, mostly from Central Americans, Haitians, and Cubans.[79] During the same period, Costa Rica received 231,679 asylum applications.[80] While U.S. attention was almost exclusively focused on its own border, the reality remained that a larger number of migrants and refugees were actually staying in the neighboring countries and testing the emerging migration and refugee policies of those countries.[81]

Since 2021, there has been a renewed migration from South America and parts of the Caribbean to the United States, as it became possible to cross the Darien Gap that had once separated South America from Central America. This combined with increased labor market demand in the United States after COVID-19 to create major irregular migration movements from and through South America up through Central America and Mexico to the U.S. border.

At the same time, the large Latin American and Caribbean diasporas, which developed in the United States, Canada, and Europe through the arrivals of migrants from the Americas, continue to shape daily life in many parts of Latin America and the Caribbean. Citizens living abroad—and sometimes even their children and grandchildren—play important roles in the economic, political, and cultural life of their countries of origin.[82] Sometimes diasporas organize in affinity groups, often tied to their hometown or region within the country of origin, while other times they participate directly in political movements in their countries of origin. The importance of remittances sent by diasporas abroad compounds this influence (see table I.4).

TABLE I.4   Amount of Remittances and Share of GDP Received by Select Latin American and Caribbean Countries, 2023.

Country	Remittances (USD in Millions)	Remittance Share of GDP
Nicaragua	4,662	26.8%
Honduras	8,968	25.7%
El Salvador	8,193	24.1%
Haiti	4,247	19.7%
Guatemala	19,978	19.6%
Jamaica	3,567	18.9%
Dominican Republic	10,619	8.9%
St. Vincent and the Grenadines	92	8.8%
Ecuador	5,452	4.6%
Mexico	66,239	3.7%
Colombia	10,112	2.8%
Peru	4,446	1.7%

Source: Authors' calculations based on data from the World Bank and KNOMAD. See World Bank and KNOMAD, "Migration and Development Brief 40," June 2024, https://documents1.world bank.org/curated/en/099714008132436612/pdf/IDU1a9cf73b51fcad1425a1a0ddicc8f2f3331ce.pdf.

Increasingly, many countries are also seeing the return of citizens who have lived abroad for periods of time, who often face challenges for reintegration but also often bring new skills and perspectives.[83] Few countries have yet to fully grapple with how to integrate returning migrants or take advantage of their skills, but a few are trying to figure this out.[84] And in many countries, particularly in the Caribbean and Central America, young male returnees who are deported often face stigma for bringing their "criminal knowledge and skills" acquired in the U.S. to disturb local communities.

Out of this complex and deeply conflicted history have emerged the contours of the countries that today exist in Latin America and the Caribbean, thirty-five independent nations plus several territories.[85] The countries in the region today are, on one hand, a testament to how nations can be successfully forged out of racial, ethnic, and religious differences. And yet they are also simultaneously a reminder of how historical patterns of settlement, slavery, and migration produce enduring patterns of social and economic inequality, racial and ethnic discrimination, and enduring conflicts. Latin America remains the region of the world with the highest inequality overall, and these inequalities track significantly across racial and ethnic identities.[86]

This essential contradiction has created a strange mix of both openness to difference, on one hand, and extreme intergroup distrust, on the other, that has been handed down until today.[87] This duality, in turn, influences attitudes towards migration and the ways that they are often incorporated into countries throughout the region. Indeed, many migrants find themselves welcomed on paper but embedded in preexisting hierarchies of race, ethnicity, and economic status that vary from country to country and often shape their degree of upward mobility.[88] And, of course, most find themselves working in informal markets where so much of the population of Latin America and the Caribbean already work.[89]

Migrants today may face more openness in legal terms on their arrival in Latin American and Caribbean countries than in North America and Europe, but they also move into societies that are profoundly stratified by race, ethnicity, gender, and social class, especially in labor markets.

So, if the first set of questions we explore in this book has to do with how governments make migration policy, the second set has to do with how well migrants and the societies at large in destination countries are doing in an era of large-scale migration. The first set of questions has to do with how and why policy is made; the second with the implications of these policies.

How are migrants actually integrating into the societies where they now live? How do their incomes compare to those of the native-born, and are they converging over time? Are there noticeable differences by gender, race, ethnicity, education level, or national origin? And how does the arrival of immigrants affect destination societies as a whole in terms of income, public security, and other indicators of quality of life? And what do the native-born think about their newly arrived migrant neighbors?

Unfortunately, the data available to date do not always allow for detailed or fully rigorous answers to these questions, since studies on integration are still few and far between and concentrated, where they exist, in only a few countries of South America.[90] However, we try to patch together the fragmentary evidence that exists so far to see if we can offer some tentative answers to these questions based on what we know so far in at least a few countries.

In the end, Venezuelan singer Alexander Beja turned out to be extremely lucky. The video that Carolay Morales had shot of the encounter between him and Mario Domm had gone viral, and the Colombian government felt pressure to figure out how to get him a passport. After all, he had become something of a poster child for Colombia's ongoing efforts to welcome Venezuelans fleeing their country, and they could not let this moment to highlight their efforts publicly pass without doing something. So eventually, the Colombian government issued Beja a "provisional passport" that he could use to travel to Mexico, even though he was not Colombian. Meanwhile, Domm succeeded in getting the Mexican government to grant him a visa, even though he was traveling on a passport of a country where he was not actually a citizen, and Domm covered the plane ticket and accommodations.

Together they recorded a song written by Mario Domm called "Hoja en Blanco" ("Blank Slate"), which became a minor hit around Latin America, and Beja appeared in two different concerts with Domm's band Camila, one in Mexico City and one in Bogotá. "He returned to Colombia a star," says Carolay Morales, who traveled to Mexico with Beja and filmed the entire process.[91]

But international stardom did not change his life completely. He earned some money from the concerts and the song, but neither were enough to catapult him to stardom, and the money was soon gone. Some of that was perhaps his own failure in managing his finances and his fame, but the COVID-19 pandemic that shut down the entertainment industry in Colombia—and much of the world—certainly played a role in limiting the chances he had to build on his initial success. Right as his first single came out, movement was grinding to a painful halt around the world.

Alexander Beja, who once seemed like a rising star, ended up going back to singing on the street as he was before. To be sure, he was often recognized by people and got far better tips than he used to, thanks to the song and the news coverage of his story in Colombian media. "When I go out skateboarding or singing, people recognize me," he says.[92] But he still found himself making a precarious living as a migrant street singer, even if his quality of life had improved after gaining some notoriety.

In 2024, however, he got an important break, even if a very tentative one. A woman he had met sponsored him to start a TikTok Live channel, where he makes money for singing several hours a day, without having to hit the street. He makes a bit more money and avoids some of the dangers and inconveniences of singing on the street. He usually has 50 to 100 people watching at a time, though he once got as high as 10,000 at one time. It is still a modest living, but it is a small step up. "I am going to fight to the end to show the world that art and music are something essential for people too," he says, explaining his commitment to keep singing.[93]

Like many migrants in Latin America and the Caribbean, Beja's fortunes have gotten better over time, but he has never become fully integrated into the local community or joined the formal economy. Beja is moving up in the world, slowly, gradually, inexorably, as migrants often do (and a bit faster than most, no doubt), but even with the magic of exceptional international support and media exposure, he remains in transition.

In many ways, Alexander Beja, despite his instant fame, is an apt representative of the millions of migrants moving throughout the Americas today. Welcomed but not always integrated. Legally accepted but not always included socially. Sometimes celebrated but still marginalized. Migrants and refugees in Latin America and the Caribbean often—but not always—receive better treatment than many migrants and refugees elsewhere in the world, both in terms of legal status and the ability to work and access some public services,[94] but this reception still has its shortcomings in practice both because of state capacity[95] and the stratified nature of the societies themselves.

In addition to explaining the migration policies that governments have pursued in the region and why they have done so, this book tries to understand the particular pattern of reception and integration of migrants in Latin America and the Caribbean today, seen through the lens of the region's unique history with migration. It is true that countries in the region are unusually open to migration and have gone out of their way to provide at least minimum access to services and often legal status to those arriving, but access to legal rights on paper does not always translate into real access to education, healthcare, or legal status in the context of weakly performing institutions that cannot always deliver what they promise and in economies that often depend on informal labor markets.

Even the openness to granting legal status—an undeniably important achievement in Latin American and Caribbean countries vis-à-vis many other regions around the world—means far less in practice when most arriving migrants find themselves working in informal sectors of the economy.[96] It also means that native-born populations often have tangible reasons to worry about the sudden arrival of new people who make claims on already overtaxed public services and join a precarious and largely informal job market.[97]

Given this context, Alexander Beja was ultimately able to overcome some of the barriers to legal access in Colombia, eventually getting his situation regularized and even obtaining a "provisional passport" when he needed it. But becoming a full member of Colombian society or entering the formal economy is a more complex process that could take years—or never happen. And this despite some very special advantages he had along the way. For many other recent migrants, other than a privileged few, the challenges are often even greater. In some ways, the openness of Latin America and Caribbean countries to recent mass migration movements seems unique, but in other ways it follows patterns that would be familiar around the world.

This book is divided into three chapters, which look at South America (chapter 1), Mexico and Central America (chapter 2), and the Caribbean (chapter 3). Each of these subregions within the hemisphere has a slightly different history, significantly different patterns of migration today, and, as a result, a different policy environment that we try to unpack. In the last chapter, we try to draw some early conclusions about the nature of migration policymaking in Latin America and the Caribbean, how and why policy is made, how and why it differs across countries, and whether it is changing over time. And we venture a few tentative answers to the questions on how migrants and destination societies are faring in this new era of migration.

It is our hope that this book helps shed light on these changing migration patterns and on the ways that policies in the region are adapting to address these. And we hope that it puts the policy decisions of Latin American and Caribbean governments and their effects at the center of international discussions on how to address migration policy sensibly.

1 South America

The Weight of Displacement,
the Possibilities of Integration

JUAN CARLOS VILORIA was examining a patient with a cough when the heartbeat he heard from the stethoscope reminded him of moments of anxiety he had in his childhood. It brought back a moment, years before, when he heard his parents arguing about returning to Colombia. Juan's parents, both engineers, had fled Colombia in 1974 due to the violence that engulfed the country and decided to try their luck in Venezuela's booming oil economy next door. Juan was born in Caracas, Venezuela, and he grew up there with a comfortable middle-class life.

But then things began to change again, and, when he was eighteen, in 2009, his parents told him to pack a few things together, mostly clothes, for a journey back to Colombia, a country he barely knew.

Juan threw a few essentials into a bag, including his clothes and a pair of shoes, but then he thought to add in the small blue cup he had used for drinking water when he first started school as a child. "We all had our little cups," he recalled. It was a reminder of the peaceful life that he was leaving behind. Even now that he is a doctor, Juan takes a sip of water from that little blue cup before heading to the hospital for rounds every day, a reminder of the past he had to leave behind.

Colombia and Venezuela, two nations sharing a border but often separated by politics and circumstance, have a history of complex diplomatic interactions. For the most part, Colombians, who were terrified by their country's descent into armed conflict in the 1970s, '80s, and '90s, moved to Venezuela, which was experiencing rapid development fueled by oil exploitation. But then, in the 2000s, a mixture of growing authoritarian control and mismanagement began to poke holes in Venezuela's success right as Colombia began to reduce the power of insurgent groups and drug traffickers that had wreaked havoc on their country.

By the time he was in his teens, Juan was witnessing Venezuela, a once-thriving country, grapple with soaring inflation, shortages of essential goods, and a deteriorating quality of life. The brief boom under President Hugo Chávez, an authoritarian but charismatic leader, had given way to a much less competent administration under his even more authoritarian successor, Nicolás Maduro. Juan's adolescence was marked by the departure of friends and family, other Colombo-Venezuelans; some of them headed back to Colombia and others to the United States or Spain. And he perceived an encroaching specter of insecurity, a growing authoritarian control of government, and the decline of basic services. The social gatherings that used to spill onto the streets had retreated into the confines of homes due to growing unease and insecurity.

It was against this backdrop that Juan's parents made the decision to leave Venezuela. They headed back to Colombia to see whether they could start life over again in their country of origin, the first wave of a growing number of Colombian nationals who gave up on Venezuela and headed back to their homeland or to other countries. But that number would soon increase dramatically.

According to the 2011 Venezuelan Census, there were about 722,000 Colombians living in Venezuela.[1] However, Colombian consulate estimates suggested that the actual number was closer to 1.3 million, highlighting a significant discrepancy between Venezuelan data and Colombian consular estimates. These consular estimates ranked Venezuela as the third most popular destination amongst Colombian immigrants (with the United States and Spain in first and second place, respectively). In addition, Colombia's Migration Agency estimated a "floating" binational population of 4.9 million individuals in 2015, a population that lived in one of the two countries but moved regularly back and forth across the border for work, study, or other activities.

In the intricate tapestry of human migration, there are moments etched in history that change the course of countless lives. The year 2015 marked such a moment in the heart of South America because the Venezuelan government decided to expel Colombians living inside its territory. The immediate cause was a skirmish between Venezuelan soldiers and Colombian paramilitaries along the shared border, but the underlying reason was that the regime in Caracas was losing control of the economy, with inflation beginning to spiral out of control, and Colombian immigrants became useful scapegoats.[2]

Venezuelan President Maduro declared a state of emergency, indefinitely closing the border with Colombia, and then deported thousands of Colombians. During this process, the Venezuelan Army marked houses with a *D* for deportation, and overnight, thousands of immigrants living in the state of Táchira, Venezuela, near the Colombian border, found themselves either crossing the Simón Bolívar River or using alternative dirt routes known as *trochas*.

People carried their bags, and sometimes mattresses and electronic devices, across the rivers and bridges to return to Colombia. Tents were set up at the border to provide nonfood items, and the newspapers were filled with images of desperation. President Maduro's actions drew criticism from human rights groups, international organizations, and foreign governments. The crisis resulted in separated families and Colombians in search of refuge, food, and shelter.

The deportations of 2015 were not isolated events, and they set in motion a chain reaction that reshaped the dynamics of migration in the region. The borderland, once a place of thriving commercial ties and cultural exchange between the two countries, was now transformed into a corridor through which people fled from desperation. The vast majority of Colombians living in Venezuela left the country, even if they had not yet been marked for deportation. Juan's family had anticipated this crisis by leaving a few years earlier, but suddenly their neighborhood in Barranquilla, Colombia, where they had returned, was filling up with other Colombians who were forced out of Venezuela too.

In 2021, the Colombian government estimated that approximately 980,000 Colombians had returned to Colombia from Venezuela, a handful before the 2015 crisis and most immediately afterwards. In some cases, these returnees brought with them children who were born in Venezuela, like Juan, some of whom had never even set foot in Colombia before.[3]

Migrating to Colombia was heart-wrenching for Juan, who had not spent much time there, though he was a dual citizen of Venezuela and Colombia since his parents were Colombian citizens. But he eventually landed on his feet and today is a doctor and a local community leader in Barranquilla on Colombia's Caribbean coast. "My relocation was not as traumatic as it was for many others," Juan admits. "Thanks to my dual citizenship and my parents' foresight, I was able to have my degrees officially certified and acquire a Colombian passport among other [personal identification] documents. Nevertheless, the emotional toll was heavy. I wept, time and again. Every day that has gone by, I've found myself longing for my home country, yearning for the companionship of my friends, and mourning the life I had to leave behind."[4]

But the migration of Colombians living in Venezuela back to their country of origin in 2015 was just the tipping point of a much bigger migration about to happen that would reshape South America more than any other population movement in decades.

When Jacqueline Perdomo and her partner Marcial first arrived in Santiago, Chile, in 2017, they began to realize how hard their exile would be. They had lived a comfortable life in Venezuela, and even though things had started to collapse around them, they had been largely immune to the chaos. The country's currency was devalued repeatedly, losing almost all its value, and prices of even the most basic goods spiked, with inflation reaching an astounding 130,000 percent in 2018.[5] Although subsequent years saw lower inflation rates, these remained alarmingly high, and meanwhile healthcare services began to implode as doctors and nurses fled the country, and medicines were suddenly in short supply.

According to an IMF study, Venezuela's economic collapse is one of the two most significant contractions of an economy in the past half century, and one of only three that are not directly tied to war, a violent change in government, or the collapse of the Soviet Union.[6] Fluctuations in oil prices, the country's main export, along with an explosive cocktail of corruption, mismanagement, and political conflict, took their toll on the well-being of Venezuelans.

An increasingly authoritarian regime under President Chávez became even more so under his successor, President Maduro, who tightened government controls on free speech and cracked down on protests. The United States, European Union, and other governments imposed crippling economic sanctions on oil exports, while government leaders and a small elite close to them extracted the country's wealth for their own benefit. Venezuelans protested in the streets, the regime tightened its grip on power, and political tensions rose to a boiling point in the period 2017 to 2020.[7] In Cucuta, Colombia, and later in other cities of the country, displaced Venezuelans sold colorful purses and wallets made out of Venezuelan bolívares, the currency that was so devalued it was no longer worth anything except as cheap material for handicrafts.

Despite this chaos, Jacqueline and her husband, who both worked for the national telecommunications company, continued to have a fairly decent middle-class life, even if the scarcity around them began to be felt. Unlike Juan Carlos's family, they did not have another country to move to, and they did not see a reason to move, since they were somewhat insulated from the chaos around them. But that was until she accidentally fell afoul of forces in the government she did not fully understand.

Jacqueline was in charge of building telecommunications infrastructure in some of the country's poorest communities, and in one project she began to discover that the cables they were installing were being stolen. The copper wire inside the cables was valuable, and someone was making off with entire rolls of cable at night. Jacqueline stopped the installation, ordered the cables locked up, and began to investigate what was going on, with help from the Venezuela military.

A few weeks later, a vice admiral in the Venezuelan Navy, with whom she had developed a friendship, called her and told her that she needed to get out of the country. He confessed that elements in the military, including some of the same ones who were supposedly helping her in the investigation, were behind the theft of the cables. They were taking the cables, melting down the copper inside them, and then shipping them to Curaçao for sale on the international market. The vice admiral warned her that she had gotten on the wrong side of some very dangerous people in her efforts to investigate the theft, and that they had a very specific and detailed plan to kill her. "You have a week to leave the country," he warned her.

Within forty-eight hours, she and Marcial took their US$1,800 in savings and bought two plane tickets to Chile. Even though they did not have any strong ties there, they were certain that with their educational and professional credentials and some money in their pockets, things would work out well, and they could send for their children and grandchild soon.

But they soon realized that what was left of their savings after purchasing the plane tickets would not last long in Chile. "My professional title wasn't worth anything, and the money wasn't worth anything either," she says, as she remembers that time. They avoided becoming homeless only because of the charity of a Chilean woman, who decided to give them temporary lodging. They were eventually able to get jobs working at toll booths in the southern city of Talca.

Over half a million Venezuelans have moved to Chile, almost all since 2015, when the crisis in Venezuela deepened. The first to arrive were people like Jacqueline and Marcial, who had college degrees and professional careers, and they were followed in later years by others who had less education but an equally strong drive to start over. A few left Venezuela on airplanes, but many others took a several-day journey through Colombia, Ecuador, and Peru, sometimes on public buses and other times managing to get free transportation on shuttles set up by international organizations that were trying to facilitate the passage of Venezuelans fleeing their country. Some even left on foot, as Jacqueline vividly recalls the images from the news, describing it as an exodus of biblical proportions. Most arrived with next to nothing and had to restart their lives from zero.

Overall, the Venezuelans who arrived in Chile had fairly high human capital. Almost three-quarters of those who had arrived by 2019 had either college or technical degrees,[8] far higher than the Chilean population on average, even if some of those arriving later were not quite as highly educated. In fact, Venezuelan migrants tend to be more educated, on average, than the native-born population in many countries in South America, including not only in Chile but also Ecuador, Peru, Argentina, and Uruguay. This is partly thanks to the high overall average level of educational attainment among Venezuelans before the displacement crisis and partly because those Venezuelans who made it further than neighboring countries were often those with slightly more resources and connections to migrants who had left earlier (and were likely to be professionals).[9] In the neighboring country of Colombia, Venezuelans migrants had similar levels of educational attainment as the native-born population, and in Brazil, another neighboring country, a slightly lower level.

But as Jacqueline and Marcial soon learned, even with professional careers behind them, migration meant starting anew in a different country. It was almost impossible for immigrants to get their professional degrees from another country recognized in Chile—or most countries in the region—or even to open a bank account or obtain a driver's license. And getting legal immigration status took time.

The Chilean government at first allowed anyone with a formal sector job to apply for an employment-based residence visa. However, in 2018, the rules changed, requiring migrants to secure employment before arriving in Chile, making the process considerably more difficult. The government would later carry out regularization campaigns in 2020 and 2022 to provide legal status to those who were already living in the country so that by late 2022, roughly three-quarters of Venezuelans who had arrived before then had managed to obtain some sort of legal status, with almost half having permanent residence.[10] However, many others, especially some of the more recent arrivals, remain in legal limbo.

Chilean law allows all children to attend public school free of charge, from primary through secondary school, regardless of their legal immigration status, which helped Jacqueline's young grandson begin his studies shortly after arriving. However, for many Venezuelan families, navigating this system proved challenging. Schoolchildren in Chile need to have a unique national identification number to enroll, as well as to receive any public benefits, like free lunches, that they may be entitled to. While the Chilean education ministry eventually created a separate school identification number that allowed children who did not have a national identification to enroll, this process took time. Even now, it does not provide access to certain benefits, meaning migrant children in some poorer communities are often the only ones bringing their own lunches, as they cannot participate in free meal programs.[11]

These modifications and challenges are not unique to Chile. Across the region, countries like Peru, Ecuador, and Colombia have had to adapt their education systems to integrate irregular migrants and those who have temporary legal status. In Colombia's La Guajira Department, for instance, a teacher at an ethnic school shared the difficult reality of rationing lunches, sometimes deciding which students will eat or splitting portions to accommodate the number of children in her class.[12] These stories reflect the broader strain that large-scale migration places on public resources and the difficult choices educators face in ensuring equitable access for all in the absence of government responses.

At the same time, Chilean government officials, under different administrations, have gradually extended health coverage to migrant families, starting at first with emergency services and medical attention for pregnant mothers and small children.[13]

Chile had once been a major country receiving migrants from abroad. Spanish, German, British, and Slovakian immigrants were encouraged to settle in the late nineteenth and early twentieth centuries, and Chile has the largest Palestinian descent community anywhere outside the Middle East. There was an intentional policy to colonize the country's south in the late 1800s and early 1990s, and immigrants were welcome, especially if they were European and white.[14] But by the late twentieth century, migration had slowed, and immigrants made up about 2 percent of the population in 2010, almost all citizens of Peru, Bolivia, and Argentina, the three neighboring countries.

The arrival of Venezuelan migrants—and a few hundred thousand Haitians, who arrived around the same time—began to transform the country. Migration policy, which had been an afterthought for more than a half-century, suddenly became politically important again. And this did not mean just visa and border policy but also issues of access to education, healthcare, housing, and financial services, all of which were set up only for those who had national identification numbers.

Jacqueline eventually learned to navigate the system. She and her husband managed to secure their legal documents, which allowed them to open a small stand selling empanadas. Slowly, they saved enough to rent a modest storefront, expanding their business to sell imported goods to immigrant families—not just Venezuelans, but also Colombians, Haitians, Peruvians, Bolivians, and others. As time passed, their business grew into a bustling enterprise, providing them with a stable income and a path to rebuilding the decent life they once knew.

And they helped start a local Venezuelan self-help organization, Migrants in Maule—the name of the region where Talca is located—which was dedicated to helping later arrivals from Venezuela and other countries obtain legal documents and get back on their feet. Juan Carlos Viloria, as a medical school student in Barranquilla, had done something similar in his new hometown. These were among the dozens of self-help organizations of Venezuelan immigrants and refugees that sprang up across Latin America and the Caribbean after 2015 to help recent arrivals. Through a course sponsored by the International Organization for Migration (IOM), several of these organizations got to know each other and, with help from the Organization of American States

(OAS), launched an international group called the Coalition for Venezuela that today spans dozens of countries around the world.

In many ways, the experience of Jacqueline's family is a huge success. They left Venezuela in precarious and dangerous circumstances but eventually got back on their feet in Chile. They are legally present, thanks to the country's relatively welcoming policies that extended legal documents to them. They run thriving businesses, and their grandson is even getting a good education in Chilean schools.

But this seeming parity masked enormous differences between some of the earlier arrivals, like Jacqueline, who are now thriving, and migrants who have arrived more recently and often still struggle to survive. And for Haitians, there remains a vast difference in income with Venezuelans, on average. According to data from the Chilean Ministry of Social Development and Family, the average monthly income of Venezuelan migrants in 2020 was 512,000 pesos (US$562), while Haitians received an average of 397,918 pesos (US$438).[15] And Haitians are far more likely to report experiences of discrimination as well.[16] In a country that once privileged whiteness in its immigration policies, this gap is hardly surprising and highlights the little-discussed but constantly present role of skin color in social relations in Latin America.[17]

Today, immigrants make up 9 percent of Chile's population, which is an increase of more than fourfold since 2010 when immigrants made up 2 percent of the population. Venezuelans compose almost a third of the 1.5 million immigrants in Chile, and they are the largest and most recent group to arrive in large numbers. In contrast, around 180,000 Haitian immigrants live in Chile according to its last census which was published in early 2021.[18]

"I know I'm never going back to Venezuela," says Jacqueline, pointing out that she still receives threats from some of the same people in the Venezuelan military who once had wanted to kill her. But she is thankful for the new life she has built in Chile. And while she has been able to keep her country and its traditions alive through both her store and the work she does with other Venezuelan immigrants, she knows that her grandson is growing up culturally Chilean.

———————————

In 2010, most countries in South America had very few immigrants, usually well under 2 percent of the total population, and few had thought much about their migration policies. Instead, as with Central America and Mexico, most migration in the late twentieth and early twenty-first centuries had been to destinations outside of Latin America and the Caribbean.

South American immigrants were almost evenly split between the United States and Europe. Unlike in the Caribbean, Central America, and Mexico, where most migrants headed to the United States and Canada (see chapters 2 and 3), South American migrants often had Europe, especially Spain and Portugal, as important destinations (table 1.1).[19] There was also some migration within the region, with Argentina and Venezuela as the principal destinations.[20]

But by 2023, the panorama had changed. For the first time in decades, most South American countries had large immigrant populations, usually somewhere between 4 to 6 percent of their population (table 1.2), with Chile closer to 9 percent and Brazil and Bolivia with a smaller percentage of their population born abroad. And all countries were struggling to figure out how to build the right foundations for their migration policies.

TABLE 1.1   South American Emigrant Population, Share, and Top Countries of Destination, 2020.

	Total Population	Emigrant Population	Emigrant Share	Top 3 Countries of Destination
Argentina	45,036,032	1,076,148	2%	Spain, United States, Chile
Bolivia	11,936,162	927,244	8%	Argentina, Spain, Chile
Brazil	213,196,304	1,897,128	1%	United States, Japan, Portugal
Chile	19,300,315	643,800	3%	Argentina, United States, Spain
Colombia	50,930,663	3,024,273	6%	Venezuela, United States, Spain
Ecuador	17,588,596	1,127,891	6%	Spain, United States, Italy
Paraguay	6,618,695	896,484	14%	Argentina, Spain, Brazil
Peru	33,304,756	1,519,635	5%	United States, Chile, Spain
Uruguay	3,429,087	367,060	11%	Argentina, Spain, United States
Venezuela	28,490,454	5,415,337	19%	Colombia, Peru, Chile

Source: Authors' tabulations of data from the United Nations' Department of Economic and Social Affairs, Population Division, "International Migrant Stock 2020: Destination and Origin," accessed September 23, 2024, https://www.un.org/development/desa/pd/content/international-migrant-stock.

TABLE 1.2 Immigrant Population in South America, by Country, 2023.

	Total Population	Immigrants	Immigrant Share
Total	431,530,048	14,558,764	3%
Argentina	45,036,032	2,269,383	5%
Bolivia	11,936,162	174,764	1%
Brazil	213,196,304	1,399,661	1%
Chile	19,300,315	1,654,177	9%
Colombia	50,930,663	2,982,435	6%
Ecuador	17,588,596	840,704	5%
Paraguay	6,618,695	174,801	3%
Peru	33,304,756	1,824,634	5%
Uruguay	3,429,087	126,298	4%
Venezuela	28,490,454	1,324,193	5%

Notes: To illustrate the extent of Venezuelan mobility across Latin America and the Caribbean in recent years, immigrant stock for 2023 combines 2020 population estimates of non-Venezuelan immigrants from the UN Department of Economic and Social Affairs (UNDESA) with 2023 estimates of Venezuelan refugees, migrants, and asylum seekers from the Inter-Agency Coordination Platform for Refugees and Migrants from Venezuela (R4V). While UNDESA methodology relies primarily on population censuses and some representative surveys to produce estimates, R4V estimates are based on a diverse set of government databases and therefore do not necessarily imply individual identification nor registration of each individual. Government sources may undercount immigrants who are in vulnerable conditions or are difficult to survey, like immigrants in irregular status. Because of methodological differences and ongoing improvements across government databases, these estimates are regularly updated and can vary. Sources: Authors' calculations based on population data estimates from UN DESA "International Migrant Stock 2020: Destination and Origin," https://www.un.org/development/desa/pd/content/international -migrant-stock, and R4V, "Refugees and Migrants from Venezuela," updated November 2023, https://www.r4v.info/en/document/r4v-latin-america-and-caribbean-venezuelan-refugees-and -migrants-region-nov-2023.

What made this all the more pressing was that a vast majority of the rising migration across South America was driven by displacement crises, especially from Venezuela, which had once been one of the top two destinations. There was a lot of other migration taking place in South America, of course, but the size, scale, and speed of displacement from Venezuela, accompanied to a lesser extent by displacement from Haiti after the 2010 earthquakes, made this a dominant focus. Venezuelans alone accounted for 71 percent of all new migrants in South America between 2010 and 2022, and Venezuelans and Haitians together accounted for 76 percent, just over three-quarters.[21]

Since 2015, roughly 7.9 million Venezuelans, about a quarter of Venezuela's population, have left, with 82 percent of them moving to other countries in South America. Nearly half of them, around 2.9 million, are in Colombia, with around 1.6 million in Peru, and around a half million each in Brazil, Chile, and Ecuador, a quarter million in Argentina, and slightly smaller numbers in the remaining countries, Uruguay, Paraguay, and Bolivia (table 1.3). The exodus that began with Colombians, like Juan Carlos Viloria, leaving Venezuela, many of them explicitly forced out by the government, was followed by a mass departure of Venezuelans, like Jacqueline Perdomo, fleeing their own country as political conflict escalated and living standards cratered.

Of course, not all immigration in South America is the result of displacement. Venezuelans are a significant percentage everywhere, but they are only a majority of the foreign-born population in Colombia, Peru, and, just by a little, Ecuador. In Brazil, the half million Venezuelans are only a third of the 2.2 million foreign-born residents in that country,[22] with significant numbers from other neighboring countries, such as Bolivia and Paraguay, as well, as well Portugal and Angola, which share a common language and colonial ties. In Argentina, 65 percent of the country's 3 million immigrants are from the neighboring countries of Paraguay, Bolivia, Chile, Uruguay, and Brazil, with a full half from just Paraguay and Bolivia. However, Venezuelan migrants do compose the largest group by far in South America, even if they are not the only immigrant population everywhere.

Betzabeth Jarramillo, a Venezuelan democracy leader who fled Caracas for Quito, Ecuador, after the government ransacked her house and arrested her father, remembers watching vast caravans of people walking from Venezuela across the continent. At one point, over 200 Venezuelans set out on foot each day from the border, aiming to reach their final destinations, whether in Co-

TABLE 1.3   Venezuelan Immigrants in Select South American Countries, 2023.

Country	Immigrant Population
Argentina	165,616
Bolivia	18,715
Brazil	626,885
Chile	532,715
Colombia	2,808,968
Ecuador	444,778
Paraguay	5,580
Peru	1,662,889
Uruguay	41,116

Source: R4V, "Refugees and Migrants from Venezuela," updated November 2023, https://www.r4v .info/en/document/r4v-latin-america-and-caribbean-venezuelan-refugees-and-migrants-region -nov-2023.

lombian cities or other countries in the region. One study conducted in July 2018 found that Venezuelans leaving the border on foot walked an average of sixteen hours a day, typically for thirteen days overall.[23] Some walked because they lacked the required documentation to fly into neighboring countries legally, while others simply could not afford bus fares.

More than 90 percent slept on the streets at some point during their journey, a story that deeply resonates with Betzabeth, who herself had spent several nights living on the street in Ecuador, sharing the experiences with other Venezuelans who were forced to sleep on cold stone benches with hunger gnawing at them. The Red Cross, the International Organization for Migration (IOM), and the United Nations High Commissioner for Refugees (UNHCR), set up tents along the continent's highways in countries like Colombia, Ecuador, and Peru. Hundreds of Venezuelans stopped by each day to drink water, have a meal, rest, and make phone calls. Sometimes they could even get a new pair of shoes to replace the ones they had worn down by walking so far over mountainous territory.

Still other Venezuelans, mostly from the eastern part of the country, crossed into the state of Roraima in northern Brazil, where UNHCR, in coordination with the Brazilian federal government, established ten shelters housing over 4,000 Venezuelans. In two of the shelters, hundreds of Warao Indigenous community members slept in colorful hammocks and prepared their own meals with provided supplies. In others, Venezuelan citizens from across the country received three meals a day and slept in white tents or special refugee housing units, an image reminiscent of refugee camps elsewhere in the world but unprecedented in recent years in Latin America.[24]

In other countries, though, there were no refugee camps. Instead, Venezuelans moved into local communities and started their lives anew, finding work, trying to put their children in schools, and trying to get legal status. It is hard to underestimate how radical a departure this is from most other displacement crises around the world, where countries house refugees in special camps, often permanently, and delegate their care and feeding—and often their legal status—to the international community, generally through UNHCR.[25] The response in South America marks a significant departure in one of the world's largest displacement crises and may, as a result, hold lessons for other regions in the future.[26]

At the same time, the Venezuelan displacement crisis would transform South American countries from mostly emigrant societies to major destination countries for immigrants. And it forced governments across the continent to figure out what their migration policies should be, often in an ad hoc manner as they responded to real events on the ground.

When Roxana del Aguila took over as head of the Peruvian migration agency in 2018, she was relatively new to the issues involved. A career public servant, she had spent most of her time innovating online processes for the country's census bureau and other agencies before she was suddenly elevated to run the migration agency.

Right as she took over the agency, Roxana found herself confronted by the arrival of tens of thousands of Venezuelans. The Peruvian president at the time, Pedro Pablo Kuczynski, was leading a regional effort to address the situation in Venezuela and wanted to show solidarity with those who fled the regime. "He wanted to give residency to all of them," says Roxana, so she drew up the first regularization program specifically for Venezuelans, known as a Temporary Stay Permit (PTP, in Spanish).[27]

The PTP was not a visa but rather a special status created by executive decree that allowed Venezuelan migrants to remain legally for a year, work, and enroll their children in school. It involved an online application, so it was relatively easy and inexpensive to set up and run, building on Roxana's passion for information technology. And eventually they managed to integrate the required police background check via Interpol into the review process so that migrants did not have to get a separate document from Interpol first.

But there was another problem. To apply for the permit, Venezuelans had to enter the country legally, and few had passports. So, Roxana worked with the Foreign Ministry to set up an asylum office in the main northern entry point to the country, and migrants who did not have passports were directed to apply for asylum at the port of entry, which then allowed them to enter the country legally and apply for the Temporary Stay Permit. Peru soon had one of the largest asylum caseloads in the world, over a half million pending cases, but only around 10,000 of the applications had even been reviewed by the end of 2023.[28] The asylum system was used primarily as an entry point with the Temporary Stay Permit becoming the de facto way that they could get legal status.[29]

Over the next five years, Roxana implemented multiple versions of the Temporary Stay Permit, and many immigrants eventually received a permanent status. But she also worked for four different presidents and eleven interior ministers, and priorities changed with each shift in national leadership. She managed to keep the temporary permit programs alive by flying under the radar and successfully navigating the country's Byzantine bureaucratic and political conflicts. On one hand, Peru's fairly open response to the arrival of displaced Venezuelans persisted. On the other hand, it never again attained much high-level political attention, which limited the possibilities for expanding or innovating the original measure.

It also meant that the migration agency was not able to get additional funds from Congress to implement the regularization programs. So to be able to carry out these efforts, the migration agency had to build efficiencies, including developing new technologies and processes. Roxana hired a team of engineers to create an entirely new workflow, which included options for applicants to submit data and documents online with key questions asked up front and biometric information checked across other databases in real time. Eventually applicants could even get their final decision and their legal documents by downloading them from an online system, rather than having to stand in line at the migration office. The migration agency, which had been a largely forgotten agency inside the Peruvian government, quickly pushed itself to do more with the same resources and became much more sophisticated than ever before. And since government funds were in short supply, Roxana struck a partnership with IOM, UNHCR, and other international organizations to help supply computers, software, and other key resources needed to make the programs work.

Across several South American countries, this same story played out in different ways. Migration agencies, which had been minor agencies within governments, suddenly had to play an outsized role, often with limited experience or resources. And they adapted and innovated, to different degrees, by automating processes and getting outside help from international organizations. Migration went from a largely secondary field within South American governments to an increasingly important element within public policy.

At the same time, the political support for Venezuelan immigrants and refugees in Peru would gradually fade, as it became politically a more visible and increasingly sensitive issue. The government eventually imposed a visa requirement on Venezuelans that tried to make it harder for them to cross the border irregularly, though the measure did not stop migration flows since the border is fairly easy to cross between ports of entry. And any hope of creating a broader national policy around integration largely disappeared, although some local governments stepped into the breach to address this. "There is still no policy on effective integration" of immigrants, she notes.

In Colombia, next door to Venezuela, the response played out somewhat differently, even if it looked very similar at first. Colombia received an even larger number of Venezuelans, eventually around 2.9 million, nearly twice the number as Peru, and millions more passed through Colombia on their way to other countries in the region. Colombian public opinion was originally quite supportive of receiving Venezuelan migrants, given the close ties between the two countries and the hundreds of thousands of Colombians who had lived in Venezuela when Colombia was in the midst of internal conflict and Venezuela's oil industry was booming.

The Colombian administration of President Juan Manuel Santos implemented a similar measure to Peru's temporary permit, called the Special Stay Permit (PEP), that granted two years of right to remain and work in the country, which was also renewable. Originally it was only for those who entered legally with a passport, but it was later extended to all Venezuelans in the country. The government would carry out six different Special Stay Permit registrations over a three-year period, addressing different groups that had come in regularly or not, and at different periods, and eventually covering over 700,000 Venezuelan immigrants.[30]

Policymakers considered using the asylum system or establishing a special visa for Venezuelan arrivals, but both options presented political and logistical obstacles. Either would be an open-ended invitation for Venezuelans to come to Colombia, which was politically difficult to do, and neither seemed feasible in practice. The asylum system, run by the Foreign Ministry, had limited capacity, and the Foreign Ministry was particularly skeptical about trying to expand asylum. Trying to pass legislation was a long process that would require significant negotiations among political leaders and multiple steps in Colombia's complex legislative process. The Special Stay Permits, implemented through presidential decree, allowed for a rapid, efficient, and politically sustainable alternative. And international organizations, funded by the U.S., Canadian, and European governments, helped cover many of the costs of the measures implemented, with UNCHR and IOM playing important advisory roles.

In contrast to Peru where governments and ministers came and went every few months, in Colombia the government was significantly more stable and successive administrations decided to maintain and even expand its policy. In December 2021, the next administration, under President Eván Duque, decided to expand the policy by offering a ten-year permit instead of the usual two-year option. According to Lucas Gómez, who served as President Duque's coordinator for migration at the time, Duque "was clear that they shouldn't do what was popular but what was right" and that it made sense to offer a ten-year status rather than force people to renew every two years. This was far more efficient, gave migrants a longer time horizon to plan their lives, and would allow for some to move into permanent residency through employment or marriage in the meantime.[31]

The subsequent administration of President Gustavo Petro, maintained the measure and extended the entry date to encourage more applicants. By summer 2024, there were close to 2.3 million Venezuelans who had the ten-year permit and several hundred thousand more who were awaiting a final decision.[32] Other

Venezuelans had obtained residency permits, through their work or marriage to Colombian citizens, so there remained only a relatively small number of recent arrivals, estimated at around 350,000, with no legal documents.[33]

Ecuador too pursued a series of regularization programs, at least three different programs at different times, while perhaps a hundred thousand or so Venezuelans obtained residency visas over time, which were available until 2022 to citizens of any South American country but were quite expensive.[34]

Meanwhile, Argentina and Uruguay, which received fewer and generally more middle-class Venezuelans, used special visas that are extended by law to all South Americans as part of their affiliation with Mercosur, a regional mobility agreement started by those two countries with Brazil and Paraguay. Although Venezuela is officially suspended from Mercosur, the Argentinian and Uruguayan governments decided to recognize Venezuelans as eligible for these visas, which are open to all South Americans, and which provide easy access to temporary and eventually permanent status.

The former Director of Migration in Argentina, Alfredo López Rita, notes that "there was no capacity in the asylum system . . . and it could no longer respond" to the number of applications of Venezuelans who were arriving in the country after 2016. However, the Argentinean government still recognized Venezuela as a member of Mercosur for purposes of trade, mobility, and other specific areas of agreement, even though the Venezuelan government no longer had voting rights in the bloc. As a result, the migration agency was able to offer Venezuelans the option of applying for the Mercosur temporary residence visa instead, which also allowed for permanent residence after two years. This only required them to prove their Venezuelan nationality, which most could do easily, and the process became much faster and more secure.[35]

Brazil, meanwhile, created a special residence visa for Venezuelans and citizens of other neighboring countries that were not part of Mercosur, which allowed them to live for two years as temporary residents and then transition to permanent residency. It granted the recipients all the same rights, at least on paper, to public services that Brazilians have, even if migrants sometimes faced specific challenges in practice. And the Brazilian asylum system issued a decision in 2019 recognizing all Venezuelans as refugees, under the Cartagena Declaration definition of a refugee (see the introduction), which allowed Venezuelan migrants to choose which path they preferred.[36] By the end of 2023, far more had received temporary residency (229,000) than asylum (50,000 recognized), but both were viable options.[37]

Brazil initiated Operação Acolhida (Operation Welcome) in 2019, a forward-thinking program aimed at relocating Venezuelans from camps to regions with more promising labor markets. Since January 2017, when recordkeeping began, up until April 2023, this program has not only facilitated the integration of over 100,000 displaced Venezuelans by matching them with labor opportunities but also signaled a shift towards a more comprehensive state policy.[38] Operation Welcome, supported by international cooperation and implemented through federal, state, and municipal collaborations, has evolved into a national policy that has persevered despite changes in administrations. It is built on three pillars: comprehensive border management, provision of basic necessities and services in border cities, and encouragement of voluntary relocation to areas within Brazil that offer greater economic and integration prospects.

Even before the Venezuelan displacement, Haitians had begun arriving in Brazil, leaving their country following the economic and political crisis that resulted from the 2010 earthquake. The Brazilian government, with support from Chile, had led the UN peacekeeping force that had been in Haiti in the period from 2004 to 2017, and this had led to expanded significant ties between the two countries. In 2011, the Brazilian government extended a special humanitarian residence permit to Haitian citizens who had moved to Brazil and lacked legal immigration status, which gave them the right to stay and work for five years. In 2012, the government decided to make a humanitarian visa available to those who applied at a Brazilian consulate before arriving. Several tens of thousands Haitians received either the humanitarian residence permit or the humanitarian visa during the 2010s.[39] By 2022, there were around 80,000 Haitians in Brazil and around 180,000 in Chile, with much smaller numbers in other countries.[40]

The reasons that governments in the region offered immigrants legal status are complex. Early on, there were strong feelings of solidarity with Venezuelans who were arriving among the general public in most countries, both as fellow Latin Americans, but also because of Venezuela's generosity to citizens of other countries who had moved there during periods of crisis in earlier decades. In Brazil and Chile, the relationship with Haiti through the UN peacekeeping mission undoubtedly had a similar effect. And for some governments, including those in Peru and Colombia (and perhaps also Brazil, Argentina, Chile, and Ecuador, at different moments), the decision to welcome Venezuelans also reflected their opposition to the regime in Venezuela. Solidarity, familiarity, and geopolitics all blended together.

The history of relatively liberal laws for residency certainly helped in some countries, including Argentina, Uruguay, and Brazil, which used or adapted existing authorities to grant legal status.[41] The spirit, if not the letter, of the Cartagena Declaration perhaps also influenced normative ideas about protection, even if most countries other than Brazil did not use asylum to do it.[42] Asylum systems were too underdeveloped in most countries to serve as an effective response mechanism, and offering refugee status automatically to all Venezuelans would have been politically complicated, but governments found ways of responding to the ethos of the Cartagena Declaration through other means.

And, of course, there was also a strong element of pragmatism, with governments realizing that it would be easier to have a population that was legally present, known to the authorities, and did not compete unfairly in the labor market as unauthorized immigrant workers. After all, the Venezuelans were already there, so it was a question of whether they stayed legally or not. And most countries in South America recognized that they had very little capacity to carry out border control if migrants were determined to circumvent official controls.

In most countries, since migration was not a significant politically divisive topic at the start of the displacement crisis, technical and political leadership within executive branches also made a significant difference. Bureaucratic entrepreneurs like Roxana del Aguila in Peru, Alfredo López Rita in Argentina, and Lucas Gómez in Colombia carried enormous weight in making decisions on what to do and shepherding the measures that were implemented through changes in administrations.[43] Many of these measures were not the result of major political decisions at high levels of governments—with the clear exception of Colombia's ten-year permit—but rather decisions made by heads of agencies and presidential advisors, sometimes with sign-off at the highest levels.

And the role of the international community mattered too. UNHCR and IOM helped provide resources, technical expertise, and political support in implementing these temporary measures, especially through a shared platform called the Interagency Coordinating Platform for Venezuelan Refugees and Migrants (also known as the Response for Venezuelans, R4V), financed by international donors. International donors also made the regularization programs feasible financially in several cases. And governments that implemented pathways to legal status often received significant positive attention for their efforts in the international community. And the creation of a shared platform among countries receiving Venezuelan migrants and refugees, the Quito Process, helped create peer pressure and even some competition among governments to grant entry and legal status to Venezuelans.

Not all Venezuelans and Haitians who emigrated to countries in South America received a legal immigration status, but a vast majority did (see table 1.4). However, many remained in temporary statuses that had no clear

TABLE 1.4 Estimates of Legal Status Measures in Select South American Countries Hosting Venezuelan Immigrants, 2023.

Country	Principal Measures for Legal Status	Population Affected as of December, 2023 (or date indicated)
Argentina	Mercosur Visas	337,000 (June 2022)
	Refugee Recognition	300 (June 2023)
Brazil	Temporary Residency Permits	229,000
	Refugee Recognition	50,000 (June 2023)
Chile	Regularization Programs	158,200
	Visas	681,000
	Refugee Recongition	30 (June 2023)
Colombia	Regularization Programs	1,627,000 (10-year permits)
	Visas	90,000
	Refugee Recognition	1,300 (June 2023)
Ecuador	Regularization Programs	92,000
	Visas	150,000
	Refugee Recognition	1,100 (June 2023)
Peru	Regularization Programs	709,000 (April 2023)
	Visas	37,000 (April 2023)
	Refugee Recognition	4,000 (June 2023)
Uruguay	Mercosur Visas	20,329 (December 2022)
	Refugee Recognition	500 (June 2023)

Source: Luciana Gandini and Andrew Selee, *Betting on Legality: Latin America and Caribbean Responses to the Venezuelan Displacement Crisis* (Washington, DC: Migration Policy Institute, May 2023), https://www.migrationpolicy.org/research/latin-american-caribbean-venezuelan-crisis.

pathway to permanence, even as it became increasingly evident that most displaced immigrants would likely never return to their countries of origin. Yet, immigrants would find that they faced other daunting challenges in starting their lives anew in these countries too, even if they had legal status.

Indeed, the generally open response to those immigrants moving throughout the region, however, does not mean that there are not significant tensions that underneath these decisions nor that their implementation is free of conflict.

While studies suggest that the arrival of immigrants is helping drive economic growth in the receiving countries, there were immediate impacts on public service expenditures, especially education and healthcare.[44] In most countries, immigrants entered into education and healthcare systems that were already short-staffed and insufficiently resourced, creating additional strains on public services.[45] Native-born residents in communities where immigrants arrived, who already worried about overcrowded classrooms and long waiting times at clinics and in hospital emergency rooms, were not always convinced that the added burdens on these systems was worth it.

The same is true of the shock to the wages of some workers. Studies in the United States show that normal migration patterns have limited impacts on the wages of the native-born, though much depends on whether immigrant workers who arrive are complements or substitutes for native-born workers. In other words, if the arriving workers bring different skills than the native-born, they tend to complement them so that the labor force becomes more productive overall, but if they have the same skills (as at least some part of the labor force) they are more likely to displace some workers, at least in the short term.[46] And studies in selected South American countries indicate that the increase in migration over the past few years is likely to boost economic growth in coming years.[47]

But there are also labor market studies in Brazil, Colombia, and Peru,[48] which suggest that there was some short-term shock to wages and employment for some workers in these countries, especially to those working in the informal economy, during the arrival of large numbers of immigrants, especially those from Venezuela who arrived in large numbers over a short period of time.[49] While these effects generally last from two to four years—the economy gradually expands allowing different workers to recover their employment and wage levels, and perhaps even increase earnings—in the short-term, the lowest wage workers may have faced some real loss in income, at least in certain cities and towns. And while migrants in South America, including Venezuelans, are generally more educated than the native-born population, they can rarely employ their full skills when they arrive, since they need to get their professional or technical education degrees recognized in the new country.[50] Adding to this, the arrival of the largest number of Venezuelan migrants happened right before the global recession caused by the COVID-19 pandemic, so migrant workers were entering the labor force right as it was contracting.[51]

In addition, the rise in migration has coincided with a period of rising crime rates, especially visible forms of violent crime, in several countries in South America, especially Chile and Ecuador and, to a lesser extent, Brazil, Colombia, and Peru. Shifting patterns in the cocaine trade and disputes among organized crime groups appear to be at the root of most of the violence.[52] In fact, the available studies all show that migrants actually have a lower arrest and conviction rate than the native-born, especially for violent crimes, in these countries.[53] However, it is also true that Venezuelan organized crime groups, especially the most visible one in South America, known as Tren de Aragua, have established a visible presence in some countries, especially Chile, Ecuador, and Peru, and that they are involved in some of the high-impact crimes that have captured public attention.[54] As a result, it may be no surprise that average citizens in some countries conflate the rise in violent crime with the rise in migration, even if empirically one is not actually related to the other.

Migration always creates some pushback in public opinion, especially when it happens on a large scale, because of the social and cultural changes that it produces. But the real effects on employment for some workers, strains on already overtaxed public services, and the persistent perception that it generates additional crime also contribute to even greater public anxiety around migration in some countries.[55] However, one extensive study by the Inter-American Development Bank's Public Perceptions Laboratory on Migration shows that public pushback against migration is particularly focused on employment and crime, while there is still broad support for legal status and access to public services.[56] That suggests that there is some nuance in the way publics respond to different migration policies, endorsing the provision of legal status and access to services, but worrying about effects on their own well-being.

Governments have responded to these concerns by trying to gain greater control of their borders and put visa requirements on Venezuelan and Haitian citizens, among others.[57] But there is little evidence that governments have reduced access to public services or legal status, as yet. And that probably points to not only the nuanced perceptions that many people in the region have on migration and migrants, but also to the low salience of the issue in politics so far. While some politicians—especially in Peru and Chile—have raised migration control as a political platform, it has yet to become a major issue of political debate in most countries in the way that other issues are.

At the same time, migrants themselves face real challenges in integrating into the countries where they have moved to in South America. While most (but certainly not all) have some form of legal status, many have only temporary rights to remain and work. Overall, adult migrants tend to have higher levels of educational attainment than their native-born peers in most countries, but they often struggle to get their professional or technical degrees recognized,[58] and they frequently end up in jobs that do not make full use of their education. Migrants actually have higher employment rates than the native-born in most South American countries and they work longer hours, but they often have lower earnings overall and are more likely to be in the informal economy, though not in all countries.[59] Over time, Venezuelan immigrants, in particular, appear to see their wages increase and are more likely to enter the formal labor market.[60] Since so much of the migration in South America is recent, it is likely that formal employment and income will improve over time.

Access to education is guaranteed in all countries of South America, regardless of legal immigration status, but immigrant children have lower attendance rates in some countries, than native-born students. This may be partially related to ongoing mobility among migrants or pressures to work at an early age, but it is also likely that there are hidden barriers to enrollment that persist despite attempts to reduce these.[61]

Access to health services varies widely. Argentina, Brazil, Ecuador, and Uruguay have almost universal access to healthcare, and Chile is relatively close. In Peru, access to public healthcare depends on the specific legal status that immigrants have.[62] In Colombia, a 2022 telephone survey revealed that 73.6 percent of Venezuelan respondents remain uninsured, a stark contrast to

3.6 percent of Colombians, even though a significant majority now have a legal status.[63] The Colombian Ministry of Health and Social Protection notes that the average cost of emergency care for nonaffiliated individuals is more than double that for those affiliated with the healthcare system.[64] In 2021 alone, Colombia accrued a debt close to US$100 million for emergency care related to the Venezuelan migrant population, so this is an issue that does not just affect migrants but also the society as a whole.[65]

There are often other barriers to full integration in host societies. Many migrants, even those with temporary status, often struggle to access bank accounts and financial services, which limits opportunities for entrepreneurship. And access to housing and other social programs may be limited for those with temporary or no legal status. Even when migrants are eligible for services, government bureaucracies are rarely designed to handle documents issued in other countries, temporary status permits, or identification numbers that are not the official national identification numbers that most native-born residents have. Countries that historically had only small immigrant populations are now having to adapt systems rapidly to a new reality in which a larger percentage of the population is not native-born.[66]

Some migrants also report discrimination in treatment by people in the communities where they live, though this varies widely from country to country.[67] There are almost certainly significant differences among migrants of different ethnic, racial, and socioeconomic backgrounds, as well as between women and men, but there are few studies to date that evaluate this fully.[68]

On balance, South American countries have proved surprisingly adept in responding to one of the largest displacement crises in modern times and adapting to suddenly large numbers of immigrants within their societies. However, their responses are often incomplete, and they have not come without significant stresses and strains on public systems. To date, immigration has yet to rise to the level of political salience in these countries that it has in some other parts of the world, especially in parts of Europe and the United States, but policymakers must contend with negative perceptions on some aspects of migration.

Most countries continue to make significant efforts to integrate immigrants who live in their countries, even if they may try to reduce future arrivals. But the tensions are real, and only the future will tell how migration issues play out in people's lives and in national debates.

When Gerardo Espíndola was elected mayor of Arica, Chile's northernmost municipality, he was an unlikely politician. A journalist who joined a small left-of-center party, he won by a narrow majority in a highly competitive field in 2017 and then went on to win reelection by a large majority in 2021.

Arica is a municipality of slightly more than 200,000 inhabitants set in an almost unimaginably beautiful place, with the Pacific Ocean on one side and the Atacama desert, a windswept plain of sand dunes that is known as the second most arid place on earth, on the other side. The city seems to emerge out of the sand, a fertile crescent of land set against the ocean on one side, the border with both Peru and Bolivia to the north, and the desert to the east and south.

Watching Espíndola in action tells a lot about why he is so unusual. Whether with his team at the municipal office or in an outside meeting, he lets others speak first and listens intently before he offers his opinion, comfortable to be both a strong presence in the room and to let others lead first. It is a skill that has come in handy in one of the most complex regions of Chile, a border community that is partly urban, partly rural, home to the largest African-descent population in Chile and one of the largest Indigenous populations, both Quechua and Aymara. There are also thousands of Peruvians and Bolivians who cross the shared border daily to work on the Chilean side, and Arica was, until recently, the principal entry point for Venezuelans coming down through the Andean route. It is a hyperdiverse border community that makes for a complicated set of needs and highly complex politics.

And the border defines Arica in multiple ways. The largest nearby city is Tacna in Peru, where Arica residents routinely go to get medical attention or sell their goods. And the agricultural economy depends on the Peruvian and Bolivian farm workers on the Chilean side. The arrival of tens of thousands of Venezuelan migrants was just the latest chapter in this constant movement across borders, although the major point of entry now moved further east. Migration and international mobility are a way of life embedded in the pattern of daily existence.

Not all migration and international mobility in South America is about displacement. In Chile, about a third of all immigrants are from Venezuela and another 12 percent are Haitian, while a full third are from the three neighboring countries, Bolivia, Peru, and Argentina (and the remainder are from a wide variety of other countries).

In the case of Chile, agreements with the neighboring countries of Peru and Bolivia have allowed for easy movement across the border with only a national identification card, rather than a passport, as tends to be true among many neighboring countries in South America.[69] However, in the case of Chile, Peruvians and Bolivians are allowed to come for only short periods, and technically, they are not supposed to work.

These limitations on employment do not actually conform to the realities on the ground. The legally permitted period for staying in Chile "doesn't coincide with the agricultural seasons," notes Espíndola, which means that some overstay their permitted stay in the country while others just return home on the weekends to make sure they do not overstay their allowed duration. Their lack of employment authorization has not stopped Peruvian and Bolivian workers from coming to Arica, of course, since the government has no way of really enforcing who is working without a visa, but it makes their status working situation and conditions a great deal more precarious, as often happens when laws do not conform to the realities on the ground.

In contrast, Mercosur not only provides immigrants passport-free travel but also the right to become temporary residents for up to two years with minimal bureaucratic requirements, after which they can opt for permanent residence. Before the Mercosur agreement, there was a great deal of irregular migration from Paraguay and Bolivia to Argentina and Brazil, although much of it was circular rather than permanent.[70] But the mobility agreement, which included Bolivia as well, made it possible for people to move and work legally. It recognized the long-standing mobility ties among the countries in this subregion.[71] Over time, Bolivian and Paraguayan migration to Brazil and Argentina, even though now legal, has actually decreased as those two countries have developed economically.

But even if the Mercosur agreement is the most extensive mobility agreement among South American countries, it is not the only one. The Andean Community—originally comprising Bolivia, Colombia, Ecuador, Peru, and Venezuela—also includes a mobility agreement that allows citizens of the five countries to cross borders with only their national identification.[72] Venezuela has been suspended from the Andean Community since 2006,[73] but the other countries approved a residency agreement in 2021 that allows citizens of the remaining countries to live and work for up to two years in any of the other countries.

Brazil recognizes the right to residency for citizens of neighboring countries that are not part of Mercosur, including citizens of Guyana and Suriname. Chile and Argentina also have a bilateral agreement to allow for easy mobility and residency in each other's countries. And, of course, Chile has agreements on mobility (though not residency) with Peru and Bolivia. Overall, there are considerable pathways for migration among neighboring countries that have been developed over time.

In 2008, all South American governments came together to create a bloc called the Union of South America, or UNASUR, and part of the initial agreement was to create a common agreement that would allow any citizen of a South American country to live in another country and to move with ease across borders. In the end, only Ecuador issued a UNASUR visa, which stayed on the books until 2022, and, for a time, this visa became the primary vehicle through which Venezuelans and other South American nationals were able to access legal status in Ecuador, including many Colombians who had moved to Ecuador to escape civil conflicts and violence in their country during the 1990s.

UNASUR collapsed after a decade, and so South American countries failed in their latest attempt to build a common mobility arrangement allowing for unfettered movement across the continent.[74] If anything, the Venezuelan displacement crisis has now probably made it harder even to have a discussion about this in the near future. But the sheer number of agreements on mobility in South America is still quite notable.

This proliferation of a regional agreements is actually part of broader trend around the world,[75] which started with the Schengen Agreement in Europe in the late 1990s and has extended to South America, Central America (chapter 2), the Caribbean (chapter 3), Africa, and Central Asia. Although much of the focus in the literature is on the hardening of borders, it turns out that borders have actually become much more fluid among many neighboring countries, and South America has been at the forefront of this movement.

When he thinks about his municipality, Gerardo Espíndola says "we're not a homogeneous city; we are quite mixed together," and the constant comings and goings across the border, embedded in tradition as well as law, are a big part of this diversity.

After Nancy Arellano, a Venezuelan public policy specialist, settled in Peru, she decided to help other Venezuelans who were arriving and had fewer opportunities than she did. As a dual citizen of Spain, Nancy was able to access legal status in Peru fairly easily, since Peru and Spain have a reciprocal agreement for issuing visas to each other's citizens, but few other Venezuelans had this option.

So Nancy embarked on a mission, founding Veneactiva, the first nonprofit group led by professional migrant women in Peru. Their goal was to monitor, assist, and empower migrants and refugees in Peru, with a special focus in the beginning to support the regularization process of the Venezuelan community, as the then new process for regularization was taking place in 2018. They aimed to bridge the gaps and foster lasting solutions, all within the framework of harmonious coexistence and productivity in the host society. And, over time, Veneactiva became particularly important as a voice for Venezuelan migrants themselves in the policy process in their new home country of Peru, advocating for measures that not only provided legal status but ensured inclusion in schools, healthcare facilities, housing, and social programs.

There are now dozens of organizations like Veneactiva across South America, mostly started by Venezuelan professionals who arrived early during the displacement crisis and decided to build organizations that could help others arriving after them. Some of these organizations are quite well established and have a strong influence on decision-making about migration policy, as does Veneactiva, while others serve as self-help organizations to help recently arrived migrants find housing and work and sometimes access legal status. Many, of course, do both.

Jacqueline Perdomo leads another Venezuelan self-help organization in Talca, Chile, and Juan Carlos Viloria helped put together a global network of these Venezuelan organizations a few years ago, which now has over a hundred affiliated organizations, called the Coalition for Venezuela. And Haitian organizations are particularly influential in Chile.

South American immigrants abroad are also often quite organized and remain involved in the politics and daily life of their countries of origin. Colombia has a representative in its Chamber of Deputies elected by Colombians abroad, Peru has two in its Congress, and Ecuador six in its National Assembly.[76] Argentinians and Brazilians living abroad do not have special seats in their national legislatures, but they influence politics by voting absentee in elections in their countries of origin.

On top of this, citizens of almost all South American countries living abroad send remittances that shape the future prospects of family members and the communities where they once lived.[77] The overall amount of remittances is far less in South America than it is in many of the countries of Central America and the Caribbean, which have even larger percentages of their populations living abroad, but it can be quite significant for some communities (see table 1.5). And, although trustworthy data are hard to find, Venezuela is probably the one country in which remittances actually do help sustain the basic survival of a significant percentage of families and the economy as a whole.

TABLE 1.5   Remittances in South America: Contribution to GDP and Total USD Flows, 2010 and 2023.

Country	Remittances as a Share of GDP (2010)	Remittances as a Share of GDP (2023)	Remittances in USD (2010)	Remittances in USD (2023)
Argentina	0.2%	0.2%	644.3 million	1.1 billion
Bolivia	4.9%	3.2%	960.2 million	1.4 billion
Brazil	0.1%	0.2%	3.1 billion	4.4 billion
Chile	0.0%	0.0%	62.3 million	69.8 million
Colombia	1.4%	2.8%	4 billion	10.1 billion
Ecuador	3.8%	4.6%	2.6 billion	5.5 billion
Paraguay	1.5%	1.7%	409.9 million	745.7 million
Peru	1.7%	1.7%	2.5 billion	4.4 billion
Uruguay	0.3%	0.2%	124.9 million	133.6 million

Notes: All remittances are in current (nominal) U.S. dollars. This means that dollar values are not constant between years. There is no reliable data available for Venezuela in 2010 and 2023. However, Manuel Orozco from the Inter-American Dialogue estimated that remittances reached $4.2 billion in 2022 and are now received by an estimated 29 percent of Venezuelan households. Source: Manuel Orozco, "Venezuela: Remittances as a Source of Foreign Exchange and Economic Survival," May 2, 2023, https://thedialogue.org/analysis/venezuela-re mittances-as-a-source-of-foreign-exchange-and-economic-survival.

There is no question that migration has become one of the areas where governments are building the foundations of public policy, but immigrants themselves are often critical actors in shaping these policies too, both immigrants who are living in those countries and those from their countries' diasporas abroad. They are not only the subject of public policy, but quite often a part of the debate on public policies too.

And there are more subtle, but perhaps even more powerful, ways that migrants are reshaping the countries where they have moved, through culture, food, language, and music. Past migrations left a powerful imprint on countries in South America, from Brazil's many musical traditions, including samba and bossa nova, which echo musical styles from Africa; to Peru's omnipresent *chifas*, restaurants that serve a fusion of Cantonese food brought by Chinese immigrants with traditional ingredients that are part of the country's Indigenous heritage; to Chile's empanadas, originally imported from Galicia in Spain; to the pizzerias throughout South America that reflect the many waves of Italian immigrants who settled across multiple countries.

Today, signs of the influence of the newest immigrants are popping up everywhere too. Venezuelan arepas can be found in any major city or even mid-sized town in South America, alongside Cuban bars and nightclubs. And immigrant street musicians bring a wide variety of musical styles to passersby at night in any large city.

Ralph-Jean Baptiste, who moved to Chile from Haiti in 2010, shortly after the earthquake there, is one of the musical innovators who has watched the tastes of his new home country change over the past few years. He has put out two albums in Chile to wide acclaim, finding his own style that mixes Afro-Caribbean rhythms, Chilean pop, and Haitian Kompa into a unique synthesis that has mesmerized audiences across Chile. While he started off in gospel music in Haiti, he says that "in Chile, I sought out my own path, my own style." His songs move easily between Spanish and Haitian Creole, sometimes with a few words of English mixed in, and you can hear strands of different musical styles playing off each other in his compositions.

Initially Ralph-Jean found himself facing significant obstacles as a Haitian musician in a country where many people had significant reservations about immigration and especially Black immigrants. "Today, the rejection that existed in other moments is less," he notes. "It's still there, but it's gone down." And he credits immigration with gradually making Chile a more open society.

Comparing it to when he first arrived, he says, "there is a much greater variety of food, many more entrepreneurs, and fruits and vegetables that you couldn't find here—and the kinds of parties, the sense of joy" has shifted.

But Ralph-Jean is hardly naïve about the future. Changes create opportunities but they also generate tensions. "Politicians are now blaming immigrants for insecurity," he says, fearing that there may be a new wave of pushback against immigrants starting up again after things had started to improve. In the end, he notes, you need a "sense of resilience" and "a desire to seek out opportunities in order to persist."

2 Mexico and Central America

In the Shadow of the United States

MOST PEOPLE IN DURHAM, North Carolina, have never heard of San Pablito, a small village built along the side of a steep mountain in the municipality of Pahuatlán in Puebla, Mexico, but the two cities are inextricably interlinked. Almost everyone who has had their house painted in Durham has met someone from San Pablito given that Mexican immigrants from that small village dominate the city's house painting industry, the result of solidified migration routes dating back to the late 1980s.[1] The connection is palpable in many ways, including every June 29 when residents from San Pablito gather to celebrate the Day of Saint Peter and Saint Paul in a mixture of Spanish and Otomí, the native language of San Pablito.[2]

Most Mexicans, too, have never heard of San Pablito, but almost all know its most famous product, *amate*, a kind of paper made from the bark of trees that is a fixture at arts and craft markets around the country. For many years, Mexican elementary schoolchildren were required to buy *amate* and do art projects on it as part of the national curriculum, as a way to celebrate and recognize important historical traditions. But few Mexicans know that *amate*, which was a centerpiece of ceremonial ornaments and writing in several Indigenous cultures in the pre-Hispanic period, largely survived thanks to the residents of San Pablito. They almost single-handedly conserved this tradition for centuries long after it was lost elsewhere. They continued to cut the tree bark and grind it into a fine paper, while the nearby Nahuatl-speaking communities perfected the art of painting on *amate*.[3]

The migration ties that bind San Pablito and Durham are, like many other pairings, a result of intersecting factors, including economic supply and demand, social networks, and policies, but also chance. Some unauthorized Mexican immigrants from San Pablito found their way to Durham when North Carolina's economy was growing in the 1980s and later adjusted their immigration status through the U.S. Immigration Control and Reform Act (IRCA), which allowed many of them to become lawful permanent residents (LPRs). With their newfound legal status, some of them started house painting businesses and began to provide employment to others from their hometown who wanted to move to Durham, following similar settlement patterns as in other emerging destinations in southern U.S. states.[4]

The ups and downs of migration from San Pablito to Durham have since generally followed rhythms of supply and demand, tied to economic cycles, as well as social networks that tie the two cities together.[5] Millions of Mexican family farmers were displaced in the 1990s as agricultural employment fell significantly with a drop in coffee and corn prices.[6] The reduction in coffee prices, a major income source in Pahuatlán, and an expanding U.S. economy thus triggered emigration from San Pablito through the early 2000s.

Then there was a sustained drop in migration as Mexico's economy improved in the 2000s and 2010s and *amate* production thrived, while at the same time it became increasingly harder to cross the U.S.-Mexico border without authorization. Finally, a recent drop in the demand for *amate*, at a time when the U.S. economy had emerged from the global recession stronger than Mexico's, led to a resurgence of migration northward from San Pablito to Durham. Each wave of migration solidifies economic, social, and cultural ties between both locations.

For well over a century-and-a-half, migration to the United States has shaped towns across Mexico, like San Pablito, each with slightly different local dynamics. This migration has created the largest diaspora shared between any two countries anywhere in the world.[7] The supply of workers in Mexico, U.S. demand for migrant labor, and significant salary differences between the two countries drove this mass movement, while the accumulated social networks that tied the two countries together facilitated the migration journey for millions of Mexicans.[8] By 2023, about 10.9 million people born in Mexico lived in the United States, roughly 9 percent of all people born in Mexico, and about 38 million people in the United States claimed Mexican ancestry, roughly 11 percent of the U.S. population.[9]

Migration helped shape the thousands of Mexican communities that saw residents—primarily working-age men—leave in large numbers, send remittances back, and sometimes return. Entire villages and towns were emptied out gradually by emigration, while others grew and prospered because of it, and many experienced a mixture of both. Migration changed livelihoods, expectations, cultural tastes, and family relationships.[10] And, of course, immigration from Mexico also shaped the United States every bit as much as it did Mexico, changing demographics, labor markets, and cultural patterns.[11]

By the mid-2000s, Mexican migration fell notably and entered a new stage of decline. The U.S. economic downturn from 2007 to 2009 caused by the Great Recession significantly reduced Mexicans' incentives to migrate, and irregular migration began to decline (see figure 2.1). And at the same time, more Mexican immigrants considered leaving the country to reunite with family.

FIGURE 2.1   Migrant Encounters of Mexican Nationals between Ports of Entry at the U.S.-Mexico Border, FY 2000–2024.

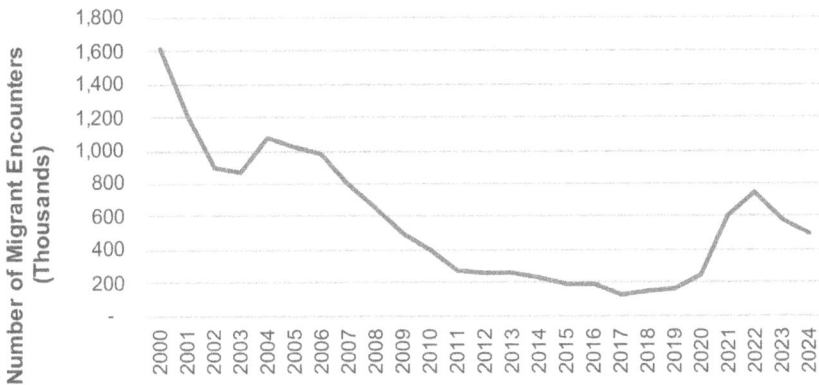

Note: Migrant encounters by U.S. Border Patrol are recorded events, not of individual people, and in some cases may count multiple attempts by the same person to enter the United States. Encounters include formal apprehensions by U.S. Border Patrol of migrants crossing without authorization plus short-term detentions and returns of migrants to Mexico under a special expulsion authority known as Title 42 that was in effect from March 2020 through May 2023.

Sources: Authors' tabulations of migrant encounter data from U.S. Border Patrol. See U.S. Border Patrol, "Total Encounters by Fiscal Year," accessed December 6, 2023, https://www.cbp.gov/sites/default/files/assets/documents/2021-Aug/U.S.%20Border%20Patrol%20Apprehensions%20From%20Mexico%20and%20Other%20Than%20Mexico%20%28FY%202000%20-%20FY%202020%29.pdf; U.S. Customs and Border Protection, "Southwest Land Border Encounters," updated March 12, 2025, https://www.cbp.gov/newsroom/stats/southwest-land-border-encounters.

In fact, more Mexicans left the United States than headed north between 2009 and 2014, reversing a decades' old trend.[12]

Other factors also contributed to this drop in Mexican irregular migration. Mexico's economy experienced sustained improvements as GDP per capita rose by 13 percent between 2009 and 2018.[13] Falling fertility rates and slow population growth, among other demographic factors, also led to emigration declines.[14]

At the same time, increasing access to legal pathways provided more Mexicans alternatives to migrating without authorization. Particularly noticeable was the expansion of temporary employment visas, through the H-2 program for seasonal agricultural and nonagricultural work, which allowed U.S. employers to recruit workers for specific jobs in the United States for several months a year (see figure 2.2).[15] Also, Mexicans who were able to adjust their immigration status under IRCA in the 1980s, including the house painting entrepreneurs in Durham, and others who were able to become lawful permanent residents and by 2010 were able to sponsor family members already living in the United States or abroad.[16] An average of 140,000 Mexicans became lawful permanent residents annually between 2010 and 2022.[17]

A series of U.S. policy changes after 2011 also contributed to the decrease

FIGURE 2.2   Number of H-2A and H-2B Visas Issued to Mexican Nationals, FY 2010–2024.

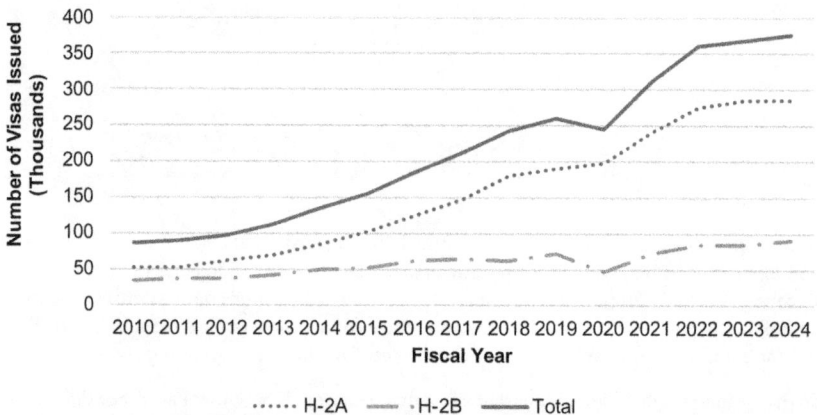

Source: Authors' calculations based on data from the U.S. Department of State, "Nonimmigrant Visa Issuances by Visa Class and by Nationality," accessed January 16, 2025, https://travel.state .gov/content/travel/en/legal/visa-lawo/visa-statistics/nonimmigrant-visa-statistics.html.

in irregular migration from Mexico. With the implementation of a new consequence delivery system, U.S. authorities identified migrants who attempted multiple times to enter illegally, prosecuted them in criminal court, and prohibited them from entering the country for five or ten years.[18] In the U.S. interior, the implementation of Secure Communities, a congressionally mandated program, required local law enforcement to screen migrants under arrest against immigration databases to identify if they were in the country without authorization and notify U.S. Immigration Customs Enforcement (ICE) to remove or return them.[19] Coupled with bilateral agreements with the Mexican government, these policies increased repatriations of Mexican migrants from the U.S. interior and the border, with approximately 210,000 deportations annually from 2014 to 2023.[20]

In the United States, the combination of these trends resulted in a net decrease in the Mexican population.[21] About 10.7 million Mexican immigrants resided there in 2022 compared to 11.7 million in 2010. Although Mexicans were still the largest national group among the 45.3 million immigrants in the United States, accounting for a little less than a quarter of all immigrants, Mexico stopped being the top country of *new* migration flows in 2013.[22] And today, slightly more Mexicans in the United States have a legal status, roughly 5.5 million, than those that do not, 5.2 million, a number that also includes about 434,000 Mexicans who are protected from deportation and have employment authorization as beneficiaries from the Deferred Action for Childhood Arrivals (DACA) program.[23]

Even as Mexican emigration to the United States ebbed and flowed, Mexico simultaneously began to come to terms with becoming a country of transit and, increasingly, of a destination for migrants. Starting in 2012 and through 2019, increasing numbers of Central American migrants of varying family composition transited through the country en route to the United States, including some that opted to stay temporarily. And after 2021, as health-related travel restrictions eased across the hemisphere and migration resumed, the number of migrants in transit rose sharply with more coming from other world regions. This required a shifting framework for managing migration, and Mexico was not the only country in the neighborhood dealing with this shift.

The unfinished hospital in San Pedro Necta is a visible reminder of why people from Guatemala migrate north. The massive complex, which is meant to serve the surrounding communities in Huehuetenango, in Guatemalan's Western Highlands, was first started in 2010, but fourteen years later it remains unfinished. There have been promises and periods of intense construction, including for a while during 2022, but so far, no government administration has been capable of finishing the project. Instead, the current regional hospital, housed in a small building on loan from the Catholic Diocese, has only limited space to meet the demand for medical care in the surrounding communities.[24]

People do not migrate from San Pedro Necta and the other communities in Huehuetenango specifically because of the lack of healthcare but because they want to improve their quality of life, much like those who leave San Pablito. And today they are much more likely to have the means to migrate because they now have family members and neighbors living across the United States who can provide them with a place to stay when they arrive and connections to employment.[25] But the hospital is a daily reminder that they should expect little future progress from their government and that their best chance of getting ahead in life is to migrate abroad and earn enough money to help their family—and have a small financial cushion in case anyone takes ill, the family crops fail, or anything else unpredictable happens.

And in San Pedro Necta, the local private high school and college also teach the same lesson as the hospital. There is no public high school or college in town, but those who are willing to migrate may be able to pay for their children to go to the private high school and college that was built a few years ago to satisfy the aspirations of migrants that their children might become professionals and not have to migrate themselves. Migration provides the pathway forward and the safety net in the absence of effective public education and healthcare opportunities or a thriving local labor market. Migration is thus understood to be a tangible, even if risky, pathway to development and opportunity.

Several countries in Central America have experienced emigration every bit as much as Mexico, and even more so in relative terms, but this process started a bit later and more gradually. While there has always been some Central American migration to the United States, the largest movements happened during the civil wars and counterinsurgency campaigns of the 1970s and 1980s, followed by significant emigration in the 1990s and 2000s during periods of economic change.[26]

On the surface, the Central American migration story over the last decade has been one of increasing irregular emigration toward the United States, driven primarily by economic factors but also changes in real and perceived levels of violence.[27] Yet even though migrants in different countries share similar motivations for leaving home, migration has and continues to shape Guatemala, El Salvador, and Honduras in different ways. Especially as these countries face increasingly diverse migrant transit flows, each one can add a new chapter to their migration story.

Seasonal agricultural work largely defined Guatemalan emigration. Due to its geographical proximity and cultural similarities, southern Mexico had historically been the most common migrant destination. More recently, however, larger numbers of Guatemalans—primarily from the Western Highlands, the country's most Indigenous and poorest region—have migrated to the United States.

Of the three countries, El Salvador has the longest and most extensive history of migration to the United States, with almost a quarter of those born in El Salvador now living in the United States. However, migration from El Salvador to the United States has slowed in recent years, partially as a result of changing demographics, since El Salvador has the lowest birth rate and most urban population of the three countries,[28] and perhaps partly as a result of improving public security conditions.[29] Meanwhile, migration from Honduras, which was once the lowest among the three countries, has ballooned and is today the most diverse in composition, with families and children accounting for large shares of migrants.

Irregular migration from northern Central America to the United States started to increase in 2012 in earnest, and then surpassed Mexican migration from 2014 through 2019, as first unaccompanied minors and then adults and families joined in the migration northward. In many ways, Central Americans are repeating a pattern once developed by Mexicans, consolidating social networks between their countries and the United States that allow them to navigate complex, often costly, and dangerous journeys and find housing and work on arrival.[30] But there is a new twist with high levels of violence in parts of the three countries that may also drive some of the migration, as well as increasing environmental pressures in some regions that may also contribute to decisions to leave.[31]

Perhaps the most recent illustrative change in irregular migration flows from the three countries started in 2018 and can be described in three stages:

pre-pandemic mobility from 2014 to 2019, restricted mobility at the onset of the pandemic in 2020, and resurgent migration as mobility restrictions were lifted after 2021.

In the first stage, uneven economic growth and rising political discontent triggered heightened levels of irregular migration. Though most Central American migrants travel on their own or with a smuggler,[32] a series of highly visible migrant caravans in 2018 and 2019 drew wide regional attention. Seeking safety in numbers as they transited Guatemala and Mexico, these caravans were primarily composed of Honduran families disillusioned by perceived high levels of corruption, stagnating socioeconomic conditions, and high violence rates.[33] Similar political pressures in Guatemala contributed to the increase of migrants seeking to reach the United States, although most of them used smugglers hired locally in their communities of origin.[34] Migration from El Salvador also increased but remained significantly lower than that of other two countries. In 2019, Mexican enforcement policies, coordinated with the U.S. government, targeted and reduced the number of caravans, but flows continued until the start of the COVID-19 pandemic.

A stage of mobility restrictions applied by the three Central American governments in 2020, though to different degrees, dramatically reduced northbound emigration flows, like in the rest of the world. Although governments provided people some economic assistance, it fell short of the existing need, especially among vulnerable groups. A series of climate disasters in late 2020, including two tragic hurricanes and accompanying mudslides, left a trail of devastation in many parts of Honduras and Guatemala, compounding existing economic pressures to emigrate for some.[35]

The third and current stage has been one of resurgent migration because of receding mobility restrictions and uneven economic recovery across Central America. Irregular migration from Guatemala, El Salvador, and Honduras reached a new record in FY 2021 with 684,000 arrivals between ports at the U.S.-Mexico border, surpassing the prior FY 2019 record of 608,000. Migration from the three countries increased in FY 2021, with Guatemalans and Hondurans accounting for most of the growth. However, as the United States and Mexico implemented additional enforcement measures in 2022 through 2024, including a significantly higher number of removals and expulsions from the United States and additional inspections and controls across known transit routes in Mexico, irregular migration from the three countries began to fall, even if it remained high compared to other nationalities (see figure 2.3).[36] By the end of FY 2024, irregular migration from the three countries combined was trending down and was below 2019 levels.

Much less noticed has been the important increases in legal migration from Central America through seasonal agricultural labor, which have also contributed to the decrease in irregular migration. Historically, Guatemalan workers have been important to agricultural labor in southern Mexico using Border Worker Visas to work in coffee plantations and other fields. Through the Temporary Foreign Worker Program (TFW), furthermore, approximately

FIGURE 2.3   Migrant Encounters of Northern Central American Nationals between Port of Entry at the U.S.-Mexico Border, by Nationality, FY 2008–2024.

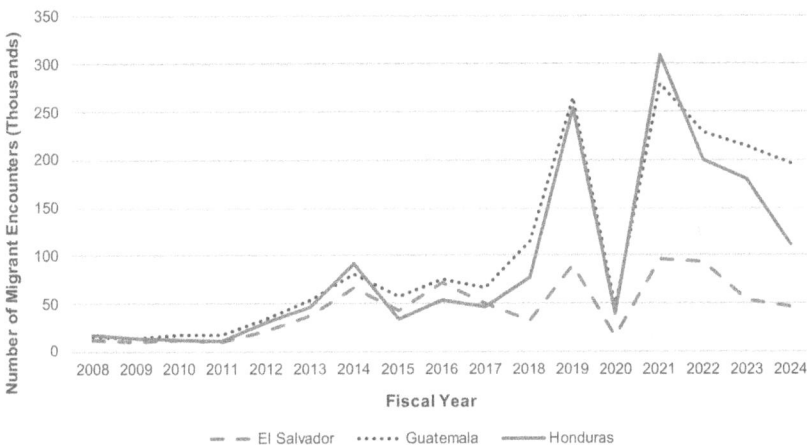

Note: Migrant encounters by U.S. Border Patrol are recorded events, not of individual people, and in some cases may count multiple attempts by the same person to enter the United States. Encounters include formal apprehensions by U.S. Border Patrol of migrants crossing without authorization plus short-term detentions and returns of migrants to Mexico under a special expulsion authority known as Title 42 that was in effect from March 2020 through May 2023.

Sources: Authors' calculations based on U.S. Border Patrol, "U.S. Border Patrol Apprehensions Nationwide by Citizenship and Sector, FY2007-2019," updated January 2020, https://www.cbp.gov/sites/default/files/assets/documents/2019-Mar/BP%20Apps%20by%20Sector%20and%20Citizenship%20FY07-FY18.pdf; Office of Homeland Security Statistics, "Immigration Enforcement and Legal Processes Monthly Tables, November 2024," updated January 16, 2025, https://ohss.dhs.gov/topics/immigration/immigration-enforcement/immigration-enforcement-and-legal-processes-monthly.

16,000 Guatemalan workers traveled to Canada for seasonal work in 2022.[37] But more recently, the largest growth in labor mobility not just for Guatemalans, but also Salvadorans and Hondurans, has been through the U.S. H-2 seasonal program for agricultural (H-2A) and nonagricultural (H-2B) workers.

Even if they compose only a fraction of all workers in the H-2 program, Guatemalan, Salvadoran, and Honduran workers have made notable gains in accessing work opportunities in the United States. Guatemalan workers have received the majority of H-2 visas in Central America, primarily for agricultural work. And despite a drop in visa issuances in 2020 due to mobility restrictions and U.S. economic instability, the number of workers from the three countries has increased sharply since then (see figure 2.4). Key to that growth have been recent U.S. government allocations of H-2B visas specifically for Guatemalan, Salvadoran, and Honduran migrant workers which have incentivized U.S. employers to hire more workers from the region.[38] It remains to be seen if this increase in legal temporary pathways will significantly redirect Central American irregular migration into regular channels, as some recent studies have suggested it could.[39]

Not all migration from Guatemala, El Salvador, and Honduras is northward. The three countries also have a long history of intraregional migration, especially in border regions, and an agreement among them and Nicaragua

FIGURE 2.4   Number of H-2A and H-2B Visas Issued to Guatemalan, Honduran, and Salvadoran Nationals, FY 2010–2024.

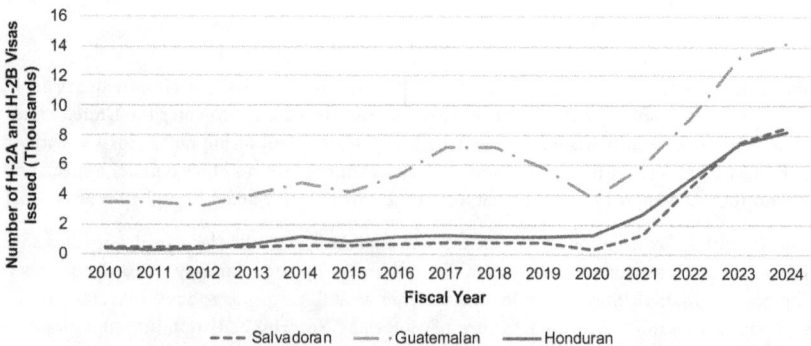

Source: Authors' calculations based on data from the U.S. Department of State, "Nonimmigrant Visa Issuances by Visa Class and by Nationality," accessed January 16, 2025, https://travel.state.gov/content/travel/en/legal/visa-lawo/visa-statistics/nonimmigrant-visa-statistics.html.

in 1991, called the Central American Convention of Free Mobility, or CA-4 agreement, has allowed for people from the four countries to cross borders with only their national identification and without a passport.[40] Some, but not all, of the governments have also created special residency programs for nationals from neighboring countries, which makes it easier for people to move and live in the country next door.[41] There were also smaller numbers of people from all three countries living in Costa Rica and Panama, but these were only a small fraction of those who headed northward or who have moved among the three countries.

The other major destination for migrants from the three countries has historically been Belize, which is both a Central American country, because of its location, and Caribbean country, because of its history as a British colony and a member of the Caribbean Community (CARICOM) (see chapter 3).[42]

By 2020, approximately 25 percent of all people born in El Salvador, roughly 1.6 million, lived abroad—and most resided in the United States. About 10 percent of Hondurans and 8 percent of Guatemalans lived outside of their birth countries, also primarily in the United States (table 2.1), but with Mexico and Belize as secondary destinations. And there was a growing number of Hon-

TABLE 2.1   Mexican and Central American Emigrant Population, Share, and Top Countries of Destination, 2020.

Country	Total Population	Emigrant Population Worldwide	Emigrant Share of Total Population	Top 3 Countries of Destination
Mexico	125,998,302	11,185,737	9%	United States, Canada, Spain
Costa Rica	5,123,105	150,241	3%	United States, Nicaragua, Panama
El Salvador	6,292,731	1,599,058	25%	United States, Canada, Guatemala
Guatemala	17,362,719	1,368,431	8%	United States, Mexico, Belize
Honduras	10,121,763	985,077	10%	United States, Spain, Mexico
Nicaragua	6,755,896	718,154	11%	Costa Rica, United States, Spain
Panama	4,294,397	139,520	3%	United States, Costa Rica, Spain

Source: Authors' tabulations of data from the United Nations' Department of Economic and Social Affairs, Population Division, "International Migrant Stock 2020: Destination and Origin," accessed September 23, 2024, https://www.un.org/development/desa/pd/content/international-migrant-stock.

durans moving to Spain as well, a movement that started in the 2010s and numbered a few tens of thousands by 2023.[43]

Whether in San Pedro Necta in Huehuetenango, Guatemala, or San Pablito in Pahuatlán, Mexico, one can always find a place to pick up the money that their relatives and friends abroad remit home.[44] There is one ATM in the largest town in each municipality for those few who use banks to receive the money, but most people pick up these remittances in their home village at convenience stores that serve as correspondent points for money transfers. The store charges a small fee in return for doling out the cash that the electronic transfer requires, which is paid by the transfer service, often Western Union or MoneyGram. In fact, remittances from migrants living abroad are so vast today across the world that they far exceed financial transfers through international development aid and, in some years, actually surpass foreign direct investment flows in their volume.[45]

Notably, remittances sent to Mexico and Central America, primarily from the United States, have increased every year for the last decade, changing how migrants send and family members receive them.[46] Seeking to enter the multibillion-dollar market of remittances, smaller firms increasingly shifting to digital money transfers (e.g., phone applications and digital wallets) are beginning to transform this landscape. Often these digital firms charge migrants lower fees, have fewer requirements, and are more accessible than traditional companies.[47] However, they may be more difficult for receiving family members to access in remote areas or where banking options are limited.

Given their economic contributions and increasing influence on domestic politics, the governments of Mexico, El Salvador, Guatemala, and Honduras have sought to develop active policies to connect with their diaspora communities abroad, although with different degrees of success. In Mexico, state governments with large diaspora communities have tried to do this for more than thirty years, as has the federal government over the last two decades. The three other countries have sought to do so more recently as the impact of remittances on their economies, which range from 20 to 26 percent of GDP (see table 2.2), has become increasingly evident, and migrant leaders living abroad have begun to be influential in domestic politics.[48]

All four countries have government bodies that are designed to help build

TABLE 2.2 Amount of Remittances and Share of GDP Received by Mexico and Central American Countries, 2023.

	Remittances (USD in Millions)	Remittances as a Percentage of GDP
Mexico	66,239	3.70%
Guatemala	19,855	19.50%
Honduras	8,800	25.60%
El Salvador	8,142	23.90%
Nicaragua	4,668	26.20%
Costa Rica	633	0.70%
Panama	530	0.60%

Source: Authors' calculations based on data from the World Bank and KNOMAD. See World Bank and KNOMAD, "Migration and Development Brief 40," June 2024 , https://documents1.worldbank .org/curated/en/099714008132436612/pdf/IDU1a9cf73b51fcad1425a1a0dd1cc8f2f3331ce.pdf.

the relationship with their citizens abroad. Mexico has an Institute for Mexicans Abroad (IME), part of its Foreign Ministry, which regularly brings together migrant leaders with Mexican policymakers. In the early 2000s, this body received considerable political attention, although its work is less visible today. And Mexican consulates in the United States, fifty-three of them as of 2023, play a particularly active role in building relationships day-to-day between local Mexican organizations and the Mexican government.[49] The other three countries have smaller but still quite active consular networks, and similar bodies that are charged with conducting outreach to diasporas abroad, although none are quite as consolidated.

Still, although the size and importance of remittances has raised the profile of migrants living abroad, no country has really found a way to strategically channel remittances into sustainable, long-term development projects. The money sent by relatives abroad plays a significant role in everyday consumption and improving housing, healthcare access, and educational outcomes, which suggests that remittances are a powerful force for improvement in livelihoods and overall social indicators.[50] Many migrant-led organizations in the United States also raise money for specific community projects, from building classrooms to paving roads to supporting youth sports, in their towns of origin, which greatly improve community infrastructure. These organizations often gain considerable influence with local governments, since they provide needed resources for infrastructure improvements and community activities, and they sometimes negotiate their specific investments with municipal and even state or departmental governments directly.

Most remittances, however, are sent directly to family members, and the recipients take the money they receive and either keep it in cash or spend it quickly on basic needs. These needs range from paying food expenses and utility bills to buying school supplies for children. In some cases, the recipients will convert them into bricks and mortar for housing improvements, since migrants both want to have a better house for their families but also tend to trust housing as an investment more than the banking system.

Efforts to channel remittances into broader and more sustainable investment in community infrastructure are rare and not available nationwide. A long-time advocate for financial inclusion in Mexico, Isabel Cruz runs a network of micro-banks and contends that if people saved a fraction of their remittances in micro-banks and cooperatives, which have a history of lending money to local communities, it could transform their communities.[51] But so far, no government has tried to create incentives for this to happen, despite the importance of remittances for the economies of all four countries. The state government of Zacatecas, Mexico, once tried matching remittances sent by migrants to start or expand small businesses with interest-free loans and thereby incentivize investments in the state, a particularly creative idea.[52]

Each of these countries has also tried to develop systems for reintegrating those migrants who return home.[53] This has taken on particular importance in the case of Mexico, where millions of Mexicans have returned voluntarily or through deportation since 2000,[54] but is also becoming particularly salient in Honduras, Guatemala, and El Salvador, where thousands of citizens return each year.[55] A growing volume of literature has documented returnees' changing needs and the socioeconomic benefits to receiving communities. One extensive study of returning migrants in Mexico shows that they bring not only quantifiable skills, such as higher education or technical degrees, but also intangible skills, such as entrepreneurship and business management skills, that are often in short supply in poorer communities and can be tapped for economic development with the right incentives.[56] Another study highlights the complexities of receiving and reintegrating migrants in Central America following the effects of the COVID-19 pandemic.[57]

The question of how to reintegrate return migrants and maximize their economic and social contributions is gaining greater focus from governments in all four countries. These governments have implemented return and reintegration programs, often with help from the International Organization for Migration (IOM) and local nonprofits, to help those who return get needed legal documents, find employment, and sometimes invest their savings.[58] But most of these efforts are still quite incipient, and until recently lacked psychosocial services to address returnees' mental health.[59]

Another consequence of return migration has been a growing number of U.S. citizens in Mexico, as those returning may bring foreign-born spouses and children with them. According to the 2020 Mexican census, there were an estimated 446,000 U.S. citizen minors living in the country, accounting for more than half of the 800,000 U.S. citizens settled in Mexico. And estimates from the U.S. State Department suggest that the U.S. immigrant population in Mexico could be up to 1.6 million.[60] Not all of these are family members returning with Mexican migrants, but many are, which raises serious bilateral interest in their successful integration in Mexico. Ensuring that U.S. citizen minors obtain lawful immigration status and personal identification to be eligible for healthcare and other basic services in Mexico, as well as enroll in school, for example, are necessary priorities, especially for those who may return to the United States in the future.[61] And though estimates of the U.S. immigrant population in Central America are not clear, it is likely that the number of spouses and children has increased in tandem with recent increases in repatriations from the United States, raising similar integration issues for this population.

———————————

Migration has been a key policy issue in the U.S.-Mexico bilateral agenda for decades, but *how* the two countries collaborate in policy design and coordinate migration management has evolved notably since the late 1990s. Once an issue that was decoupled from other priorities in the bilateral agenda because of its political divisiveness, migration policy today is arguably the leading issue that finds its way into all diplomatic negotiations between Washington, DC, and Mexico City.

In fact, efforts to manage the transit of irregular migration through Mexico have been front and center as migrant flows have ballooned in recent years, raising the visibility of diplomatic negotiations. Former U.S. President Barack Obama visited Mexico four times—tied with France for the most abroad visits—to discuss migration management with his Mexican counterparts during his two terms in office. Former U.S. President Donald Trump visited Mexico during his political campaign and hosted former Mexican President Andrés Manuel López Obrador at the White House. And former U.S. President Joe Biden met with López Obrador three times in person and numerous times over the phone.

But the U.S.-Mexico bilateral agenda actually started to evolve in the early 2000s. Experts contend that the implementation of NAFTA in 1994 brought about closer diplomatic relations between the United States and Mexico, leading to the establishment of new mechanisms for consultation and cooperation years after, including a Binational Study on Migration.[62] This policy opening was a welcomed change given the complexity of migration collaboration that characterized the 1990s as a period of limited cooperation and infrequent congruence in the bilateral agenda.[63]

By the early 2000s, migration policy discussions largely focused on Mexican migration to the United States. Former Mexican President Vicente Fox and former U.S. President George W. Bush reached a framework agreement on migration in 2001 that would have offered legal immigration status to unauthorized Mexican immigrants living in the United States, expanded lawful pathways for migration between the two countries, and reinforced controls at the shared border to reduce irregular migration. The deal fell through after the 9/11 terrorist attacks, and there were mixed views on whether the deal could have passed through the U.S. Congress as outlined, but these three elements would frame migration discussions between the two countries for more than a decade afterwards. The U.S. Congress made at least three major bipartisan efforts to pass Comprehensive Immigration Reform, as it came to be called, in 2006, 2007, and 2013, but failed each time due to insufficient majority support and political divisions. Notably, however, the Mexican government played a major role in indirectly supporting each effort, seeking to improve conditions for Mexicans in the United States and setting a marked difference from its prior approaches of the 1990s.

It was in 2014 when irregular migration from Central America increased significantly that the focus on migration enforcement resurfaced and began to change U.S.-Mexico collaboration once more. Tens of thousands of unaccompanied minors, primarily from Guatemala and El Salvador, transited through Mexico without authorization, exposing U.S. and Mexican institutional limitations to detain and repatriate minors. In response to this and other changes in Central American migration, both governments committed to modernizing security and technology at their shared border and improving migration controls in Mexico and along its border with Guatemala, with a U.S. investment of $100 million dollars in training and equipment under the Mérida Initiative.[64] U.S. policy changes and Mexican enforcement, among other factors, reduced the transit of Central American minors, but irregular migration continued.

A series of large groups of migrants, primarily from Honduras, traveling in "caravans" transited through Mexico in 2018 and 2019, testing U.S.-Mexico diplomatic relations and intensifying migration policy negotiations. Threatening to impose tariffs on Mexican imports, the Trump administration pressured the López Obrador administration in 2019 to accept the return of non-Mexican migrants to remain in Mexico until the resolution of their U.S. asylum hearings, a major shift in policy for both countries.[65] The program was mired in litigation and later suspended by the Biden administration, but it set the course for additional bilateral cooperation on migration enforcement.

Shifts in the diversity of nationalities and the scale of migration flows since 2021 turned the focus of U.S.-Mexico migration policy cooperation to reducing the irregular transit of migrants coming from other parts of the Western Hemisphere and the rest of the world. Mexico imposed visa travel restrictions for migrants from Brazil, Ecuador, Peru, and Venezuela and required Colombians to preregister for travel.[66] And as result of negotiations with the Biden administration in May 2023, Mexican authorities agreed for the first time to accept formal U.S. removals of Venezuelans, Cubans, Haitians, and Nicaraguans to Mexico in May 2023.[67] In return, the U.S. government opened legal migration pathways for an equal number of migrants from these four nationalities.

At the same time, Mexico's National Institute of Migration (INM) significantly expanded its enforcement operations across its territory with the assistance of the National Guard, and since 2023 with more participation from the Mexican Army and Navy. The combined effects of these efforts raised migrant encounters by Mexican authorities to record levels (see figure 2.5) and contributed to a decrease in irregular migrant arrivals at the U.S.-Mexico border through 2024.

FIGURE 2.5   Migrant Encounters by Mexican Authorities, by Country of Origin, 2014–2024.

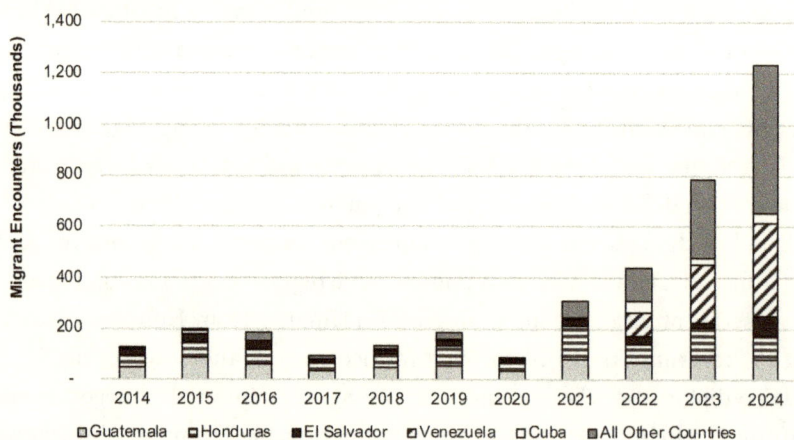

Source: Authors' calculations based on data from the Mexican Ministry of Interior (SEGOB). See SEGOB, "Boletín Mensuales de Estadísticas Migratorias," accessed May 24, 2025, http://portales.segob.gob.mx/es/PoliticaMigratoria/Boletines_Estadisticos.

Despite that the number of irregular arrivals of Mexican migrants at the U.S.-Mexico border also increased after FY 2021, surpassing half a million each fiscal year through 2024,[68] it did not become a major point of tension. Bilateral discussions continued to center almost exclusively on citizens of other countries transiting through Mexico. In addition to economic demand in the United States that attracted migrant labor during this period of recovery after the COVID-19 pandemic, heightened violence in parts of Mexico undoubtedly drove some of this emigration, especially from the states of Guerrero and Michoacán.[69] Additionally, rising violence and internal displacement in some Mexican states likely contributed to the increase in emigration,[70] especially of those traveling in families from certain areas of the country.

Of particular concern for the Mexican government was the rise in migration of children and families transiting the country after 2021. To reduce the negative impacts on children, a reform of Mexico's migration law in 2021 prohibited the detention of migrant children and their family members and instead required they be transferred to support centers under the purview of Mexico's National System of Integral Development for the Family (DIF) while the Prosecutor Office for the Child and Adolescent Protection (PPNNA) determined the minor's best interest.[71] However, due to lack of funding and DIF shelter space, the implementation of these reforms was underwhelming, and reports suggested that children, mostly from Central America, were still being detained and repatriated.[72]

Not surprisingly, these changes in the volume and composition of irregular migrants in Mexico placed significant pressure on INM's limited capacity to hold and process them humanely. Across its fifty-four detention centers, INM had an estimated capacity to hold approximately 6,000 migrants at any one time in 2023.[73] Following a tragic fire that killed thirty-nine migrants in a detention center in Ciudad Juarez, Chihuahua, which revealed significant mismanagement if not outright criminal neglect,[74] INM closed thirty-three centers pending an investigation by the National Commission for Human Rights (CNDH) to certify their conditions meet required standards.[75] As of March 2024, INM operated seventeen detention centers with a capacity to hold nearly 4,800 migrants, most located in Mexico City; Tapachula, Chiapas; Acayucan, Veracruz; and Villahermosa, Tabasco.[76] At this capacity, INM was unable to detain every migrant it encountered long enough to process them for repatriation—nearly 4,000 per day on average through July 2024—and instead it transported many migrants to southern Mexico with the option to stay and seek protection or leave the country.[77]

As it became more difficult for migrants to transit irregularly through Mexico, more of them appeared to consider staying in the country even if temporarily, adding to the immigrant population already living in the country. Although the immigrant population residing in Mexico increased from 1 million in 2015 to approximately 1.2 million in 2020,[78] the widest pipeline of settlement in the country had been the asylum process. As a signatory of the Cartagena Declaration, Mexico can provide complementary protection to asylum seekers who flee generalized violence but do not meet the traditional eligibility requirements under the 1951 Refugee Convention and 1967 Protocol.[79] This has allowed many to find safety and refuge in parts of Mexico where they can make valuable contributions. Others have used the asylum process to regularize their status temporarily before trying to migrate to the United States.[80]

In fact, the number of migrants seeking asylum in Mexico rose through 2019 and reached a historic level in 2023, before falling in 2024. In 2021 alone, the Mexican Commission for Refugee Assistance (COMAR) received about

130,000 asylum applications from migrants. That was nearly twice as many as it received in 2019 (see figure 2.6), ranking Mexico third in the world according to asylum requests, only after the United States and Germany. And it also ranked third in the world in 2023 with 141,000 asylum requests.[81] In 2024, asylum requests fell to 79,000 as migrants' access to lawful pathways to the United States improved and Mexican asylum processing slowed.[82]

The Mexican government partnered with United Nations High Commissioner for Refugees (UNHCR), IOM, and the private sector to relocate recognized refugees to parts of the country where there are significant labor needs, providing transitional housing and connections to employers. Over 30,000 refugees have been relocated through the program with over half employed within a month and more than 90 percent within six months.[83]

The convergence of these new migration realities cemented Mexico's identity as a country of emigration, transit, and destination and underscored its central role in regional migration management—with and without the United States. Across regional forums, like the Los Angeles Declaration on Migration and Protection, the Mexican government sought to become a key actor

FIGURE 2.6   Asylum Applications Submitted to Mexico's Refugee Agency, 2013–2024.

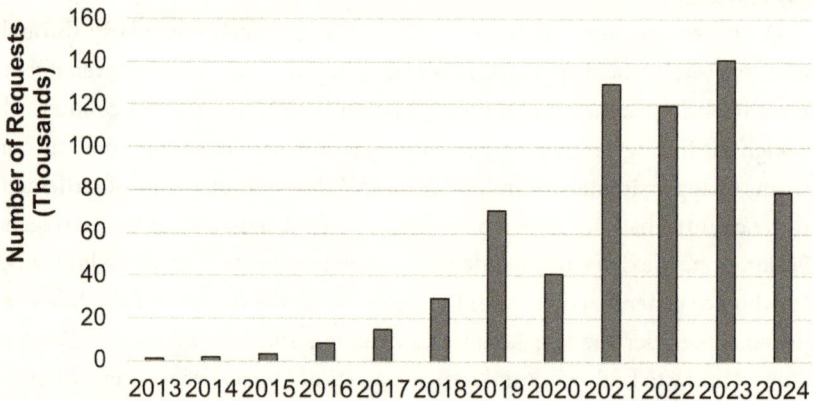

Note: The humanitarian protection requests include applications for refugee status, which are processed by Mexico's Refugee Agency (COMAR), but not political asylum, which is granted by the Foreign Affairs Ministry.

Source: COMAR, "Solicitudes de Refugio al Cierre de Diciembre 2024," accessed January 3, 2025, https://www.gob.mx/cms/uploads/attachment/file/964580/Cierre_Diciembre-2024.pdf.

in hemispheric migration discussions, advocating for stronger protection systems, expanding lawful mobility pathways, and investing in the root causes of irregular migration, while also strengthening border controls.[84] In doing so, the López Obrador administration managed a difficult balancing act: simultaneously seeking to slow the number of migrants from other countries that pass through its territory while championing for more lawful migration options for Mexicans and other migrants.

Towards the end of the administration, the foreign ministry led an interagency planning process that produced the Mexican Model of Human Mobility, the country's first comprehensive strategy to address the different aspects of migration for the Mexican government, including maintaining ties with the diaspora and assisting those who return to the country; integrating migrants who stay in Mexico; controlling irregular migration throughout the country; and investing in countries that are the source of migration. It remains to be seen if this strategy will have an impact on policies down the road, but it was a major step forward in acknowledging Mexico's complex position as a sending, receiving, and transit country.[85]

The Mexican government increasingly began to negotiate migration policy with other countries in the hemisphere, starting with its nearest neighbors in Central America. It committed to lead a regional committee on labor mobility, working with Guatemala and El Salvador, as well as Haiti, the United States, and Canada.[86] Seeking to reduce the need for irregular migration, the López Obrador administration also implemented two social welfare programs—Sowing Life and Youth Building the Future—first in El Salvador and Honduras and subsequently in Guatemala, Belize, and Cuba.[87] These programs offered direct small grants to generate jobs and provide training for farmers and youth. Early program results suggested Salvadoran and Honduran participants' intentions to emigrate decreased, but these have not been independently evaluated yet to understand their long-term effects across countries.

By the end of 2024, as managing migration was becoming a hemispheric affair, Mexico's strategic importance was palpable unlike any time before. Its proximity to and collaboration with the United States raised pressures to respond quickly to changes in northbound migration flows. Its long history of emigration had set a benchmark for addressing migration through a human rights lens. And its broader diplomatic relations with countries like Venezuela, Cuba, and Nicaragua expanded its influence in countries of emigration.

But Mexico was not the only country coming to terms with the new reality of transit migration. Broader use of routes to traverse the Darien Gap and new air routes to Nicaragua complicated Central American countries' ability to respond and adapt to these flows, generally with a fraction of the institutional capacity and resources of Mexico. Honduras, for instance, recorded that approximately 520,000 migrants transited the country in 2023, compared to 174,000 in 2022.[88] And this mismatch between rising transit migration and governments' protection and processing capacities extended further south.

––––––––––––––––

When you walk through the streets of La Carpio, a large neighborhood on the outskirts of Costa Rica's capital of San José, you could easily think that you are in Nicaragua. The accent on the street changes as soon as you enter the neighborhood, and signs outside storefronts boast the names of Nicaraguan towns where their owners once lived. At a local community center, SIFAIS, dedicated to arts and sports education, the staff teach courses on woodworking, ceramics, textiles, and entrepreneurship to recently arrived migrants from Nicaragua, and they provide legal assistance to help Nicaraguan asylum seekers navigate the complexities of obtaining protection in Costa Rica. The neighborhood was once considered one of the most dangerous in Costa Rica, a ramshackle slum that most people who did not live there avoided. But today it is relatively safe, well-organized, and quite livable, a testament to the organizational capacity of the neighborhood's residents, who have built a tight-knit community of exiles.[89]

Costa Rica and Nicaragua, two countries of roughly comparable population size with about 5 to 7 million residents each, have had a symbiotic but asymmetric relationship for decades. Costa Rica has emerged as an oasis of peace, stability, and relative economic success in an otherwise difficult region marked by civil conflicts, deep inequality, and frequent economic crises. After a civil war in the 1940s, the country abolished its armed forces, and it has seen a peaceful transition of elected authorities since then. In 2023, Costa Rica's GDP per capita of roughly $28,000 in purchasing power parity terms was almost four times that of Nicaragua and Honduras and more than twice that of Guatemala and El Salvador. It was even slightly ahead of that of Mexico.[90]

The only Central American country that was comparable in economic terms to Costa Rica was Panama, which had a higher GDP per capita. It is probably no surprise that Costa Rica and Panama were therefore the only Central American countries with very little emigration. In fact, only around 3 percent of the population of each country lived abroad, while both countries attracted many immigrants and refugees from other countries. As of 2023, the best available estimates suggest that immigrants and refugees compose between 13 and 16 percent of Costa Rica's population, with nearly two-thirds of them from Nicaragua, and 7 percent of Panama's population.[91]

Costa Rica and Nicaragua have long had divergent development outcomes, but migration from Nicaragua to Costa Rica did not really pick up until the 1970s when a first wave of Nicaraguans fled during a civil war that eventually led to the overthrow of the long-running Somoza dictatorship and brought the Sandinista Front to power. A second wave of emigration took place during the 1990s as Nicaragua went through a deep economic crisis and Hurricane Mitch devastated parts of the country, which led to the establishment of La Carpio, among other smaller Nicaraguan communities in Costa Rica. And a third wave began in 2018 when the Nicaraguan government, now under a regime led by Sandinista leader Daniel Ortega that turned out to be as dictatorial as the Somoza regime it once replaced, cracked down on protests by students, professional associations, and rural organizations, and began a long campaign to imprison and exile all those seen as opposed to the regime.[92]

Costa Rica went to great lengths to receive Nicaraguans fleeing their government's growing autocracy and spiraling economy, offering education and emergency healthcare. Most Nicaraguans were able apply for asylum, which allowed them to work legally while their applications were processed. From 2018 through July 2024, approximately 275,000 Nicaraguans had applied for asylum in Costa Rica,[93] while many others likely arrived without seeking asylum. In contrast, about 361,000 Nicaraguans were encountered by the U.S. Border Patrol at the U.S.-Mexico border from FY 2018 through May 2024. This suggests that despite the lure of the United States, many Nicaraguans took advantage of existing family and community ties to move south to Costa Rica rather than north to the United States.

Costa Rica has long been a refuge for asylum seekers and others fleeing turmoil at home. In fact, it was one of the world's largest recipients of new asylum claims in 2022 with 87,000 applications, over 90 percent of them from Nicaragua.[94] Smaller but notable numbers of Venezuelans and Cubans also sought protection in the country. Compared to other Latin American and Caribbean countries, Costa Rica has a well-developed asylum system, which includes an appeal process through an administrative tribunal, but the system has been overwhelmed by the influx of applications submitted in recent years.[95]

Changes under the administration of President Rodrigo Chaves Robles starting in 2022, however, sharply restricted access to asylum. The administration argued that unfounded applications for protection overloaded the system and slowed processing for cases requiring assistance. As of July 2024, asylum seekers are no longer able to receive employment authorization until their cases are resolved, and the number of applications has fallen substantially to about 14,000.[96]

Though far behind the number of Nicaraguans, Venezuelan and Colombian migrants have also sought asylum at different times due to political instability in their countries. Many of them, however, entered the country through employment-based or family-based visas, even if they may have had protection needs.[97] These visas are relatively easier to access for migrants with professional degrees or those who are employed in high-skilled occupations, and they provide a faster pathway to lawful status.

But not all those who move to Costa Rica are displaced populations seeking protection. U.S. nationals were among the top immigrant communities residing in Costa Rica, seeking employment opportunities, remote work, or retirement. And tens of thousands of other immigrants move to the country for employment or for a better quality of life.[98] Indeed, Costa Rica was one of the first countries to create a remote work visa in the aftermath of the COVID-19 pandemic to attract workers.[99]

Also as a recovery response after the health pandemic, Costa Rica updated its labor migration program to make it easier to hire Nicaraguan workers in agricultural industries. A Costa Rican-Nicaraguan agreement, the General Protocol to Address Labor Migration sought to improve worksite and living conditions for temporary migrant workers. It also established a digital migration management system, the Migratory Labor Traceability System (SITLAM), that allows workers to petition to change employers, who can access seasonal labor visas for agricultural work, construction, domestic work, and other sectors of the economy. And due to its success in 2024, the Costa Rican government was considering expanding the program to other industries and immigrants from beyond Nicaragua.[100] Outside of agricultural work, Nicaraguans can also access other kinds of temporary work visas for domestic work, construction, and other sectors of the economy.

Notably, for years Costa Rica and Panama have had special provisions for Indigenous people who live alongside the Costa Rica-Panama border, allowing them to cross back and forth for health and work reasons. In 2019, the Costa Rican government began to issue citizenship to members of the Ngobe-Bugle Indigenous peoples who live on this border to allow them to move even more easily between the two countries.[101]

Perhaps the biggest challenge in Costa Rica's migration policy framework, like in many other Latin American countries, is integrating its immigrant population. Despite enacting a law to promote immigrant integration in 2019, migrants face many obstacles to do so. A key example is that for migrants to become affiliated with the country's healthcare system, the Social Security Fund, they must have a permanent legal status and pay a monthly fee.[102]

Like Costa Rica, Panama next door has long attracted immigrants from around the world seeking employment opportunities. But unlike Costa Rica, Panama has a very restricted asylum system, and relatively few migrants seek asylum there.[103] Panama's visa system is also famously sclerotic, working only slowly to grant visas to those who arrive for work. And the Panamanian government dismantled much of the country's security apparatus, after the fall of long-time strongman Manuel Noriega in 1989, and never fully rebuilt the parts related to migration that had been within that apparatus.[104]

These institutional weaknesses complicate migrant workers' access to lawful immigration status despite the interest from many world regions due to the country's economic dynamism. Venezuelans and Colombians have commonly migrated to Panama, but also many others from the United States, China, and Spain. The government has relied on frequent ad hoc regularization programs, instead of broader immigration reforms, to provide cohorts of migrants a regular status.[105] Since 2010, three regularization programs—two directed at all foreign-born people without legal status and one specifically at Chinese nationals—have provided legal residency to approximately 146,000 migrants.[106] This compares to 312,000 migrants who received legal residency through ordinary visas, which suggests that regularization measures have supplemented the regular visa system not just for displaced populations but for many immigrants from a wide variety of nationalities. And while the administration of former Panamanian President Laurentino Cortizo sought to bolster the visa system during his 2019–2024 tenure, its efficiency was not yet clear as of the end of 2024.[107]

Panama's legal framework is also unique due to its very strict labor law, which was modified several times in the 1950s to prohibit foreign-born residents, even those legally present, from working in over fifty different occupations, from nurses and doctors to lawyers and engineers. There were a few narrow exceptions to the law, but it largely restricts employment options for many immigrants who have lived in the country for years.[108] At the same time, Panama has a regime of exception for workers in foreign-owned industries that have headquarters in Panama, which allows them to hire immigrant workers, who can also bring their families to the country with them.[109]

In addition, Panama and Costa Rica are quite culturally distinct, despite their economic similarities. Costa Rica has historically been a large European-descent society, with a large African-descent population on the Caribbean coast, and Indigenous populations near the Panama border, but with comparatively less mixing among different groups than in most other countries in Latin America and the Caribbean.[110] As Costa Rican migration expert Maria Jesús Mora found in interviews with Costa Ricans and Nicaraguan migrants, skin color and accents serve as markers that often lead to discrimination against Nicaraguan migrants.[111]

Panama, by contrast, is a highly racially and ethnically diverse society thanks in large part to the Panama Canal, which attracted Afro-Caribbean immigrant labor in the early twentieth century, large Chinese and European immigrant populations after that, and a permanent population of U.S. immigrants of all racial and ethnic backgrounds tied to the Panama Canal Zone, which remained under U.S. control until 1999. However, the U.S. influence in Panama also led to significantly less fluid racial and ethnic boundaries in Panama than other parts of the region, with studies indicating that self-identification is often closer to U.S. categories that identify separate categories of whiteness and blackness than is true elsewhere in the Americas.[112] Unlike in Costa Rica, immigrants are not always immediately identifiable by their physical appearance, but the effects of race, ethnicity, and social class interact in complex ways that affect the way they are incorporated in Panamanian society.

Today Panama and Costa Rica are facing a new set of challenges around irregular migration, which has attracted worldwide media attention to their borders and escalated public pressure for the governments to better manage migration. For years, a few risk-taking migrants tried to cross the Darien Gap, an almost impenetrable forest between Colombia and Panama. From 2010 to

2014 roughly 2,400 migrants tried crossing each year, increasing to 30,000 annually in 2015 and 2016, and then dropped back again to a few thousand through 2020.[113] The composition of migrants who crossed the Darien Gap has always been diverse, coming from across South America and as far as from Asian and African countries.[114]

Starting in 2021, however, migrant crossings at the Darien Gap rose significantly, first with Haitians living in South America composing the vast majority of crossers, and later Venezuelans and significant numbers from other countries. Setting a historic record, over a half million migrants crossed in 2023, followed by a notable decrease in 2024 (see figure 2.7).[115] International organizations and others have extensively documented the dangers of crossing the jungle, from the natural hazards of steep mountainous areas and strong rivers to deadly wildlife encounters and exposure to diseases to robbery, kidnapping, and sexual harassment at the hands of criminals and smugglers.[116] Additionally, the sheer number of migrants crossing the jungle have created positive and negative spillover effects for the Indigenous communities living there. On one hand, some of these communities have experienced economic gains from selling goods and services to migrants, at times at a cost of expanding criminal networks. [117] On the other hand, it has brought about unprece-

FIGURE 2.7   Migrant Crossings at the Darien Gap, by Country of Origin, 2014–2024.

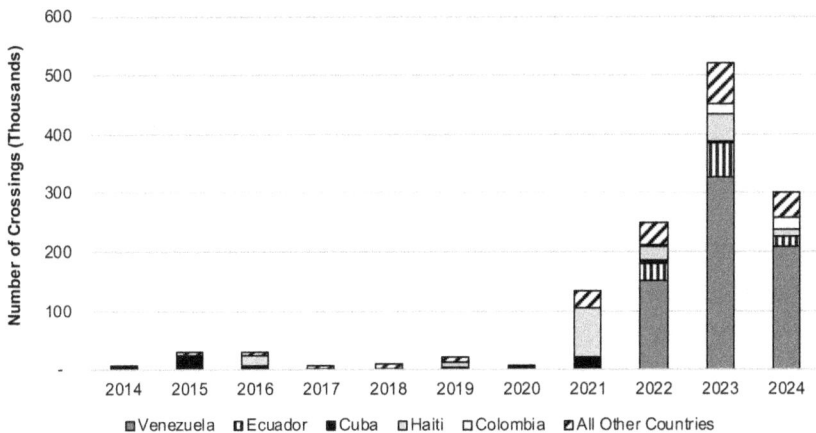

Source: Authors' tabulations of data from Panama's Migration Authority, "Tránsito Irregular por Darién, 2024," accessed January 5, 2025, https://www.migracion.gob.pa/estadisticas.

dented ecological damage through human waste and contamination in what was once one of the most pristine rainforests in the world.[118]

Throughout Central America and Mexico, the public and government reaction to large numbers of migrants passing through their countries has been decidedly mixed, with some solidarity for people in dire circumstances but also discomfort at the sheer size of the population movements. For many countries, other than Mexico, this is the first time that large numbers of people have visibly transited their countries on their way to the United States, and it has created more than a little disconcertion as people camp out in public spaces along the route.

Lack of institutional infrastructure to provide migrants long-term shelter and other services in Panama and Costa Rica, as well as public pressures from urban hubs where migrants would otherwise congregate, led the governments to enact a policy of "controlled flow." Designed with the U.S. Department of Homeland Security (DHS), this policy allows governments to monitor and screen migrants against criminal and terrorist databases when they arrive at the Panama-Colombia border and at the Costa Rica-Panama border. Panamanian and Costa Rican officials collect migrants' biometric information and, if they are approved to continue, provide access to buses that transport them northbound. Fingerprints are shared with the DHS to determine if migrants are potential security threats or dangerous, and the few cases that get a positive match have generally been repatriated. However, the policy was designed for a few thousand crossings a year, not for the hundreds of thousands that transited through the region in 2023 and 2024.

Governments along the route almost uniformly have indicated that they want to deter flows of migrants transiting their territory without authorization en route to the United States. A U.S.-Panama agreement in 2024 to implement a new removal flight program by Panamanian authorities using U.S. funding was among the most important developments in the region. And though the Panamanian government repatriated about 200 migrants in a span of two weeks, including a flight to India, the number was still a fraction of total crossings at the Darien Gap.[119] With additional institutional capacity and resources, this U.S.-Panama agreement could be expanded in the future. Other governments have tried similar efforts with minimal success. We return to this topic, which has policy implications across not only Central America but the hemisphere as a whole, in the final chapter of the book.

3 The Caribbean

The Uneven Search for Integration

WHO IS CARIBBEAN? Before his improbable journey from popular singer to president of Haiti to controversial public figure in his post-presidency, Michel Martelly recalled Haitians' contribution as the first free Black republic of the Caribbean (and the world) when singing passionately in a troubadour-style: "neg nwa ki fè lindependans, ki invente la libète, pa janm mache tet bese mem lè peyi nou an danje" ("Us Black people who did the revolution, we invented freedom, keep your head up, even when your country is in trouble").

And there's no doubt that Jamaican cultural ambassador Bob Marley is an international symbol of Caribbean culture; the parallel between Buffalo Soldiers in the United States and that of Black Caribbean people is obvious in his lyrics: "Stolen from Africa, brought to America . . . fighting on arrival, fighting for survival . . . driven from the mainland to the heart of the Caribbean."

Further confirmation of the predominance of African heritage for most Caribbean people is the steel pans heard at Trinidad and Tobago's Carnival, but Caribbean identity is also captured by popular Indo-Caribbean Chutney music of Trinidadian legend Sonny Man and Guyanese singer Terry Gajraj. And who can deny the Latin Caribbean spirit of Marc Anthony and Gente de Zona, as they call out in "La Gozadera" the cultural contributions of Puerto Rico, Cuba, the Dominican Republic and the Caribbean coasts of Mexico, Colombia, and Venezuela, proudly reminding the world of their presence in the lyric "y del Caribe somos tú e yo."

From an outsider's perspective, the definition of the Caribbean is simple:

it is made up of islands with hundreds of wonderful beaches ripe for tourism, where people of similar cultures live a simple life. Yet a closer look reveals a number of contrasts, rooted in its geography—not all Caribbean nations are islands, and those that are vary greatly in size and topography—as well as people, cultures, and wildly different institutional and economic systems. The region's legacy of colonialism, in many cases passing from one colonizer to another, makes it an especially disparate region today. Yet, a Caribbean culture and obvious commonalities have transcended these differences. The move towards a unified region has been both natural and intentional and has come from both inside and outside forces.

The socioeconomic impact of colonialism is multifaceted, and still visible today, albeit at various degrees. The disastrous consequences of slavery to people's humanity are a fundamental element in the region's development. It is important to understand how significant this region was for colonial powers between the sixteenth and nineteenth centuries, and the early extractive nature of colonialists' interest in Caribbean land. Indigenous cultures, mostly annihilated and enslaved people from Africa, were brought as labor to extract primary resources from the lands to be exported to European countries. As such, the governments of Spain, the United Kingdom, France, Portugal, the Netherlands, Denmark, and eventually the United States established competitive systems to dominate the triangular trade between the Caribbean, North America, and Europe. The nature of this trade system, while focused on goods, also involved the (mostly forced) movement of people between Africa, Europe, the Americas, and later South and Southeast Asia as well.

The intrinsic nature of colonial powers' competition in the region meant that institutional and economic systems in each colony were geared towards countries outside of the region, not with neighboring Caribbean islands, and that colonial powers imposed their own language, culture, legal systems, currency, and norms in their respective colonies, exacerbating islands' distance from one another. Meanwhile, maintaining slave systems and later indentured servitude from South and Southeast Asian countries, meant that contact among islanders was discouraged so as to avoid the spread of attempted rebellions, which were a common occurrence.

What does this all mean for migration? Historical evidence suggests that despite rigid institutional barriers, Caribbean populations moved across the region, thanks to geographical proximity, slim opportunities for islanders who were not enslaved to move to other islands, and, in many cases, as an act of rebellion to escape slavery. For instance, the British possessed a set of islands, among which movement could occur more easily. However, parallel movements from one European-controlled colony to another would generally occur as acts of defiance.

Haiti, the first country to gain independence in the Caribbean through a revolution led by both enslaved and mixed-race descendants of the French and enslaved Blacks, immediately afterwards sought to liberate other countries from slavery. In this quest, Haitian leader General Jean-Jacques Dessalines sent troops throughout the Caribbean and Latin America to spread the word that the French had been defeated. This prompted other colonial powers to tighten the grip on their colonies, refusing to recognize Haitian independence for decades (until 1862 in the case of the United States). More than a century later, Cuba experienced a similar fate of international isolation after Fidel Castro's successful Communist revolution in 1959, which aimed to regain control of the islands' resources by pushing out growing U.S. financial interests.

The triangular trade system left behind Caribbean economies designed for external trade relations with the United States and Europe. Raw materials were extracted from the Caribbean and exported to the United States and Europe for assembly and processing; then the finished products were imported by the Caribbean (and the world). This production model was most apparent in the sugar, coffee, and lumber industries. These trade patterns have largely shaped todays' patterns of mobility in goods, services, and people: for nearly all Caribbean nations, the main commercial partner, and first destination of their emigrants, is the U.S. or a European country. Moreover, there is a persistent lack of connectivity between neighboring islands—there is no regional ferry boat system or Caribbean airline. Air travel from one Caribbean nation to another usually involves going through the Miami hub, controlled by U.S.-based airlines. This is a disincentive for intraregional travel of Caribbean nationals, not only because it is costly and time-consuming, but because it involves stricter visa requirements.

The plurality of colonial systems and different decolonization experiences also left behind an array of legal and political systems that are not always compatible, which undoubtedly hinders the movement of Caribbean nationals within the region. The end of colonialism and what replaced it further exacerbated differences between countries. From Haiti's abrupt early independence from France in 1804 to St. Kitts and Nevis's recent independence from the UK in 1983, a spectrum of experiences indicates that a more gradual transition to modernize economies and gain political control occurred in some of the Commonwealth nations, while others transitioned to modern forms of colonialism, as exist today in a number of French, British, Dutch, and U.S. territories and dependencies. The lack of autonomy of some nations and significant development challenges for others mean that external actors, particularly former colonial powers, are still heavily involved in the region's affairs, including in the area of human mobility. To this day, the region heavily depends on international development aid for capacity to build financing and policy coordination between nations.

Despite their differences, the region's leaders have long recognized the need to join forces given their geographic proximity, relatively small population size, cultural affinity, shared history, and mutual interests in facing major challenges like global inequality and climate change. The Caribbean Community (CARICOM) and other subregional agreements have contributed to a legal framework and an ambitious vision to facilitate trade and the movement of people within the region. Today, the region is characterized by high mobility both from outside the region, primarily due to tourism, and from within the region, thanks to mobility agreements and an increase in the movement of migrants with protection needs.

The data on immigrants living among the thirty Caribbean nations, fifteen of which belong to the Caribbean Community (CARICOM) reveal a surprising set of facts about who moves to or within the Caribbean that are not always what we might expect.[1] Haitians, Americans (from the continental United States), French, Venezuelans, Dominicans, and Guyanese are the most likely to be living as foreigners in Caribbean countries (table 3.1).

Haitians represented nearly a third of the 1,810,344 foreign-born living in the region in 2020, the largest share for any single nationality, and they were in the top three nationalities in The Bahamas, Dominica, the Dominican Republic, Guadeloupe, St. Maarten, and Turks and Caicos. Haitians are, not surprisingly, highly concentrated in the neighboring Dominican Republic, where as many as 517,000 Haitians lived in 2020 (table 3.2). The 2010 earthquake in Haiti, followed by disastrous hurricanes and social and political turmoil, have

TABLE 3.1   Immigrant Population in Caribbean Countries, by Country of Origin, 2020.

	Number of Immigrants	Share of Immigrant Population
All Countries	1,839,189	100%
Haiti	590,100	32%
Other Countries	502,401	27%
United States	235,642	13%
France	131,779	7%
Venezuela	119,160	6%
Dominican Republic	77,174	4%
Guyana	49,726	3%
Jamaica	36,139	2%
Suriname	33,190	2%
United Kingdom	21,773	1%
Netherlands	21,426	1%
Dominica	20,679	1%

Source: Authors' tabulations of data from the United Nations' Department of Economic and Social Affairs, Population Division, "International Migrant Stock 2020: Destination and Origin," accessed September 23, 2024, https://www.un.org/development/desa/pd/content/international -migrant-stock.

TABLE 3.2 Immigrant Populations in Caribbean Countries and Territories, Shares, and Top Countries of Origin, 2020.

	Total Population	Immigrant Population	Share of Immigrants Out of Total Population	Caribbean Immigrant Population	Share of Caribbean Immigrants Out of Immigrant Population	Top 3 Countries of Origin of Immigrants
CARICOM Member States						
Antigua and Barbuda	92,664	23,670	32%	23,621	80%	Guyana, Dominica, Jamaica
Bahamas	406,472	63,583	16%	42,520	67%	Haiti, U.S., Jamaica
Barbados	280,693	34,869	12%	15,762	45%	Guyana, SVG, UK
Belize	394,921	62,043	16%	621	1%	Guatemala, El Salvador, Honduras
Dominica	71,995	8,284	12%	4,839	58%	Haiti, UK, US
Grenada	123,663	7,213	6%	4,356	60%	T&T, USVI, SVG
Guyana	797,202	31,169	4%	1,348	4%	Venezuela, Suriname, Brazil
Haiti	11,306,802	18,884	0%	5,088	27%	Venezuela, DR, US
Jamaica	2,820,436	23,629	1%	6,546	28%	US, UK, T&T
Montserrat	4,500	1,379	31%	878	64%	Dominica, Guyana, US
Saint Kitts and Nevis	47,643	7,725	16%	3,632	47%	USVI, Guyana, Montserrat
Saint Lucia	179,237	8,338	5%	4,990	60%	Guyana, US, UK
Saint Vincent and the Grenadines	104,633	4,738	5%	3,081	65%	T&T, UK, Grenada
Suriname	607,065	47,801	8%	13,557	28%	Guyana, Brazil, China
Trinidad and Tobago	1,518,147	78,849	5%	33,211	42%	Venezuela, Guyana, Grenada

Other Caribbean Islands or Nations Associated with the Caribbean

Other Caribbean Islands or Nations Associated with the Caribbean						
Aruba	106,585	53,593	50%	13,704	26%	Venezuela, Colombia, Netherlands
Anguilla	15,585	5,715	37%	3,220	56%	SKN, DR, Jamaica
British Virgin Islands	30,910	22,164	72%	15,523	70%	Guyana, SVG, Jamaica
Cayman Islands	67,311	29,242	43%	13,359	46%	Jamaica, US, UK
Cuba	11,300,698	3,024	0%	116	4%	Spain, Italy, Russia
Curaçao	189,289	57,210	30%	20,275	35%	Venezuela, Netherlands, DR
Dominican Republic	10,999,664	603,794	5%	505,372	84%	Haiti, Venezuela, US
French Guiana	290,970	119,249	41%	28,684	24%	Suriname, Brazil, France
Guadeloupe	395,642	90,206	23%	28,967	32%	France, Haiti, Martinique
Martinique	370,391	68,624	19%	12,922	19%	France, Guadeloupe, St. Lucia
Puerto Rico	3,271,565	247,132	8%	60,554	25%	US, DR, Cuba
Sint Maarten	43,622	28,845	66%	23,342	81%	DR, Haiti, Jamaica
Turks and Caicos Islands	44,277	25,748	58%	18,083	70%	Haiti, DR, US
United States Virgin Islands	100,443	56,753	57%	38,688	68%	US, SKN, Dominica

Note: Caribbean total includes UN classified Caribbean countries + Belize, French Guiana, Guyana, and Suriname.

Source: Authors' tabulations of data from the United Nations' Department of Economic and Social Affairs, Population Division, "International Migrant Stock 2020: Destination and Origin," accessed September 23, 2024, https://www.un.org/development/desa/pd/content/international-migrant-stock.

pushed thousands of Haitians to establish themselves in the Dominican Republic. Though circular migration of Haitian workers to the Dominican Republic had long existed, this more recent migration reached even higher levels and presents unique challenges for Dominican authorities. Haitian migrants have faced a hardening of immigration policies after a brief welcoming attitude in the aftermath of the earthquake, when removals were temporarily suspended and greater access to healthcare services was granted to victims of the earthquake and their families.[2]

Perhaps more surprisingly, as many as 235,642 U.S.-born citizens from the continental U.S. lived in the Greater Caribbean in 2020, ranking second after Haitians in terms of largest immigrant groups.[3] Moreover, these U.S.-born citizens were the most dispersed nationality in the Caribbean: they appear in the top three nationalities of foreigners in eleven of the thirty Caribbean nations. In Puerto Rico and the U.S. Virgin Islands, both territories that are part of the United States, Americans born in the continental U.S. were the largest group of foreign-born. Many of these Americans may be retirees taking advantage of the Caribbean's proximity, great weather, and financial benefits,[4] but there are also U.S.-born descendants of the Caribbean diaspora in the U.S. who have chosen to return to the Caribbean.

Similarly, there is a notable presence of nationals from European countries in nations that are still tied to European countries. As a result, in the French overseas departments of French Guiana, Guadeloupe, and Martinique, French citizens represented the third largest group of foreign-born overall, after Haitian and U.S. citizens. The Dutch were concentrated in the territories of Aruba and Curaçao, which are still part of the Kingdom of the Netherlands though highly autonomous. On the other hand, while the British represented a small percentage of all foreign-born in the region (around 1 percent, similar to the Dutch), they represented a significant share of the foreign-born in several nations, including CARICOM countries Barbados, Dominica, Jamaica, St. Lucia, and St. Vincent and the Grenadines, all of which were once British territories but are now independent nations.

In 2020, as many as 119,000 Venezuelans were settled in the Caribbean, or about 6 percent of all foreign-born in the Caribbean, a number that had increased significantly by 2023 to around 213,000.[5] Following the collapse of Venezuela in 2016, at least 7.5 million Venezuelans left their country, most settling in neighboring Colombia (2.9 million), but a significant number headed to newer destinations, including the Dominican Republic, Trinidad and Tobago, Aruba, Curaçao, and Guyana. The majority live in the Dominican Republic, such that the country now hosts the two largest groups of migrants with protection needs in the Caribbean (Haitians and Venezuelans). Though the flows of Venezuelans are smaller in the other Caribbean nations, the arrival of thousands of Venezuelans over a short period of time has represented tremendous challenges, in part because these countries lack experience with receiving humanitarian populations. Also, the small size of some of these islands—Trinidad and Tobago has a population almost nine times smaller than that of the Dominican Republic and its territory is far smaller—poses unique challenges for these nations' capacity to manage large migrant flows.

About 4 percent of all foreign-born in the region were from the Dominican Republic in 2020. Aside from neighboring Haiti, Dominicans are primarily established in nations outside of CARICOM (of which it is not a member) including Anguilla, Curaçao, Puerto Rico, St. Maarten, and Turks and Caicos. Puerto Rico has long been a destination for Dominican migrants, starting in the mid-1960s and accelerating in the 1980s as Dominican migrants would attempt to reach Puerto Rico in small, overcrowded boats, known as yolas, through the dangerous Mona Passage. Puerto Rico, an intended gateway to the United States, attracts many Dominicans because of its significantly higher wages. Dominican women are more likely to find jobs than men, particularly in the domestic sector where they tend to work for years and send remittances back home to sustain their families.[6] Immigrant advocacy organizations and several reports describe the heightened vulnerability of Dominican women, who are often subject to sexual harassment and abuse along the journey to Puerto Rico, but also as workers without protection.[7] It is estimated that close to 30 percent of Dominicans living in Puerto Rico today are unauthorized.[8]

After U.S. citizens from the continental United States, Guyanese were the most dispersed nationality in the Caribbean. Although in smaller numbers overall, they featured in the top three nationalities of foreign-born residents in eight Caribbean nations, seven of which are CARICOM member states: Antigua and Barbuda, Barbados, Montserrat, St. Kitts and Nevis, St. Lucia, Suriname, Trinidad and Tobago, and the British Virgin Islands. As Guyanese Ambassador Zulfikar Ally notes, decades of political instability and dictatorship following independence in 1966, lack of basic social infrastructure, and economic uncertainty drove many Guyanese to migrate, mainly to the United

States, Canada, the United Kingdom, and neighboring Caribbean nations.[9] Although since 1992, democratic elections have been held regularly, Guyana remains a migrant-sending country, due in part to its relatively lower standards of living, Guyanese seeking to reunite with their families abroad, and searching for better opportunities for their children.

When oil and gas were discovered in 2015, the Guyanese government anticipated rapid economic growth and a need for migrant labor to fill jobs. Projections were that the country would need at least 100,000 migrant workers to reach full economic potential and reap the benefits of the newly discovered resources.[10] While it is still too early to know what will happen, indicators suggest that Guyana may in fact be in a position to reverse its economic trajectory, and by the same token, shift from a migrant-sending to a migrant-receiving country. After the start of gas and oil production in 2019, the country's GDP grew from 5 billion dollars in 2020 to 8 billion dollars in 2021, and to an impressive 15 billion dollars in 2022. As the Guyanese economy tripled during a period that coincided with the COVID-19 pandemic and a slowdown of all other economies in Latin America and the Caribbean, the unemployment rate fell from 15 percent to 12 percent, and the rate of out-migration slowed significantly compared to earlier years.[11] In addition to attracting members of its own diaspora, Zulfikar notes that the government hopes to attract migrants from other Caribbean countries. With the right plans in place, a new corridor of heightened regional mobility within CARICOM could emerge.

Overall, Caribbean countries tend to have very high immigrant-to-population ratios, due in part to their small populations and long history of foreign presence. In several non-CARICOM nations, more than half of the population is foreign born, including in Aruba, U.S. Virgin Islands, Turks and Caicos, St. Maarten, and the British Virgin Islands (see table 3.2). Many of these economies rely heavily on migrant workers. For instance, in the tourism sector of the Cayman Islands, British Virgin Islands, and Turks and Caicos, migrants make up at least 60 percent of all workers. In CARICOM nations, the shares of foreign-born out of total population tend to be lower but still quite high compared to other countries in the Americas. For example, the shares of immigrants were 16 percent each in The Bahamas, Belize, and Saint Kitts and Nevis, and were the highest in Montserrat (31 percent) and Antigua and Barbuda (32 percent), higher than in any country in Central or South America.

Intraregional mobility is high, including in non-CARICOM nations. Half of the people living in the Greater Caribbean in 2020 were from another country in the region.[12] In Antigua and Barbuda, British Virgin Islands, the Dominican Republic, St. Maarten, and Turks and Caicos, seven in ten foreign-born, or more, were from another Caribbean nation.

In contrast, the shares of Caribbean migrants were particularly low in Aruba, Belize, and Cuba, where no Caribbean country featured in the top three countries of origin of migrants. Aruba, a country within the Kingdom of the Netherlands, has become an important destination for Venezuelans who are now the largest immigrant group. In Belize, a small CARICOM country, which is also a member of the Central American System (SICA), just 1 percent of its immigrant population came from the Caribbean. Meanwhile, migrants from neighboring Guatemala, El Salvador, and Honduras represented 77 percent of the country's immigrant population in 2020.

Among Caribbean nations, Cuba had the second smallest number of immigrants, only 3,000 after Montserrat's 1,400, but Cuba's population is 2,500 times larger than Montserrat's, and that means that less than 1 percent of Cuba's population is foreign born today. It was also the only country where the top three countries of origin of immigrants (Spain, Italy, and Russia) were outside the Latin American and Caribbean region. Moreover, only 4 percent of immigrants in Cuba were from the Caribbean.

Taken together, these data would suggest that Cuba has few relations with the Caribbean, but this would not be accurate. Since 2002, CARICOM-Cuba Summits have taken place every three years. The Cuban government has an explicit policy of external cooperation that is based on capacity building, and it has made cooperation with CARICOM a priority. Cuba's cooperation programs have primarily been in the areas of education, health, and disaster assistance.[13] Medical and health cooperation agreements have been established with Jamaica, Haiti, and the Dominican Republic. After the 2010 earthquake in Haiti, the Cuban government made Haiti a priority for several cooperation programs, particularly for its medical and health services.[14] Moreover, CARICOM states that were part of the Alianza Bolivariana para los Pueblos de Nuestra América (ALBA), created in 2004 by Cuba and Venezuela, were also eligible for favorable treatment in receiving service provisions at a discounted price.[15] Despite ongoing financial pressures, the Cuban government has maintained its policy of proximity and exchange with the Caribbean. During the pandemic, many CARICOM countries sought medical support from Cuba due to a shortage of medical resources and staff.[16]

While regional mobility agreements have created legal pathways for residence in other countries, in some cases, migration is still through irregular pathways. By nature, irregular migration is difficult to estimate. But an assessment by the International Organization for Migration (IOM) suggests that the total number of irregular migrants across the Caribbean exceeds the number of regular migrants.[17] The inability to count and recognize migrants in irregular status makes it difficult for host countries to measure the extent of the phenomenon and how to address it.

Moreover, many countries lack autonomy over border management. In fact, among CARICOM countries, only Jamaica and Belize maintain their own border management system.[18] Most of the other nations use the services of a foreign-owned private-sector company to help manage their borders. This lack of capacity to manage borders, particularly for islands that have challenging geographies, like the archipelagos of The Bahamas and St. Vincent and the Grenadines, has implications for national and regional security as it presents opportunities for bad actors to exploit vulnerable migrants, especially women and children, and use them as merchandise in human smuggling networks. As a region, CARICOM has in place a mechanism, the Implementing Agency for Crime and Security (IMPACS), to identify elements of transnational crime and develop strategies to address them. Still, the lucrative business of human smuggling, which combines both illegal and legal aspects of migration, has boomed in the last years, along with drug and arms trafficking routes originating in or going through the Caribbean.[19]

Most Caribbean countries have a large percentage of their migrant population working informally, including in the Dominican Republic, The Bahamas, and Trinidad and Tobago, which are also the primary countries of destination for Haitians and Venezuelans. In the Dominican Republic, where Haitian migrant workers have been present in the agricultural industry since the early 1900s, only a small percentage are registered with a work permit.[20] Several reports have highlighted the deplorable work conditions of Haitian workers in the Dominican sugar industry.[21] The uniqueness of the shared island of Hispaniola explains in part its particular migration patterns, including both circular and noncircular labor migration originating in Haiti.[22] Today, Haitian workers represent important shares of the labor hired in the Dominican agricultural, construction, tourism, and commercial sectors.

The Dominican Republic has conducted an extensive regularization program for Venezuelan migrants, but not for Haitians, while Curaçao and Trinidad and Tobago did the same for Venezuelans, though with very limited criteria and short periods for legal status. Overall, regularization programs have been less common in the Caribbean than in Latin America.[23] For example, since 2000, at least ninety-two extraordinary regularization processes have been implemented in eighteen of twenty-six Latin American countries, of which two have taken place in Suriname and Trinidad and Tobago.[24]

In the face of irregular migration, Belize has taken a proactive approach by implementing a regularization program for migrants without legal status. As a small nation neighboring Mexico and Guatemala, Belize has long experienced influxes of Central American migrants and refugees. Belize was a British colony that gained independence in 1981. The majority of its population was primarily made up of Black descendants of enslaved people from the Caribbean (Creoles), the Afro-Indigenous Garifuna people, and the descendants of Mestizo and Mayan Mexicans.[25] Between the late 1970s and 1991, increased Central American arrivals during the civil conflicts in those countries, and sustained out-migration of Afro-Belizeans to the United States, resulted in a noticeable demographic shift, with Mestizos making up close to half of the population today.[26]

The government of Belize has generally been welcoming to foreigners despite the high number of irregular migrants—IOM estimated that there were at least 10,000 unauthorized Central American migrants by 1996, a trend that has continued with many Central Americans moving to Belize to work in agriculture. Belize also has a small seasonal agricultural worker program in which around 3,000 participants, mostly from Guatemala, work in the citrus industry each year.[27] Over the years, a series of regularization initiatives have provided a pathway to permanency for irregular migrants who arrived in the country as children, extensions of work permits for irregular migrant workers already in the country, and regularization of dependents of regular migrants and spouses, children, and parents of Belizean nationals.[28]

Unlike prior regularization programs tailored for Central American refugees and asylum seekers, Belize's more recent regularization program, launched in late 2021, aimed to grant status to irregular migrants from all countries who entered before 2017 and met specific educational, work, or family reunification requirements.[29] As former Belizean Minister Gilroy Middleton remarked, this program differs from prior initiatives because it is embedded in national law and was designed and implemented with a vision to encourage "safe, orderly and regular migration, via cooperation with local, regional and international organizations and institutions."[30] Although the government launched a wide campaign to encourage migrants to come out of the shadows, and several extensions to the application date, only 12,765 migrants applied for amnesty, far below the 40,000 to 60,000 that were estimated as potentially eligible. Sources have indicated that the initial estimates may have been inflated by an inaccurate count of migrant exits, and as such, the regularization should still be considered a success. Applicants were from thirty-two countries, the large majority from Guatemala, El Salvador, and Honduras. While their application is pending, applicants may work and reside in Belize without fear of removal.[31]

When the HMT *Empire Windrush* docked in Essex harbor in June 1948, bringing over 1,000 people from Jamaica, Trinidad, British Guiana, Bermuda, and what were then still British territories in the Caribbean to the United Kingdom, it marked a new era in mobility between the Caribbean and Europe, this time with Caribbean workers filling jobs in the British labor market in the post–World War II period. This migration, coupled with similar arrivals from South Asia and Africa, forever changed the United Kingdom, helping give birth to the increasingly multiracial, if unequal, society that persists there today. But some of this migration also proved surprisingly short-lived.[32]

After 1962, the British Parliament restricted the arrival of migrants from former colonies, responding to a rise in anti-immigrant sentiment among voters.[33] Although arrivals continued through family ties and, to a lesser extent, through job offers, the largest movement from the Caribbean shifted from Europe to North America, as the United States and Canada changed their immigration laws to attract new arrivals in the 1960s. In the United States, the 1965 Hart-Celler Act privileged the arrival of relatives of those migrants already living in the United States, which was supposed to encourage immigration from Europe. However, the small number of Caribbean migrants who had already established themselves began to bring relatives, while others arrived through specific employment visas targeted at workers in healthcare and other industries.[34] Meanwhile, Canada shifted from a series of restrictive immigration laws (some discriminating against applicants by nationality, race, or ethnicity) to immigration laws in 1962 and 1976 that ended discriminatory practices. These new laws allowed for the implementation of a points system based on skills and family relations and more welcoming policies for refugees.[35] While many Caribbean migrants would still end up in former colonial powers—the United Kingdom, France, and the Netherlands—far more would find their way northward to the United States and Canada in ensuing decades.

The Caribbean has a long history of out-migration. In 2020, nationals living abroad represented at least half of the country's total population of Dominica, Grenada, Guyana, Montserrat, St. Kitts and Nevis, St. Vincent and the Grenadines, and Puerto Rico (see table 3.3). Diasporas from Dominica, Montserrat, and Saint-Kitts and Nevis were larger than the respective populations in the home countries. In the case of Montserrat, whose diaspora was at least five times larger than the country's total population, mass emigration was caused by volcanic activity that started in 1995, which decimated the country's capital, Plymouth. It is estimated that two-thirds of the population (approximately 8,000 people) left the island over a five-year period.

Today, most CARICOM nationals who live abroad are in the United States, with the exception of Surinamese, for whom the Netherlands remains their principal destination. (Emigration is far less prevalent from non-CARICOM nations, except for Puerto Rico—see table 3.3).

The Caribbean diaspora has made its mark in the arts and entertainment industry in North America and Europe. Several Caribbean bands and artists have achieved greater success by leaving their homeland and bringing their art form to the diaspora. For instance, while its origins may be contested, the rise of salsa music can be traced back to Cuban and Puerto Rican stars living in New York City, such as Tito Puente and Hector Lavoe. By playing for the diaspora, these artists helped create a global platform for salsa originating in Latin American and Caribbean countries. Some Caribbean nationals have effectively capitalized on their influence abroad to reenter their home country in a different light. One example is how political novice Michel Martelly—better known then as the exuberant carnivalesque Kompa singer Sweet Mickey—

TABLE 3.3 Caribbean Emigrant Population, Shares, and Top Countries of Destination, 2020.

CARICOM Member States	Emigrant Population	Share of Emigrant Population out of Total Country Population	Top 3 Destinations of Emigrants	Share of Emigrants living in Top 1 Destination
Antigua and Barbuda	66,561	72%	United States, United Kingdom, U.S Virgin Islands	69%
Bahamas	53,793	13%	United States, United Kingdom, Canada	87%
Barbados	99,611	35%	United States, United Kingdom, Canada	52%
Belize	52,756	13%	United States, Canada, Mexico	81%
Dominica	78,191	109%	United States, United Kingdom, France	46%
Grenada	62,204	50%	United States, United Kingdom, Canada	41%
Guyana	438,413	55%	United States, Canada, United Kingdom	55%
Haiti	1,769,671	16%	United States, Dominican Republic, Chile	40%
Jamaica	1,118,931	40%	United States, Canada, United Kingdom	71%
Montserrat	24,582	546%	United Kingdom, United States, Antigua and Barbuda	40%
Saint Kitts and Nevis	50,285	106%	United States, United Kingdom, U.S Virgin Islands	55%
Saint Lucia	71,227	40%	United States, United Kingdom, Canada	48%
Saint Vincent and the Grenadines	55,525	53%	United States, Canada, United Kingdom	27%
Suriname	273,209	45%	Netherlands, France, French Guiana	67%
Trinidad and Tobago	330,519	22%	United States, Canada, United Kingdom	63%

Other Caribbean Islands or Nations Associated with the Caribbean				
Anguilla	2,505	16%	U.S Virgin Islands, United Kingdom, Sint Maarten	39%
Aruba	21,456	20%	United States, Netherlands, Curacao	45%
British Virgin Islands	5,355	17%	U.S Virgin Islands, Sint Maarten, Saint Kitts and Nevis	18%
Cayman Islands	1,908	3%	United Kingdom, Canada, Australia	66%
Cuba	1,757,300	16%	United States, Spain, Italy	78%
Curaçao	7,611	4%	Aruba, Sint Maarten, Netherlands	36%
Dominican Republic	1,608,567	15%	United States, Spain, Italy	73%
French Guiana	4,595	2%	Martinique, Guadeloupe, Brazil	44%
Guadeloupe	12,542	3%	Martinique, French Guiana, Sint Maarten	48%
Martinique	12,963	3%	Guadeloupe, French Guiana, Canada	67%
Puerto Rico	1,850,529	57%	United States, Dominican Republic, U.S Virgin Islands	99%
Sint Maarten	2,191	5%	Aruba, Curacao, Venezuela	36%
Turks and Caicos Islands	2,689	6%	Bahamas, Mali, United Kingdom	62%
United States Virgin Islands	3,908	4%	Antigua and Barbuda, Grenada, Saint Kitts and Nevis	19%

Note: Caribbean total includes UN classified Caribbean countries + Belize, French Guiana, Guyana and Suriname.

Source: Authors' tabulations of data from the United Nations' Department of Economic and Social Affairs, Population Division, "International Migrant Stock 2020: Destination and Origin," accessed September 23, 2024, https://www.un.org/development/desa/pd/content/international-migrant-stock.

was able to build on his popularity with the diaspora to launch a credible, and eventually successful, presidential campaign in Haiti.

In the United States, the Caribbean diaspora (and their descendants) has also been highly visible in social justice issues and politics. From contributions to the civil rights movement from Harry Belafonte and Sidney Poitier—descendants of Jamaicans and Bahamians, respectively—to the 2020 historic election of Kamala Harris as vice president of the United States, a second-generation Jamaican, Caribbean immigrants have shown a great capacity to integrate abroad, while preserving and sharing their cultural heritage.

In addition to contributing to their countries of destination, the Caribbean diaspora maintains strong ties to their home countries through remittances, investments, entrepreneurship, and many nonfinancial forms of cooperation including skills transfer and social and community projects led by hometown associations.[36] In terms of remittances, available data suggest that these sizable money transfers have become important levers of Caribbean economies, by way of boosting consumption and increasing opportunities for economic development. Caribbean nations are among some of the largest recipients of diaspora remittances globally. For example, despite the COVID-19 pandemic, remittances represented close to a quarter of Jamaica's GDP and a fifth of Haiti's in 2021. That same year, remittances from the United States to the Dominican Republic totaled about 10.4 billion dollars, representing one of the top twenty-five largest remittance corridors in the world.[37]

Although there are many benefits to having a significant Caribbean diaspora established in advanced economies, Caribbean experts contend that brain drain remains an issue of concern for the source countries. For decades, youth with tertiary education and high-skilled workers have left the region, and there is no sign of this trend slowing down. Nursing and teaching, which are predominantly female-dominated industries, are professions where brain drain is visible. Nurses receive high-quality training paid for by Caribbean governments, and there still are important unmet needs for nurses in several countries in the region.[38] Yet, active recruitment by firms in the United States, United Kingdom, Canada, and some neighboring countries offering higher wages and attractive packages are important pull factors, particularly for women, to migrate along with their families.

"We believe that this is a fundamental part of the integration architecture," said Dominica's Prime Minister Roosevelt Skerrit at the conclusion of the CARICOM's fiftieth anniversary meeting in Trinidad and Tobago in July 2023, "and at fifty, we could not leave Trinidad and Tobago and not speak about the core of the regional integration movement, that is, people's ability to move freely within the Caribbean Community."[39] With these words, he gave notice on behalf of the thirteen member states participating in the CARICOM Single Market and Economy (CSME) that they would try to update and vastly expand the existing mobility agreement before the next meeting in March 2024. "The idea of free mobility in the Caribbean is connected with the need to create a productive platform that ties our countries together," notes Leo Preville, director of the CARICOM Single Market Unit, which oversees the implementation of the economic and migration agreements within CARICOM.

Caribbean nations have long pursued regional economic integration, including free mobility for the participating member states. In 1973, Barbados, Guyana, Jamaica, and Trinidad and Tobago established the Caribbean Community (CARICOM) through the original Treaty of Chaguaramas—with the goal of attaining freer movement of capital and labor.[40] Over the years, eleven other nations joined the agreement: Antigua and Barbuda, The Bahamas, Belize, Dominica, Grenada, Haiti, Montserrat, Saint Kitts and Nevis, Saint Lucia, Saint Vincent and the Grenadines, and Suriname. CARICOM also has six associate members: Anguilla, Bermuda, British Virgin Islands, the Cayman Islands, Curaçao, and Turks and Caicos Islands. Commitment towards regional integration and the free mobility regimes for CARICOM nationals were further solidified through the Revised Treaty of Chaguaramas (2001), which launched CSME. In article 45 of the revised treaty, CSME member states committed themselves "to the goal of free movement of their nationals within the Community."[41]

During the fiftieth anniversary of CARICOM in July 2023, the heads of governments announced plans to work towards full free mobility by March 2024 for all CARICOM nationals except Haitians due to the country's condition at the time.[42] Consultations among member states will determine how this move will take place, but certainly, the CSME will be at the center of CARICOM's expanded mobility plan. The CSME currently provides for movement for economic purposes (skills[43], services, and right of establishment). Importantly, all CARICOM nationals are entitled to a six-month definite stay in

CSME member states.[44] Moreover, in the case of certain categories of skilled professionals, free movement has been achieved. Through the skills certificate regime, there exists a mechanism for twelve categories of professionals to have their skills recognized, thereby granting authorization to move to any CSME country to seek work and stay indefinitely. The skills certificate is one of life-long duration while the work permit is limited in time. This indefinite right of establishment extends to the skilled professionals' dependents. CARICOM nationals also have the right to move as service providers and under the right of establishment.

Although they are full members of the community, The Bahamas and Montserrat do not fully partake in the CSME. The Bahamas has abstained from the agreement, and Montserrat has yet to fully implement it.[45] Montserrat has been facilitating movement under the CSME while other countries have been facilitating the inflows of Montserrat nationals into their nations.[46] In fact, while several CSME countries have implemented measures to facilitate the six-month stays and skills certificates regime, administrative and legal challenges persist in some cases due in great part to limited resources and capacity, and a lack of full incorporation into national migration laws.[47]

Application for a CARICOM Skilled Certificate can be done from the country of origin or from the destination country, and unlike a work permit, the right to stay does not depend on securing employment or having an employer-sponsor ahead of time. Even in the best cases where the CSME is ratified and the skills certificate regime is implemented, access to true free mobility is limited to certain CARICOM nationals. University graduates, artists, musicians, media workers, and sportspersons were the initial five categories as documented in article 4 of the revised treaty.[48] Since 2006 more categories have been added, resulting in greater inclusion and expanded access for less-skilled workers.[49] Still, skills certificate applications can take a long time to be approved, leading some potential recipients to opt instead for less-comprehensive work permits.

While the CMSE has included only limited mobility to date—and likely will even after the renegotiated agreement—one subregion of CARICOM, the Organization of Eastern Caribbean States (OECS), has found more success in implementing free mobility for its nationals. Established in 1981 by the Treaty of Basseterre, the OECS includes protocol members Antigua and Barbuda,

Dominica, Grenada, Montserrat, Saint Kitts and Nevis, Saint Lucia, and Saint Vincent and the Grenadines. OECS associate members include the territories of Anguilla, the British Virgin Islands, Martinique, and Guadeloupe.

Through the OECS Economic Union (ECEU), ratified in January of 2011, nationals from the seven protocol member states have access to complete free movement, including indefinite stay and work authorization.[50] Although the absence of a regional data system makes it difficult to assess the extent to which OECS nationals use the ECEU, information available on the ease of movement suggests that system works quite well in practice. According to Clarence Henry, senior technical officer at the OECS Secretariat, there is little bureaucracy involved in moving from one protocol member state to another.[51] Individuals only need to prove their citizenship at the port of arrival—often via a passport, though other forms of photo identification are acceptable—and immigration authorities will immediately grant them indefinite stay. In most countries, this translates into a passport stamp indicating an indefinite stay. Once admitted, the individual can register with the Social Security Office to obtain their work authorization.

The 2020 data reviewed suggest that there is high mobility within the OECS and between the OECS and its associate members. Henry highlighted that St. Lucia, where the OECS Secretariat is located, tends to be a pole of attraction, and so are Antigua and Barbuda and St. Kitts and Nevis, which are higher-income and tourism-driven islands.

Could the OECS's experience be transferable to CARICOM's move towards full free mobility? On one hand, close to half of CARICOM's membership is part of the OECS subregion and potentially has in place systems or practices to build on. According to Deputy Program Manager of Free Movement and Labour Wanya Illes at the CARICOM Secretariat, the issue of scale may pose some limitations to this transferability.[52] Full free mobility within CARICOM involves countries with far larger populations and diverse economies, thus triggering concerns that are less likely among the smaller OECS economies. However, Mr. Henry points to the European Union's tiered system of integration that has allowed countries with different capacities to fully participate in the economic union. "It is feasible for CARICOM to have full free movement with all its member states, but the issue is often overcomplicated by governments' (often unfounded) anxieties. Evidence-based discussions, awareness building and regular and timely analysis of data would help many countries understand the benefits of free mobility, in the context of long-existing push and pull factors of migration."

Moreover, as Henry highlights, there is a fundamental difference in the approach of the ECEU and the CSME that explains the relative success of the former: from its inception, the CSME has adopted a restrictive approach by easing movement only for skilled persons. Not only has this effectively limited the number of people who can move freely, but it has also created a cumbersome system where people must prove their skills before obtaining the right to move freely. Whereas the ECEU approach is a far simpler and inclusive one; people only need to prove their citizenship at arrival, such that there is no need for additional bureaucracy or extensive national legislation. In this context, free movement becomes the default standard for all nationals, and it can be facilitated by administrative measures allowing immigration officers to grant the necessary permissions to stay and pursue work authorizations.

CARICOM's regional project is admittedly an ambitious one: it depends on integrating a high number of economies that exhibit important differences in terms of size and levels of development. Haiti, had a population of 11.6 million in 2022, exceeding that of all other fourteen CARICOM member states put together. At the same time, Haiti is also a country plagued with deep political and socioeconomic challenges: in 2022, its GDP per capita was US$1,748, and 29percent of its population lived on less than $2.15 a day.[53] That same year, The Bahamas, with a population of 406,000, had a GDP per capita eighteen times higher (US$31,458). Recognizing these differences, article 4 of the Revised Treaty of Chaguaramas designates countries based on their capacity to meet their regional economic obligations. Under this article, the most developed countries (MDCs) are: The Bahamas, Barbados, Guyana, Jamaica, Suriname, Trinidad and Tobago, and the less developed countries (LDCs) are Antigua and Barbuda, Belize, Dominica, Grenada, Haiti, Montserrat, St. Kitts and Nevis, St. Lucia, and St. Vincent and the Grenadines.

As a result of their vast differences, it is not surprising that the status of implementation of commitments to regional integration remains uneven across countries. Leo Preville, director of the CARICOM Single Market Unit, considers that the commitment to CSME is strong as evidenced by the regular renewal of CARICOM's vision by the heads of state, but that differences in access to human resources and financial and technological capacity explain in great part why some countries have not implemented all their commitments.[54] In the case of Haiti, political instability and a weak institutional framework have slowed the codification into national laws of some of its regional commitments. In other countries, lack of political will under specific administrations or special circumstances have played a role in the region's slower-than-anticipated integration. This ambiguity is even more likely in countries experiencing high unemployment and indebtedness that have limited fiscal capacity to accommodate non-nationals.

Some elements of contingent rights remain unresolved, and work is ongoing. The Contingent Rights Protocol establishes the ability of a CARICOM nationals' spouse and dependents to migrate alongside the principal beneficiary. However, none of the CSME countries have implemented provisions protecting the contingent rights of migrants' spouses and immediate dependent family members. Even within the OECS where free movement has been working well, contingent rights for relatives from third countries, in other words, the spouses of non-OECS citizens to indefinite stay and work authorization are seldom implemented in practice. According to Henry, some governments worry about cases where spouses coming from more developed economies, such as Europe or North America, will take up job opportunities that should go to nationals.

When Hurricane Maria struck the Commonwealth of Dominica in 2017, it almost finished the country off: 95 percent of houses were destroyed, and a third of the population of 78,000 was suddenly living in shelters. At least a fifth of the population left in the weeks afterwards, since they had nowhere to live. And the cost of the recovery was put at a staggering 200 percent or more of GDP, essentially two years of Dominica's economic production.[55]

Just a few days after being hit by Hurricane Maria, then Prime Minister Roosevelt Skerrit vowed that Dominica would seize the opportunity to become the world's first climate resilient nation. Today, Dominica is close to this reality. With the support of various international partners, it has rebuilt its housing stock and infrastructure resistant to hurricanes and other climate risks, and it has developed sophisticated hazard data systems to help its people plan and respond in emergency situations.[56] And as the country rebuilt, most of those who had left eventually returned. Such investments have also helped connect local communities, including the Indigenous Kalinago people, by providing better access to services (water, roads), and engaging the nation in decisions to balance tourism expansion with the preservation of cultural and environmental heritage. As a small island developing state (SIDS), Dominica's journey is an example of how deep investments in climate resilience can help locals find alternatives to migration.

But at a time when climate change is making many countries in the Caribbean even more vulnerable to natural disasters than in the past, most people have little recourse to leaving their countries if tragedy strikes. Those who fled Dominica after Hurricane Maria were comparatively lucky to those displaced by other climate emergencies elsewhere in the world. Thanks to the region's mobility arrangements, Trinidad and Tobago accepted many Dominicans through the CSME six-month stay, as did Antigua and Barbuda, Grenada, Saint Lucia, and Saint Vincent and the Grenadines through the ECEU's indefinite stay provision.[57]

Nearly all Caribbean countries lack institutions and regulatory frameworks for asylum and refugee protection, much less for those forced out of their countries by natural disasters. This has become more apparent in recent years with the rise in asylum seekers and other populations in need of protection. Recent humanitarian movements have included the mass arrival of Venezuelan migrants and their challenges with regularization and integration, natural disasters and political crises that have pushed Haitians to seek refuge, primarily in the Dominican Republic, and an increase in the number of Cubans and Africans arriving due to desperate conditions by boat to nontraditional destinations like the Cayman Islands, Antigua and Barbuda, and Dominica, among others. Some evidence also suggests that migrants may be migrating to overseas territories as a gateway to Europe. For example, French Guiana is a key transit point for migrants and asylum seeker from Suriname, Syria, and Yemen, and increasingly more for Haitians, Venezuelans and Cubans.[58] In December 2020, there were an estimated 20,000 asylum seekers in French Guiana, equivalent to 7 percent of the population.[59]

Of the more than 7.5 million Venezuelans that fled their country between 2016 and 2022, 6.5 million have settled in the Latin America and Caribbean region, with just over 200,000 in the Caribbean. As new migrants to the region, the arrival of so many Venezuelans in a short time to nations that have little experience with refugees has posed important challenges to migratory systems. But it has also presented an opportunity to learn about border management and immigrant integration. Thanks to regional coordination mechanisms such as the Quito Process and the Interagency Coordinating Platform for Venezuelan Migrants and Refugees (R4V), Caribbean countries with large numbers of Venezuelans receive assistance through United Nations High Commissioner for Refugees (UNHCR), IOM, and other agencies to help this population.

In addition to support for short-term emergency response, regional awareness and initial expressions of solidarity towards Venezuelans migrants have meant that, according to an Migration Policy Institute study, an estimated 50 to 75 percent have secured some form of legal status in Latin America and the Caribbean.[60] However, the same study suggests that in the Caribbean, the rates of regularization are lower than the hemispheric average: Curaçao (30–45 percent), Dominican Republic (30–40 percent), Guyana (60–90 percent), and Trinidad and Tobago (30–55percent), with few options in Aruba.[61] While notable, the higher rates of regularization in Guyana come with a caveat: Venezuelans receive a temporary permit that must be renewed every three months, representing a burdensome process. Still, the status does grant access to education and public health services, and although it does not come with a work authorization, the current boom in labor demand likely means that Venezuelans can still find jobs in the informal sector.

Access to education and healthcare is not a given in the other Caribbean nations. For example, in Aruba and Curaçao, where rates of regularization are on the lower end, education is technically available for everyone, but the foreign-born must pay for special insurance and have a native-born sponsor. These two conditions are difficult to meet for Venezuelan migrants with fewer means and no local connections. Moreover, public healthcare is only available for those with legal status.

In Trinidad and Tobago, healthcare is open to everyone, but education is only accessible to those with permanent status, meaning that Venezuelans who obtained temporary status are generally not eligible. Just in July 2023, the government announced it would begin integrating migrant and refugee children in the national elementary school system.[62] In the absence of an asylum system, Venezuelans in Trinidad and Tobago rely on UNHCR's refugee status determination screenings to be designated as refugees. However, the government does not recognize these designations, and consequently does not provide internationally recognized refugee benefits.

The Dominican Republic has a full asylum system but seldom uses it.[63] In the case of Venezuelans, the government has used a combination of regular resident visas and a regularization program launched in 2021 to grant temporary status measures.[64] Until recently the law made both education and healthcare accessible to all individuals regardless of status. However, recent changes in the laws, primarily targeting Haitian migrants, have restricted access to healthcare services to those with legal status.[65] In response to the public's perception of migrants taking advantage of the Dominican Republic's health system, including Haitian pregnant women crossing the border to obtain prenatal care, the government introduced a highly controversial law barring hospitals from assisting women who are over six months pregnant. Anecdotal evidence suggests that in practice, this law is strictly applied to Haitians, but spillover effects of this anti-immigrant stance could eventually impact the thousands of Venezuelans who continue to be without status.

Looking at the past two decades, the most consequential natural disaster has been the 2010 earthquake in Haiti, which triggered important displacement. Thousands of Haitians immediately headed to neighboring Dominican Republic for emergency assistance. The Dominican Republic also provided special protection, allowing special entry to certain groups of Haitians, granting humanitarian visas to allow relatives to visit Haitians in the Dominican Republic who had been affected by the earthquake and were receiving medical attention, and suspending deportations of Haitians for a few months.

Haitian migrants face significant challenges with obtaining and maintaining legal status in the Dominican Republic, where, according to UNHCR, there is the most important crisis of statelessness in the Americas. Three years after the earthquake, a Dominican high court issued a ruling that stripped an estimated 210,000 Dominicans of Haitian descent of their citizenship and pushed many into irregularity. Moreover, the Dominican Republic has engaged in large-scale deportations of Haitians, despite a U.N. plea in November 2022 to stop deporting Haitians due to the difficult country conditions. Vulnerable groups are also being deported without the possibility of requesting asylum, including pregnant and breastfeeding women, the elderly, and a significant number of unaccompanied children.[66]

Despite these challenges, the region's unique mobility regimes have, to some extent, helped facilitate the movement of displaced people and response workers during times of environmental crisis. However, governments' lack of resources and fiscal space are among the most cited barriers to address climate-related migration challenges in the Caribbean region. In regional consultations with stakeholders and experts in the migration space, various experts have highlighted the need to establish a regional fund to strengthen Caribbean nations' capacity to support climate-displaced populations. This fund could mimic the already functioning Caribbean Catastrophe Risk Insurance Facility (CCRIF), a structure into which member states contribute. The 2022 Bridgetown Initiative, led by Barbados, calls for a revamping of the global financial system geared towards climate action and attaining the UN's Sustainable Development Goals. Moreover, during the 2023 COP28, nations agreed to fund a loss and damage fund to help low-income countries address climate-related loss and damage, a major step forward for Small Island Developing States.[67] These initiatives, among others, are relevant for Caribbean stakeholders given the mounting evidence that climate-related events and natural disasters exacerbate existing development challenges and increase the risk of community displacement and disappearance of certain cultures.

Anxieties around human mobility underlie the absence of further measures to deal with displacement in the Caribbean. Many small islands have major fiscal constraints, are facing population decline, and fear a loss of native culture. There is also very limited reliable data throughout the region on irregular migration, which makes it difficult for countries to assess whether they have significant populations in irregular status. Engagement with communities to counter growing accounts of xenophobia, which challenge migrants' access to rights and basic services, has become increasingly necessary. With the more recent arrivals of Haitians and Venezuelans, there is a need for accurate information on the contributions and needs of humanitarian populations, as well as the costs associated with receiving them.

"Despite their hesitancy," says Clarence Henry of the OECS, "Member states realize that it's better to be in the regional system than out." Anxiety aside, Caribbean nations, particularly CARICOM member states, have invested decades in a free mobility regime that has yet to reach its full potential, but they have a foundation to build on. CARICOM's 2023 mandate to move towards full free mobility presents a unique opportunity to revamp regional instruments, implement mobility agreements into national laws, and abandon counterproductive practices. Almost everyone involved in ongoing discussions on mobility in the Caribbean agrees that as a first step, a thorough assessment of the status and impact of the CSME in individual countries is critical. The region, with support from IOM, has embarked on a series of dialogues to assess and reimagine its migratory institutions.[68] Few countries have (or have shared) the necessary data to assess whether the CSME has been successful or not. The uneven implementation of CSME's free mobility provisions means that some Caribbean nationals move more freely than others. It may be that a radical change in approach is necessary, like adopting as a starting point the OECS's indefinite stay and work authorization scheme for all categories of CARICOM nationals, rather than try to expand the CSME's skilled-worker approach.

To manage large inflows of migrants over a short time, most Caribbean nations have used ad hoc temporary status measures for Venezuelans, less so for Haitians. By their temporary or sporadic nature, these approaches have come with integration challenges, with more serious consequences for Venezuelans in Trinidad and Tobago and Haitians in the Dominican Republic. The lack of protection mechanisms also means that vulnerable groups, particularly women and children, are subject to being victims of human trafficking networks. Reports of sexual exploitation and prostitution of Venezuelan women have multiplied in Trinidad and Tobago and Guyana, where it has become increasingly visible to the public eye. Moreover, suspected human smuggling of Haitian women and children have garnered the attention of the governments of Belize, Guyana, and The Bahamas—resulting in temporarily suspending Haitians' right to visa-free stays in the first two countries.

As visa requirements are imposed to slow the flow of these populations, continued integration challenges also mean that migrants—with or without status—are likely to make more and more dangerous journeys to move to other destinations. Data on migrant flows in the Americas, including from the perilous jungle of the Darien Gap, show not only that Venezuelans and Haitians are still leaving their country in great numbers, but that secondary migration from nations where they are not well integrated is also underway. As such, a more proactive and holistic approach to immigrant admission and integration would benefit the region as a whole.

The Caribbean diaspora, due to its geographic proximity and strong ties, represents a pool of opportunity and talent that can contribute to revamping the region's migratory institutions. Emigrants and their descendants are well recognized for their role in channeling much-needed financial support to their families in the Caribbean through remittances, but other forms of investments beyond remittances could strengthen the region's development-focused migration agenda. The diaspora's engagement with their countries of origin also takes the form of business development and job creation, direct investments, and strengthening social and professional networks. Involving the Caribbean diaspora could be an important element of a wider strategy to engage Caribbean nations on challenging topics like government modernization, humanitarian protection, and climate-induced migration. In many ways, the diaspora strengthens Caribbean identity: in big multicultural cities in North America and Europe, several groups that do not typically live together in the Caribbean, like Haitians and Dominicans, discover their commonalities and are more likely to seek collaboration in both destination and home countries.

Guyanese Ambassador Zulfikar Ally shares how Guyana's new vision of increased engagement with its diaspora in North America and the Caribbean can contribute to growth in a manner that is not exploitative, but inclusive of all Guyanese. For those interested in returning to Guyana, the government offers a piece of land, one duty-free car, and one duty-free container to facilitate the move. So far, Guyanese residing in the Caribbean have been the most likely to take advantage of this option. For those who want to invest but remain abroad, a government office will counsel the investor to match their skills or financial investment with an identified need in Guyana. Ally notes that Guyana is currently building six modern hospitals and sees medical tourism as an important business of the future. The country has needs for medical personnel—many of which are in the diaspora and could contribute, even on a temporary or seasonal basis—but the country also needs expertise in high tech and legal skills to ensure compliance with international standards. Overall, Guyana is building its hard and soft infrastructure and needs labor at all levels of skills. The government hopes that its diaspora and other Caribbean nationals, especially those from CARICOM, will be a part of this expansion. Early signs are showing that job postings in Guyana are gaining traction for workers in Trinidad and Tobago.

As Caribbean nations continue to face important migration-related challenges, dialogue through the region's established institutions and enhanced hemispheric cooperation provide a path towards adapting Caribbean migratory systems, while ensuring that migration policies account for the concerns of sending and receiving countries.

CONCLUSION
Changing Migration Patterns, Changing Policies

IN A ONCE LITTLE-KNOWN tropical forest, along the Caribbean Sea between Colombia and Panama, the three subregions of Central America, South America, and the Caribbean meet. This forest known as the Darien Gap consists of 10,000 square miles of dense forest and raging rivers, so thick that for centuries it has formed a natural barrier between the southern and northern parts of the Americas. There is evidence that the hemisphere's original inhabitants had some trade across this stretch of nearly impenetrable forest, but this was relatively limited by the difficulty that crossing through it represented, which led to sharply different Indigenous cultural patterns in North and South America.[1] Centuries later, when the Pan-American Highway was built from Canada to Argentina, starting in the early twentieth century, the intended route from north to south remained unbuilt for over 100 kilometers (60 miles) across the Darien Gap.

The Darien Gap also shaped migration within the region. People in Central America and Mexico were connected to the United States and Canada through shared borders, even if it was often hard to cross them, but those in South America and the Caribbean faced natural barriers to reaching the United States. Many did through airplanes and boats, but this meant that most people from those regions needed visas to arrive or they had to face even more harrowing journeys by sea. There were essentially three distinct migration systems in the Americas, one each in the Caribbean, South America, and

Central America and Mexico. They connected occasionally but had significantly distinct patterns.

Of course, the Darien Gap was never completely impenetrable, despite the difficulties in crossing it. It was home to a few tens of thousands of mostly Indigenous inhabitants, and every year a few thousand people made the dangerous trek north from one end to another. Between 2010 and 2020, there was an average of 11,000 migrants crossing the perilous strip of land per year, many of them Haitians and Cubans.[2] And in the 2010s, not all of those who crossed the Darien Gap were from South America or the Caribbean. In the 2010s, a growing number of Africans and South Asians, from a wide variety of different countries, made the journey through the Darien Gap as part of a particularly long journey across continents.[3]

In 2021, however, these patterns started to change. That year, almost 100,000 migrants born in Haiti, most of whom had been living in Chile and Brazil, decided to brave the Darien Gap to reach the United States.[4] The end of COVID-19 mobility restrictions, the economic turmoil created by the global recession, long-standing patterns of discrimination in South America, and the perception that U.S. authorities were allowing most Haitians to enter the country probably all contributed to this surge. Suddenly the three distinct migration systems in the Americas were connected through this dense and dangerous strip of land between Colombia and Panama.

The U.S. government started deporting Haitians and the numbers dropped, but then the number of Venezuelans increased, some coming from Venezuela, others from different countries in South America where they had settled.[5] By 2023, there were over half a million crossings through the Darien Gap, almost two-thirds of them Venezuelans.[6] This shift, in turn, meant that those arriving at the U.S.-Mexico border during 2022 and 2023 reflected a growing number of countries who transited through South America and then headed north through Central America and Mexico, making a journey through multiple countries.[7] A few others, especially Cubans, arrived in Nicaragua by plane and headed north.[8]

If the story of migration in Latin America and the Caribbean from 2010 to 2020 was largely about migration within the region, the story after 2021 also included renewed migration to other parts of the world, with the United States as the principal destination. Spain, which received around 100,000 asylum applications from Latin American and Caribbean citizens in 2022 alone, became an important secondary destination.[9] Most citizens of Latin American countries could enter Spain without a visa and then either apply for asylum or simply remain in the country beyond their visa period, later adjusting status through Spain's rolling regularization program.[10] Migration within Latin America and the Caribbean continued to be significant, but there was renewed attention to emigration from the region to other parts of the world again.

This shift had several causes. The first is, undoubtedly, the uneven effects of the global recession in the Western Hemisphere. The United States rebounded quickly from the recession, with an increasingly tight labor market that by 2023 featured 9 to 10 million jobs that remained open from month to month, creating a powerful pull factor for immigration.[11] European countries, which are aging quickly, also emerged from the pandemic with significant labor needs.[12]

In contrast, Latin American and Caribbean countries often suffered far deeper and longer-term structural damage to their economies, something that affected both the poor and the precarious middle classes. For many displaced migrants from Venezuela, Haiti, Nicaragua, and other countries, who had already moved once but were struggling to get by, the recession pushed them to seek better options further abroad.[13]

In some cases, especially in Caribbean coastal areas and Central America's dry corridor, climate change may also be compounded economic drivers to move. Growing evidence suggests that rainfall is becoming more unpredictable, with both more frequent dry seasons and hurricanes, making always precarious livelihoods in rural areas even more precarious.[14] So the period since 2021 saw an increase in the demand for labor in the United States, right at the same time that many people in Latin America and the Caribbean were dealing with the deep effects of the global recession, struggling to adapt to shifting climate patterns, and enduring long-term displacement.

The second cause of the shift undoubtedly has to do with changes in transportation and communication. More extensive flight networks across multiple countries, mobile technology for mapping routes, and social media, which allow people to know how others travel in real time, all helped potential migrants visualize different options for migration than they could have conceived of before. And migrant smugglers also adapted their practices by selling their services on social media, reaching potential clients in real time. Almost all migrants who took long irregular journeys through multiple countries had to avail themselves of smugglers to get through key points—the Darien Gap, the Costa Rica-Nicaragua border, and the Mexico-U.S. border—plus often other points along the way, although it appears that only the privileged few had a single smuggling operation guiding them across the entire journey.[15]

Smugglers are sometimes both facilitators, helping migrants achieve their dreams, and predators, taking advantage of migrants' desperation. They play a complex role in the larger ecosystem of irregular migration. There has been a growing sophistication and expansion of these smuggling networks along the route from points of origin in South America, the Caribbean, and countries outside the hemisphere to the United States. And most of these smuggling groups maintain ties to larger criminal organizations, especially drug trafficking organizations, often paying for the right to move people through territory that these larger groups control.

In many cases, these long-distance journeys mix regular and irregular migration patterns, with migrants crossing some borders with permission and other clandestinely. Moreover, some are asylum seekers, who are entitled to a hearing on their claim for protection, while others are unauthorized migrants, and the distinctions are not always clearly delineated. And the services migrants access—from guides to lodging, food, and transportation—are often a mix of legal and clandestine businesses.

In the world of irregular migration, there is actually a complex mix of legality and illegality, permission and rejection, aboveboard and underground sources of support, and confusing and often contradictory legal regimes. Criminal actors take advantage of this ambiguity to build their networks, often bringing perfectly legal providers of services into these exchanges that often benefit these providers economically but simultaneously enmesh them in the tentacles of criminal operations. In many countries, fears around the power of migrant smuggling operations and the larger criminal groups that facilitate them have come to dominate policy concerns. And this is true not just on the route to the United States, but also on the routes that Venezuelans use to reach other countries in South America and Haitians and other migrants use to move within that region. Smuggling has become a permanent feature of irregular mobility and a lucrative new source of income and corruption across the Americas.

The third factor that motivated large-scale out-migration was almost certainly the relatively better chances that migrants faced on succeeding in entering the United States. As U.S. border authorities became overwhelmed after 2019, they had little choice but to release most migrants into the country with a notice to appear at a court date in the future. Between the U.S. fiscal years 2021 and 2023, roughly 70 percent of family units that reached the U.S. border without documents were allowed to enter the country, and that number rose to 81 percent in fiscal year 2023. This increasing porousness of the U.S. border was not so much a shift in policy as the result of a long-term trend of decreasing effectiveness of U.S. border management efforts, which had been designed for single Mexican men on their way to work, rather than families from multiple countries who often sought asylum—the population arriving after COVID-19.[16]

After a particularly large spike in border encounters in December 2023, the U.S. and Mexican governments reached an agreement to slow the numbers arriving, with the Mexican government adopting more active enforcement and the U.S. government changing asylum policy to make it harder to request protection between ports of entry.[17] A new Panamanian government also began conducting limited deportations after June 2024, with support from U.S. authorities. The number of migrants apprehended between ports of entry at the U.S. border dropped noticeably from January through June 2024 and then precipitously after that, reaching the lowest number in four years by September 2024.[18]

The drop was particularly noticeable among Cubans, Haitians, Nicaraguans, and Venezuelans who have access to the largest number of legal ways of entering the United States, which suggests that is was not merely enforcement that worked, but the combination of enforcement and legal pathways working in tandem.

Indeed, the U.S. government had opened up a series of legal pathways for migration as the numbers surged. These included the CHNV Sponsorship Parole program, which allowed people legally present in the United States to sponsor Cubans, Haitians, Nicaraguans, and Venezuelans for admission to the United States for two years with work authorization, with 30,000 slots per month; an online processing system, called CBP One, which offers entry for up to 1,280 migrants who make an appointment through the system to enter the country and pursue an asylum or other claim; increased H-2 seasonal agricultural visas; al agricultural visas; sped-up family processing for citizens of some countries in the hemisphere; and Safe Mobility Offices, that process refugee resettlement in four countries in the region.[19] Between CBP One and CHNV alone, these allowed for around 700,000 additional planned entries to the United States a year, targeted overwhelmingly at Cubans, Haitians, Nicaraguans, and Venezuelans, which also reduced pressures for irregular migration.[20]

It remains to be seen if these measures, both increased enforcement along the route and expanded channels for lawful migration to the United States, will produce a long-term shift in irregular migration patterns. And migration within Latin America and the Caribbean also remained high during this period, though it did not return to the levels seen before the global recession. But patterns were clearly shifting yet again.

One June 10, 2022, in a conference hall in Los Angeles, a group of twenty-one heads of state and foreign ministers gathered to sign the Los Angeles Declaration on Migration and Protection, the first hemispheric statement on how they wanted to manage migration collectively. The signing was taking place on the margins of the Summit of the Americas, which had been a fractious and exhausting affair, with several heads of state staying home either in solidarity with the Cuban, Venezuelan, and Nicaraguan governments, who had not been invited to the Summit, or because of their own difficult relationships with the hosts. But despite the fireworks around the Summit itself, the signing of the Los Angeles Declaration proved to be something of a bright spot.

The twenty-one signatories—which later grew to twenty-two—pledged to manage migration jointly by supporting countries that host large displaced populations, expanding legal pathways and protection systems, coordinating migration management, and creating joint emergency responses.[21]

A declaration like this would have been unimaginable only a few years earlier, because most countries in the hemisphere saw themselves predominantly as migrant-sending countries. There were a few key destinations in the Americas, including Argentina, The Bahamas, Barbados, Belize, Costa Rica, and, until 2015, Venezuela, but most of the nations in Latin America and the Caribbean were primarily countries of emigration with their citizens headed abroad, far more than of immigration.

What shifted in the period from 2010 to 2020 was that almost all countries in the Americas became destination countries for migrants for other nearby (or even more distant) nations. The specific displacement crises in Haiti, Venezuela, and Nicaragua accounted for roughly three-quarters of this movement, but others moved to take advantage of opportunities in other countries across Latin America and the Caribbean. Robust economic performance and labor market needs encouraged some of this movement, while mobility agreements helped facilitate it.

It remained unclear how well the twenty-two countries would be able or willing to implement the principles laid out in the declaration, but the fact that it existed at all was a testament to the real shifts taking place in migration patterns in the region. The seven countries that played the largest role in writing the declaration included three long-standing destinations for migrants and refugees—Canada, Costa Rica, and the United States—and three countries that had only recently become major destinations—Chile, Colombia, and Mexico.[22] And both United Nations High Commissioner for Refugees (UNHCR) and the International Organization for Migration (IOM), which had become indispensable allies for countries grappling with rising migration pressures and protection needs, also weighed in on the process along the way, which reflected their increasingly prominent role in the hemisphere.

If the Los Angeles Declaration was the most recent agreement on migration and protection in the hemisphere and the first to include countries in every subregion—North, Central, and South America and the Caribbean—it was certainly not the only one. In fact, Latin American and Caribbean countries have been creating frameworks, forums, and agreements that help them manage migration and displacement for many decades, even before it was the prominent issue that it has become today. Felipe Muñoz, who served as Colombia's presidential migration coordinator through two administrations and is one of the most astute observers of changes in the region, says that there was a "creation or renovation of regional mechanism, both new ones and those that already existed."[23]

Perhaps the most developed of these are some of the regional mobility agreements, especially those in Mercosur, the CARICOM Single Market and Economy (CSME), and the Organization of East Caribbean States, which all allow for significant mobility among members, although with quite different criteria in each case. Similarly, the Andean Community and the Central America-4 agreements also had elements that allow for extensive mobility and sometimes residency in other member countries, while many other bilateral agreements whether for mobility or residence also exist. And despite the significant asymmetries in development and economic size, even the North American Free Trade Agreement (NAFTA) and its successor, the U.S.-Mexico-Canada Agreement (USMCA), includes provisions for mobility and residency across the three member countries for certain professionals (though not broader groups).

Latin American and Caribbean countries had also developed an active response to the Venezuelan displacement crisis through two crucial forums, the Quito Process and the Interagency Coordinating Platform for Venezuelan Refugees and Migrants (generally known as R4V). The Quito Process, which is a group of thirteen governments (and a few other observer governments), has met twice a year with a rotating chair to share responses to the Venezuelan displacement crisis. While it has not turned into an institutional forum that can make decisions, it has helped provide a space for sharing government responses and flagging future challenges. At the same time, the R4V, coordinated by UNHCR and IOM with over 200 UN agencies and international development and humanitarian organizations, has become the major conduit for international aid, which is channeled through these organizations to provide support for displaced Venezuelans, host communities, and key policy responses. There has been nothing similar to date for the Haitian displacement crisis, although it too affects multiple countries that could benefit from a more coordinated response.[24]

One of the long-standing institutional frameworks in the region is the Cartagena Declaration Process, which meets every ten years to evaluate the original agreement signed by fifteen Latin American and Caribbean countries in 1984. The Cartagena Declaration on Refugees committed member states to protect "persons who have fled their country because their lives, safety or freedom have been threatened by generalized violence, foreign aggression, internal conflicts, massive violation of human rights or other circumstances which have seriously disturbed public order, a far broader group of people than those protected under the 1951 refugee Convention." Thirteen governments have incorporated this broader definition of refugees into their domestic laws and regulations.[25]

However, there is significant variation on whether and how these provisions are applied, with a few countries (including Brazil, Mexico, Costa Rica, and to a lesser extent, Ecuador, Argentina, and Uruguay) using their asylum systems to respond to regional displacement crises, and other countries opting to use immigration policy tools as a primary response.[26] The Cartagena Declaration and its ongoing process, which involves more than just the original signatory countries, appear to have informed an ethos of protection that has shaped policy responses to displacement in Latin America and the Caribbean, but the actual tools developed under the aegis of the declaration have not always been the ones used.[27]

In Mexico and Central America (including Belize), there is also an ongoing process known as the Marco Integral Regional para la Protección y Soluciones (MIRPS) in which governments meet regularly to discuss their humanitarian protection policies and institutions, and which serves as a forum for donor governments to support their efforts. This platform has helped strengthen asylum processes across that subregion, with noticeable enhancements in almost all the countries, including Mexico and Costa Rica, which already had active systems, and Belize, El Salvador, Guatemala, Honduras, and Panama, whose systems were far less well developed.[28]

And there are at least three other consultative bodies that have played a role in sharing ideas and strengthening cooperation on broader migration policies in Latin America and the Caribbean. The Regional Migration Conference (CRM), originally known as the Puebla Process, brings together governments from Central America (including Belize), Mexico, the Dominican Republic, Canada, and the United States to periodically review key issues in migration policy. It tends to include a mixture of foreign ministry and interior ministry officials from each country (or their equivalents). The South American Migration Conference (CSAM) is the analogous body for South American governments, and the two bodies have started to meet jointly from time to time since 2022. Finally, the Red Iberoamericana de Autoridades Migratorias (RIAM) brings together migration institutions from Spanish- and Portuguese-speaking Latin American countries and the government of Spain.

UNHCR and IOM play a vital role in almost all of these bodies. UNHCR helps provide technical support to the Cartagena Declaration Process and MIRPS, while IOM provides the technical secretariat for the Quito Process, the Regional and South American Migration Conferences, and RIAM, while also supporting the mobility regimes in CARICOM and Mercosur as an external partner. And both UNHCR and IOM together convene the R4V platform.

The Organization of American States (OAS) and its affiliated organization, the Pan-American Development Foundation (PADF), are the secretariat of the Los Angeles Declaration.

In some other regions of the world, especially Africa, the Middle East, and parts of Southeast Asia, UNHCR and IOM play outsize roles in housing refugees and internally displaced migrants.[29] However, in the Americas, these two organizations play a much more facilitative role by helping build cross-national institutions and supporting individual governments in developing their own policies. Their role is extremely important, but it largely focuses on creating capacity within and among governments, as well as strengthening civil society. Historically, developing countries leaned on the international community to take care of refugees and displaced populations, while developed countries were responsible for their own decisions.[30] In the case of Latin America and the Caribbean, governments have taken primary responsibility for decisions on refuge and displacement, with UN agencies playing an important but auxiliary role, much as in developed nations.

Over time, Latin American and Caribbean countries have developed an overlapping set of institutions, agreements, and platforms that link them together in different configurations around shared concerns and commitments on mobility, migration, and humanitarian protection. Most of these are far from consolidated, and they are highly uneven in their coverage, consolidation, and impact. But they represent an increasing recognition of the importance of shared management of migration and protection issues, an awareness developed over time but reinforced since the surge of migration and displacement in the region since 2010.

International cooperation has been critical in facilitating these efforts, especially some of the platforms supported by UN agencies and the investments made by international financial institutions, especially the Inter-American Development Bank, the World Bank, and the Development Bank of Latin America and the Caribbean (CAF).[31] But the initiatives for their creation and maintenance have largely come from countries in the region. This speaks to a growing belief that migration and displacement issues require regional and subregional cooperation, even if the reality of how they are dealt with in practice often falls far short of this recognition.

National governments across the region have had to make a series of decisions on migration during the period since 2010 as migration has increased across the Americas. These decisions are hardly uniform, but there are four domains along which governments have made decisions, and some common patterns emerge.

The first policy domain has to do with building relationships with their own citizens living abroad and their descendants, in other words, the diasporas. Most countries in Latin America and the Caribbean have at least some citizens living abroad, and some have a significant percentage of their population abroad. Several countries have created specialized agencies to liaison with their diasporas, encourage them to invest, or help them if they want to return home. Other countries, such as Colombia, Ecuador, and Peru, have special seats in the national legislature for representatives elected by citizens living abroad. And there have been sporadic attempts in some countries, such as Mexico, to create matching funds for remittances invested in specific purposes, such as infrastructure and small businesses.

These efforts are largely driven by self-interest. Politicians want to tap the remittances and investment that successful migrants abroad can send because it helps the economy. In some cases, countries, like Guyana, hope to encourage migrants to return to meet domestic labor needs. These efforts are often seen as integral parts of development strategies, especially in the Caribbean and Central America.

But there is also an important symbolic component in reaching out to citizens abroad, since so many families have family members living in other countries and embracing them is often good domestic politics. Finally, there has long been the hope in some countries that the presence of their citizens outside the country may serve them in negotiations with host countries, a kind of indirect lobby for their interests or, at least, soft power that raises their country's profile.

The second policy domain is setting policies for legal migration.[32] These have included changes to visa systems in some countries, with some countries such as Chile, Mexico, and Peru pursuing major legal reforms during this period. In other cases, changes in legal migration have come through bilateral and regional mobility agreements. The most developed of these, the Mercosur Residence Agreement, preceded this period by a year (2009), but it has continued to adapt with countries adjusting their domestic legislation to provide visa access to other members that are party to the agreement. The CARICOM Single Market and Economy agreement (CSME) also precedes this period, but governments are now negotiating an expansion of the terms of the agreement to facilitate greater mobility among (most of) the fourteen countries (excluding Haiti). Meanwhile, the Organization of Eastern Caribbean States (OECS) implemented a quite extensive mobility and residence agreement among its seven members states in 2011, while the Andean Community (CAN) did the same in 2021. Only the Central American-4 (CA-4), which allowed for passport-free travel but not residence in the member countries, has become somewhat more constrained since migration increased over the past few years.

These agreements were the result of the efforts of governments in subregions to create economic communities that would lower trade barriers and position themselves in the global economy. In some cases, they also represented important recognition of existing symbolic subregions that have long historical, social, and political ties. The mobility agreements were generally a result of the economic integration, but what is interesting is that these efforts have largely continued forward and deepened, even during a time of higher than expected migration (with the exception of the CA-4). It is perhaps not surprising that the mobility agreements are more developed and more likely to offer pathways to residence in other countries where there is greater similarity among the economies of the participating members, so there is no likely effect of mass migration to any one country.

The third policy domain—and perhaps the most distinctive for Latin America and the Caribbean—has been decision-making around receiving and integrating displaced populations, especially Haitians, Nicaraguans, and Venezuelans (and sometimes irregular migrants from other countries). "There was an immense legal creativity to generate mechanisms and pathways for regularization," say Muñoz, the former Colombian presidential advisor, who now heads the Inter-American Development Bank's Migration Unit.

The countries that received the smallest numbers of displaced migrants compared to their total population—Argentina, Brazil, Mexico, and Uruguay—have been far more likely to provide pathways to permanence. Argentina and Uruguay have used the existing Mercosur residence agreement, while Brazil created a special pathway for neighboring countries based on the Mercosur residence agreement, which in all three cases required some adaptation of existing policies to receive displaced Venezuelans. In the case of

Mexico, most of the Venezuelans who sought to stay in the country were professionals who were able to apply for existing employment-based visas (which also happened to some extent in Chile, at least initially).

In other countries, governments have created new categories of status through executive decree to provide temporary residence. The Colombian, Ecuadorian, and Peruvian governments have made extensive use of residence permits issued by executive decree, with the Colombian governments eventually issuing a ten-year permit for residence. In some cases, these have been focused only on Venezuelans, but in other cases they have included other nationalities. Chile has conducted two regularization campaigns (for all nationalities) and provided access to already existing temporary visas through these. Meanwhile, Curaçao, the Dominican Republic, and Trinidad and Tobago have offered residence permits on a more limited basis through regularization campaigns, while Guyana has issues special residence permits to all arriving Venezuelans, though without the right to work.

Traditional instruments for humanitarian protection have played far less of a role in these decisions. Most countries in Latin America, though not the Caribbean, have asylum systems, but these have been used only in exceptional cases in most countries. The exceptions are Brazil, Costa Rica, and Mexico, which have more consolidated asylum systems. In all three countries, the processes are slow because of the quantity of applications, but many migrants with protection needs apply and are often granted refugee status eventually. Brazil and, until recently, Costa Rica allowed asylum applicants to work once they applied for refugee status, so these became important pathways to de facto legal status even before final decisions are made.

Scholars have questioned why governments did not use their asylum systems more actively during periods of mass displacement.[33] Undoubtedly, the answer partly has to do with capacity constraints, since asylum systems in most countries were not developed with these levels of displacement in mind. But there was also a practical reason for using executive decrees to provide other forms of legal status. In most countries, governments wanted to provide legal status to displaced populations without issuing an open-ended invitation to stay or to have to start a complex political discussion with national legislatures. These temporary measures turned out to be wildly successful by some measures, since they allowed for the fast adjudication of claims for large numbers of people, but they also raise serious questions about how displaced migrants will be able to stay permanently as it becomes clear that conditions are not likely to exist for them to return to their countries of origin.[34]

In essence, Latin American and Caribbean countries have provided minimal direct support to displaced populations and sometimes only short-term status, but they have generally allowed them some form of legal stay in their countries, the right to work, and access to education and sometimes healthcare.[35] Unlike traditional refugee reception in the developing world, where governments tend to delegate their response to UN agencies, governments in the Americas have taken responsibility for their own responses. And while these are often less generous to those arriving in precarious conditions, they are much more generous in the long-term in allowing displaced migrants to begin their lives over again as part of the new communities where they live.

In many cases, it has been up to cities to provide many of the most important services that help migrants make the adjustment in adapting to their new communities and entering the labor market. In Colombia, the Intégrate Centers, which are one-stop shops for integration resources, supported by municipalities, international donors, and the national government, have been particularly successful. In Mexico City, the city government provides a special local identity card that allows migrants to access public services. In Costa Rica, cities big and small have a provided a range of integration services and access to job opportunities. Indeed, in most countries, city governments and nongovernmental organizations have provided the missing link for helping recent migrants adjust, when this happens at all.[36]

The fourth policy domain is immigration control. Almost all countries have increased their efforts to control who enters their countries as migration has become a more visible political issue. Haitians and Venezuelans, in particular, have the most entry requirements across the region.[37] This is a clear response to the numbers arriving and the desire to regulate their entry. But in addition to these specific restrictions, most governments have invested in border control, sometimes using national police or the military as auxiliaries in these functions.

Along the route most commonly used by Venezuelan migrants, Ecuador, Peru, and Chile have all increased their controls at borders, including demanding passports and valid visas for entry, with the Chilean government even reinforcing border crossing with military personnel. At times, the Ecuadorian, Peruvian, and Chilean governments have conducted deportations of migrants with criminal records. The Peruvian and Ecuadorian governments at times have talked about expelling Venezuelans without legal status, but they have not had the capacity to follow through on these threats as of yet. And at the same time, those same governments have continued to offer pathways to legal status for Venezuelans already living in the country, which suggests a differentiated approach between new arrivals and those who have already settled.

In Central America and Mexico, governments have tightened visa restrictions for certain nationalities that migrate in large numbers and increased inspections at airports and bus stations for migrants even from countries that do not need a visa (such as Colombians and Brazilians in Mexico). These efforts are largely driven by geopolitical concerns with the United States placing pressure on governments in the region to control large-scale migration movements north. However, they also reflect a growing desire by policymakers in some of these countries to bring the numbers crossing through their country down as public opinion becomes less positive towards large-scale crossings.[38]

In June 2024, a new administration in Panama started occasional deportation flights of those detained crossing the Darien Gap without required documentation, reflecting both the government's stated desire to reduce irregular crossings in the country, which emerged as a theme during the presidential election in 2024, as well as growing cooperation with the United States.[39] And several countries in South America, including Ecuador, Peru, and Brazil, have imposed visa restrictions on citizens of some countries outside the hemisphere when their citizens start crossing through the Darien Gap in large numbers, largely as a result of negotiations with the U.S. government.

These decisions on border control represent a mix of geopolitical pressure from the U.S. government—for countries in Central America and Mexico—and domestic shifts in public opinion almost everywhere, which have become less favorable to large-scale arrivals.[40] However, the shift to greater border control does not mean that governments have abandoned commitments to legal migration or mobility agreements, providing legal status for displaced populations, or conducting outreach to diasporas, the other three policy dimensions. In fact, governments are acting along all four of these policy dimensions simultaneously, with some leaning into one or more of these more than others, which creates a tapestry of different measures across the region.

For some migrants it is getting easier to enter neighboring countries if they are covered by bilateral or regional mobility agreements, while for other migrants it is getting harder. There is an increasing distinction between efforts to provide legal status and access to public services to those migrants already living in countries in the region, and making it harder for new migrants from the same countries to arrive. And almost all countries continue to be deeply engaged in outreach to their diasporas.

The foundations of migration policy that are being built in Latin America and the Caribbean represent a desire to control entry, expand legal pathways to certain countries perceived as neighbors, incorporate those who have fled displacement in at least temporary ways, and conduct outreach to diaspora populations with needs and influence. These foundations are being built in response to shifting public opinion, as migration becomes a more visible issue; a desire to build new approaches to subregional integration with specific neighboring countries; normative ideas of protection and solidarity; and the influence of geopolitical concerns and pressures.

These elements provide broad outlines of what appear to be some common policy directions in migration policymaking across Latin America and the Caribbean. There are, undoubtedly, some similarities that carry across most countries in the region, but there are also significant differences in emphasis from country to country and sometimes over time.

The general pattern of decision-making appears to be quite different—for now—than the liberal paradox in some traditional destination countries in Europe and North America, where conflict among interest groups dominates migration policymaking.[41] In Latin America and the Caribbean, most key decisions have been carried out by executive branch action with limited public or legislative debate. Migration issues have risen in salience, but they have yet to stay among the top issues in any country, other than the Dominican Republic, where the relationship with Haiti is central to national identity. This does not mean that countries in the Americas will not eventually develop their own version of the liberal paradox as the issues around migration become more visible, but so far it has yet to happen in a significant way.

Instead, there are other factors driving decisions around migration. They variably pull for openness and closure on migration, sometimes with differential impact on policies towards specific groups.

The first is the recent and generalized experience with emigration, which has impacted most countries in the Americas, although not all equally. Governments are particularly focused on their own diasporas, and this has often been a particular priority for migration policymaking. In some countries, this has almost certainly led to a desire to model domestic migration policies on how they wish other countries would respond to their diasporas abroad.

This recent history of emigration has likely also created a degree of solidarity in the general population with other migrants who pass through or arrive to stay in their countries. While solidarity can be fleeting and impermanent, it is often an important early factor in migration decisions that can have profound consequences over time, since initial decisions (such as allowing visa-free entry or providing legal status) may create a pattern for other decisions taken later.

The second factor has to do with the symbolic construction of common regions of shared history and culture. There have been attempts to construct a common sense of unity in the Caribbean, based on shared histories of colonization, slavery, and social ties, as well as in Latin America, around shared history, language, and culture. In some cases, these efforts have focused on smaller subregions, such as the Eastern Caribbean, South America, the Andean countries, and Central America. As political efforts they have not always prospered, but they have left a symbolic legacy that still resonates with people in some of these regions and subregions and creates imagined communities that tie people together across international borders.

In some cases, when these symbolic communities have been part of a political or economic project, such as building common economic markets in the Caribbean, the Southern Cone, the Andean subregion, and Central America, it has led to institutional structures with real measures that allow for movement among countries. In other words, what started as symbolic communities turned into real communities that allow for easier mobility across multiple countries and sometimes access to residence in them.

This sense of community identity has also mattered in responding to displacement crises. Colombians initially felt a strong sense of solidarity with Venezuelans, their next-door neighbors who had taken in hundreds of thousands of Colombians during their time of need, and who shared a perceived common history. Other Latin Americans undoubtedly responded positively to Venezuelans for the same reason, as citizens of a closely related nation, which had also taken in some of their own during times of need. While these emotional ties of solidarity may not be sufficient to explain long-term decisions to provide legal status to displaced populations, they are crucial at early moments when the first migrants arrive, and that sometimes helps set the template for future actions.

Something similar was almost certainly at work with Caribbean countries who took in migrants from other Caribbean nations (such as Guyanese in Trinidad and Tobago or Haitians in The Bahamas); with Costa Ricans accepting the arrival of Nicaraguans; and with Mexicans agreeing to take refugees from Central America. These bonds of solidarity may not always survive over time, but they are often important for those initial decisions that then have longer term consequences. And solidarity may continue to be one of many frameworks in debates over time, even as other frameworks, such as the need for greater order and border control, come to the fore.

However, shared identity and symbolic communities cut both ways, since they explicitly include migrants from some countries while excluding those from other countries. In the Dominican Republic, the relatively generous response to displaced Venezuelans, from another Spanish-speaking Latin American country, contrasts with the far more restrictive response to displaced Haitians, from the country next-door who are defined as the outgroup against which Dominican identity has been built.[42] Similarly, Trinidad and Tobago has been a privileged destination for many migrants from other Caribbean nations but has much more restrictive policies towards displaced Venezuelans.

Within the national distinctions, there may also be significant differences in how people perceive migrants of different socioeconomic, racial, and ethnic backgrounds in countries across the Americas. Existing studies of earlier migration waves suggest that poorer migrants, those with darker skin, and those who speak languages other than Spanish (whether Haitian Creole or Indigenous languages) often face particular barriers in Latin American countries.[43] These patterns echo the existing literature on racial and ethnic stratification in Latin America.[44]

But overall, migration discussions in Latin America and the Caribbean have generally been "less about identity," notes Muñoz, than in other parts of the world. People's perceptions of migration come down to more concrete elements, like competition for jobs and public services or perceptions of changes in public security, rather than threats to their identity and way of life, especially when it involves people arriving from neighboring nations. "And what really animates the conversation is more transit than integration," he notes, with the most vocal pushback on migration having to do with the perception of chaos around migrants who are either just arriving or passing through in large numbers, rather than those who are settling in.

A third factor that has shaped migration policies in the region is inequality. Populations in many destination countries may have personal sympathies with migrants in their countries, given shared identities and the common experience of migration, but they also worry about very real competition for scarce resources. Indeed, many of the key flashpoints against migration seem to come around the perception that already underfunded public services, such as schools and healthcare facilities, are being overtaxed by the arrival of desperate low-income migrants. In countries with chronic underfunding of public infrastructure, these concerns are hardly irrational. There is also some evidence that the sudden arrival of large numbers of displaced Venezuelans in some of the countries in South America almost certainly had an impact on the incomes of informal sector workers, who suddenly faced a large influx of other workers in the informal economy.[45] Studies indicate that there may be long-term economic benefits to the countries in the region from migration,[46] but the fear of labor market competition may have a very real basis in the short-term. If regional solidarity and recent experience with migration help facilitate a degree of openness to migration in the Americas, concerns about competition for jobs and public services push towards greater skepticism and closure.

A fourth factor shaping migration policies in the region is crime, which has been on the increase in some countries in the Americas during the same period as the rise in migration. Indeed, studies of public opinion consistently show that this is among the largest fears that people in Latin America and the Caribbean express around migration.[47] The limited available evidence in Latin America indicates that migrants are generally less likely to commit crimes than the native-born populations in most countries, although more research is needed to confirm this.[48] However, the simultaneous rise of migration and crime in many countries since 2010, in a region already known for having some of the highest crime rates in the world, makes it appear that these are connected phenomena.[49]

Moreover, there are real connections between migration and crime, even if it may not be the ones that many observers think. Venezuelan crime groups, especially the Tren de Aragua, a large organized crime syndicate, often followed the migrants, first as migrant smugglers and later to extort migrant-owned businesses. In some countries, such as Chile, Colombia, Ecuador, and Peru, these groups have now become quite visible within the domestic crime scene. In some countries, such as Chile, they appear to account for a significant number of the most visible violent crimes, even if Venezuelan migrants, on average, are quite law-abiding.[50] The same has been true of Colombian drug traffickers in Ecuador, who followed the drug trade across the border, even while most Colombian migrants in Ecuador commit relatively few crimes.[51]

A fifth factor that has shaped migration policies in the Americas is geopolitics. For many governments, decisions on accepting displaced migrants has often had to do with their political positions towards the government they are fleeing. Costa Rica takes in Nicaraguans in part to show its opposition to the growing authoritarianism of the Nicaraguan regime of long-time president Daniel Ortega. Leaders in Argentina, Brazil, Chile, Colombia, Ecuador, Panama, and Peru have framed their willingness to take in displaced Venezuelans as part of their strategy to promote democracy in Venezuela. Brazil and Chile, the two countries of destination in South America for the largest numbers of displaced Haitians, were the two countries that had led the UN Stabilization Mission in Haiti, building up a sense of responsibility for events in that country that was activated when the earthquake struck in 2010. Domestic migration policies have often followed on foreign policy considerations, especially early on.

The relationships with the U.S. government is another element in many governments' geopolitical calculations. The U.S. government has negotiated with multiple countries along the migration route from South America to the U.S. border to restrict entry at their borders to those without documents. The U.S. and Mexican governments have ongoing—and sometimes daily—consultations on migration management.[52] The U.S. and Panamanian governments have collaborated on starting deportations of those crossing the Darien Gap without legal authorization, with the U.S. government supplying the funding. Multiple countries have changed visa policy to reduce irregular migration, partly as a result of negotiations with the United States. It would be a mistake to think of these only as U.S. leverage against these countries, though that is certainly part of the equation. In many cases, the U.S. government is pressuring governments in the region to do things they are already disposed to do, since they would also like to see fewer irregular border crossings in and out of their countries.

Geopolitical pressures also play out in other ways. UN agencies have provided funding and exerted international pressure for countries to provide legal status to displaced populations. While the decisions have always been sovereign choices of the governments themselves, the incentives provided by external funding and the perception of getting international credit for their policy choices have undoubtedly helped with particular decisions. And U.S. funding (as well as European Union funding), through international organizations, has often been a critical factor in these efforts. Again, these are negotiations that lead to outcomes that governments probably already want to implement for their own reasons, but the external incentives matter too.[53]

Finally, a sixth factor in migration policy decisions has to do with capacity. Governments in Latin America and the Caribbean have the ability to make their own decisions on migration policy, including responses to displacement and irregular arrivals, but they also face constraints in what they can do, which shapes the specific decisions. Governments may want to restrict irregular arrivals but cannot feasibly do so, especially in the face of displacement crises, so they sometimes have to make a virtue out of necessity by pursuing policies that provide legal status, even beyond when they might initially want to. At the same time, they may want to provide more robust legal pathways (such as asylum or permanent residence) but cannot because they simply lack the capacity, political support, or even legal authorities to do so. Or they may implement policies partway but never fully carry them out because their institutional capacity does not allow for a full implementation process.

Indeed, it is worth thinking about capacity limitation as the source of both the immense creativity and noticeable limitations on policy implementation in many countries. The decision to grant temporary status to millions of displaced Venezuelans across multiple countries benefited from the lack of policy and institutional development in most countries, which allowed executive branch officials to create new categories by decree with limited public or legislative debate. At the same time, these measures have rarely covered everyone they are intended to cover because governments simply do not have the capacity to reach into every corner of the country, simplify processes sufficiently, or staff efforts as needed.

The same is true of migration control. Most countries in the Americas have very limited ability to detain and deport migrants, unless they are convicted of a crime, and then only to some countries. And most have only skeletal border authorities that are devoted to detecting and deterring those who enter between official ports of entry. And even those governments that have invested somewhat in these institutions, such as the Mexican government, find these easily subverted and suborned by well-funded smuggling organizations. Migration policy decisions often come down to the art of the possible, not to a set of optimal choices.

So is there a Latin American and Caribbean model of migration? Probably not. At their best, countries in the region have shown that they can absorb large migrant populations, including displaced populations, with less drama than many other places around the world. Several countries have a real story to tell on how they have done this. Generally, they have allowed migrants to start their lives over by accessing legal status, the labor market, education, and sometimes healthcare, while city governments and nongovernmental organizations have handled the limited integration efforts that exist.

For many, this has provided a true opportunity to start over in conditions of dignity. But migrants also face real barriers to integration, from formal barriers in accessing services to less visible but no less real social barriers reflecting actual patterns of discrimination based on nationality, socioeconomic background, race, ethnicity, and gender. Policies providing legal status have often been expansive, but the real experiences of integration vary widely.

And the countries in Latin American and the Caribbean have been particularly active in building regional and bilateral mobility agreements, allowing at least some people in nearby countries to move (somewhat) freely to other countries. At the same time, most countries have sought to enhance control over migration and borders, with mixed degrees of success, in hopes of creating orderly processes for entry as migration becomes more visible.

Over time, countries will have to come to terms with a new reality, which is that Latin American and Caribbean countries are aging and families are having far fewer children. "Demography matters," says Muñoz. And studies show that many countries in the region will soon begin to shrink in population without migration, which will have a significant impact on their labor markets and economic growth.[54] "Labor mobility is the way to continue discussing the issue," he adds. Countries with low population growth, including Barbados, Brazil, Chile, Guyana, and Mexico, will need to create legal pathways in the future, not to manage displacement but to ensure the arrival of workers they need for their own economic growth.

And almost all governments continue to build ties to diasporas living abroad in hopes of involving them in development efforts in their countries. In many countries, migrants living abroad play an outsized symbolic and economic role in the life of local communities, which pushes policymakers to think of how to connect with them more effectively.

Taken together, these elements do not constitute a single model for migration policymaking. But this made clear that all countries in Latin America and the Caribbean were actively engaged in trying to build the foundation of migration policy as politics and circumstances on the ground change.

––––––––

As this book was going to print, the inauguration of Donald J. Trump as president of the United States in 2025 shook the hemisphere's nascent migration policy foundations. The Trump administration had begun to rewrite U.S. foreign policy strategy across the hemisphere, demanding other governments' full cooperation to receive deportations of their citizens and, in some cases, third-country nationals, as well as to end irregular migration. Most governments showed deference and respect to the Trump administration to avoid reprisals, while also asserting their own leverage in these negotiations.

The new U.S. administration quickly terminated Biden-era humanitarian parole and refugee programs that had allowed hundreds of thousands of migrants, primarily from Venezuela, Haiti, Nicaragua, and Cuba, to enter the country with the option to seek asylum. The idea of mixing legal pathways with enforcement as a migration management strategy seemed to be over in favor of an enforcement-first strategy.

Regional migration trends as of March 2025 demonstrated that the Trump administration was initially succeeding in keeping irregular border arrivals low, but it was struggling to fulfill its campaign promise to conduct massive numbers of deportations. Still, many countries in Latin America and the Caribbean were preparing plans to receive large numbers of their citizens and developing strategies to reintegrate them, knowing that the numbers of returnees might increase eventually. Some countries were also trying to integrate migrants from other countries who had decided to stay in their countries instead of continuing north.

Lost, of course, was the moment of shared dialogue and coordinated strategies across the hemisphere, which had been built through the Los Angeles Declaration and other regional processes. It was clear that the U.S. government would act alone, independent of the interests of other countries in the hemisphere. Lost too was much of the funding for programs that had helped countries promote the integration of displaced populations, as the U.S. government cut back on foreign aid.

The current moment marks a shift. Flows have declined, but mobility is more volatile. Some migrants are returning; others seeking new routes; and reverse migration is rising. Mass deportation plans are reshaping the conversation and perhaps sidelining integration efforts. While migration intentions remain high, people face uncertainty and are testing alternative strategies in a fragmented landscape. The narrative is shifting from movement onward to return and from visibility to uncertainty.

With these changes, migration policies within the hemisphere become more important than ever. Governments and societies across the Americas will have to grapple with what they want out of migration, wrestling with a series of policy questions around integration, borders, and returns, and deciding how to manage mobility according to their national interests and values.

Notes

Introduction

1. Interview with Carolay Morales, RCN journalist, on May 12, 2021, by one of the authors. See also the video, Carolay Morales, "Un año después del sueño de Alexander," RCN Television, August 13, 2020, https://www.youtube.com/watch?v=LIBzmjlM1UI, which provides both the original footage of the encounter and follow-up on what happened afterwards.

2. Interview, Alexander Beja, August 2024.

3. Diego Chaves-González and Natalia Delgado, *A Winding Path to Integration: Venezuelan Migrants' Regularization and Labor Market Prospects* (Washington, DC: Migration Policy Institute, 2023), https://www.migrationpolicy.org/sites/default/files/publications/mpi-iom_venezuelan-regularization-2023_final.pdf.

4. Natalia Banulescu-Bogdan, Haim Malka, and Shelly Culbertson, *How We Talk About Migration: The Link Between Migration Narratives, Policy, and Power* (Washington, DC: Migration Policy Institute, Metropolitan Group, Rand Corporation, and National Immigration Forum, 2021), https://www.migrationpolicy.org/sites/default/files/publications/narratives-about-migration-2021_final.pdf. See also Inter-American Development Bank, Laboratorio de Percepción Ciudadana y Migración, *Análisis de la Percepción Ciudadana Frente a la Dinámica Migratoria Regional* (Washington, DC: IDB Unit on Migration, 2023). There is considerable research on public opinion around migration in Europe and North America, but much less on the developing world and recent migration destinations.

5. Diego Chaves-González and María José Mora, *Costa Rican Migration and Asylum Policy* (Washington, DC: Migration Policy Institute, forthcoming); Elvira Cuadra Lira and Roberto Samcam Ruíz, *De la represión al exilio: Nicaragüenses en Costa Rica* (San

José, Costa Rica: Fundación Arias por la Paz y el Progreso Humano, 2019), https://arias
.or.cr/wp-content/uploads/2019/05/1De_la_represion_al_exilio_vercompleta.pdf.

6. Jessica Bolter and Caitlyn Yates, *African Migration in the Americas* (Washington,
DC: Migration Policy Institute, forthcoming).

7. Alexandra Haas Paciuc, Elena Sánchez-Montijano and Roberto Zedillo Ortegas,
eds., *Cohesión social: Hacia una política de integración de personas en situación de movilidad en México* (Mexico City: CIDE, 2000).

8. Milagros Ricourt, *The Dominican Racial Imaginary* (New Brunswick, NJ: Rutgers
University Press, 2016); Laurent Dubois, *Haiti: The Aftershocks of History* (New York:
Metropolitan Books/Henry Holt, 2012).

9. On this point, see also the introduction by the editors in *Routledge History of
Modern Latin American Migration*, ed. Andreas E. Feldmann, Xóchitl Bada, Jorge
Durand, and Stephanie Schütz (New York: Routledge, 2024).

10. Bolter and Yates, *African Migration in the Americas.*

11. On the numbers and origins of migrants, see Colleen Putzel-Cavanaugh and
Ariel G. Ruiz Soto, "Shifting Patterns and Policies Reshape Migration to U.S.-Mexico
Border in Major Ways," Commentary, Migration Policy Institute, October 2023, https:/
/www.migrationpolicy.org/news/border-numbers-fy2023. While it is true that there is
some double-counting in the official U.S. Customs and Border Patrol statistics on
border "encounters"—the number of people apprehended or held briefly and returned—
there are also a significant number of migrants who manage to cross the border and are
not encountered by U.S. authorities. Since these two numbers largely offset each other,
it is a reasonable estimate that more than 2 million migrants tried to cross the U.S.-
Mexico border in both fiscal years 2022 and 2023, and closer to 1.5 million in fiscal year
2024, though these are not exact numbers.

12. Andrew Selee, Valerie Lacarte, Ariel G. Ruiz Soto, Diego Chaves-González,
Maria Jesus Mora, and Andrea Tanco, "In a Dramatic Shift, the Americas Have Become
a Leading Migration Destination," *Migration Information Source*, April 11, 2023, https:/
/www.migrationpolicy.org/article/latin-america-caribbean-immigration-shift.

13. On each of these crises, see the discussions in chapters 1–3.

14. In 2010, there were 8,326,588 migrants living in Latin American and Caribbean
countries, of which 831,154 were from Haiti, Nicaragua, and Venezuela. In 2020, there
were 14,794,623 migrants, of which 5,686,711 were from Haiti, Nicaragua, and Venezuela, a number which has since grown even further. Authors' tabulations of data from the
United Nations' Department of Economic and Social Affairs, Population Division, "International Migrant Stock 2020: Destination and Origin," accessed September 23, 2024,
https://www.un.org/development/desa/pd/content/international-migrant-stock.

15. Hein de Haas, *How Migration Really Works: The Facts About the Most Divisive
Issue in Politics* (New York: Basic Books, 2023).

16. For a systematic analysis of climate impacts on migration in Central America
specifically, see Andrew Linke, Stephanie Leutert, Joshua Busby, Maria Duque, Mat-
thew Shawcroft, and Simon Brewer, "Dry Growing Seasons Predicted Central American
Migration to the US from 2012 to 2018," *Scientific Reports* 13, article no. 18400 (2023),
https://doi.org/10.1038/s41598-023-43668-9.

17. Fernando Riosmena, "Environmental Change, Its Social Impacts, and Migration Responses Within and Out of Latin America: A Theoretical Inquiry," in Feldmann et al., *Routledge History of Modern Latin American Migration*.

18. On this point, see de Haas, *How Migration Really Works*, 112–14, and also Hein de Haas, "A Theory of Migration: The Aspirations-Capabilities Framework," *Comparative Migration Studies* 9 no. 8 (February 2021).

19. Dany Bahar, "The Often Overlooked 'Pull' Factor: Border Crossings and Labor Market Tightness in the US," Working Paper 695, Center for Global Development, May 2024, https://www.cgdev.org/sites/default/files/Bahar_Border_Crossings_and_Labor_Markets_Working_Paper_Final.pdf.

20. Bahar, "The Often Overlooked 'Pull' Factor"; de Haas, *How Migration Really Works*. Even in the case of displacement crises, people may choose to leave out of necessity, but where to go is sometimes based on opportunities. Those opportunities include where people can feasible get to, whether they have social connections at the destination that allow them to find work, and whether there is a likelihood of getting work.

21. de Haas, "A Theory of Migration." See also, de Haas, *How Migration Really Works*. This framework is built on the aspirations-capabilities approach developed by Amartya Sen. See Amartya Sen, *Development as Freedom* (Anchor Books, 2000).

22. On this point, see also Michael Clemens, "The Emigration Life Cycle: How Development Shapes Emigration from Poor Countries," IZA Discussion Papers 13614, Institute of Labor Economics, 2000.

23. de Haas, "A Theory of Migration." On the importance of social ties as part of this equation, see Douglas S. Massey, "The Social and Economic Origins of Migration," *Annals of the American Academy of Political and Social Science* 510, no. 1 (1990).

24. Massey, "The Social and Economic Origins of Migration."

25. Michelle F. Ferris-Dobles, "New Communication Technologies and People's Movement," in Feldmann et al., *Routledge History of Modern Latin American Migration*.

26. Silvia E. Giorguli-Saucedo, Victor M. Garcia Guerrero, and Claudia Masferrer, "Demographic Environment and Migration Perspectives in Latin America and the Caribbean," in Feldmann et al., *Routledge History of Modern Latin American Migration*.

27. On the way demographics is reshaping global mobility, see Paul Morland, *The Hidden Tide: How Population Shaped the Modern World* (New York: PublicAffairs, 2019).

28. For a quick introduction to the challenges of "mixed migration," see Nicholas Van Hear, "Mixed Migration: Policy Challenges," Oxford Migration Observatory, March 24, 2011, https://migrationobservatory.ox.ac.uk/resources/primers/mixed-migra tion-policy-challenges/.

29. On mixed migration flows, see de Haas, *How Migration Really Works*. For an approach that separates out refugees, survival migrants (forced migrants), and other migrants, as a series of concentric circles, see Alexander Betts, *Survival Migration: Failed Governance and the Crisis of Migration* (Ithaca, NY: Cornell University Press, 2013).

30. For a comprehensive overview of migration policies in the Americas, see Diego Acosta and Jeremy Harris, *Migration Policy Regimes in Latin America and the Carib-*

bean: Immigration, Regional Free Movement, Refuge, and Nationality (Washington, DC: Inter-American Development Bank, 2022). See also, Maria Jesús Mora, Ariel G. Ruiz-Soto, and Andrew Selee, *Building on Regular Pathways to Address Migration Pressures in the Americas* (Migration Policy Institute and International Organization for Migration, June 2024), https://www.migrationpolicy.org/sites/default/files/publications/mpi-iom_regular-pathways-americas-2024-final.pdf.

31. Luisa Feline Freier, "The Regional Response to the Venezuelan Exodus," *Current History* 118, no. 805 (February 2019); and Luciana Gandini, Fernando Lozano Ascencio, and Victoria Prieto, eds., *Crisis y migración de población venezolana: Entre la desprotección y la seguridad jurídica en Latinoamérica* (Mexico City: Universidad Nacional Autónoma de México, 2019).

32. Acosta and Harris, *Migration Policy Regimes in Latin America and the Caribbean.*

33. An early formulation of the "liberal paradox" can be found in James F. Hollifield, *Immigrants, Markets, and States: The Political Economy of Postwar Europe* (Cambridge, MA: Harvard University Press, 1992). A more recent formulation can be found in James F. Hollifield and Neil Foley, "Introduction," in *Understanding Global Migration*, ed. James F. Hollifield and Neil Foley (Stanford, CA: Stanford University Press, 2022).

34. Hollifield and Foley, "Introduction."

35. Terri Givens and Rahsaan Maxwell, eds., *Immigrant Politics: Race and Representation in Western Europe* (Boulder, CO: Lynne Rienner, 2012); Sasha Polakow-Suransky, *Go Back to Where You Came From: The Backlash Against Immigration and the Fate of Western Democracy* (New York: Bold Type Books, 2017).

36. On issue salience and its effect on political decision-making, see Timothy J. Hatton, "Public Opinion on Immigration in Europe: Preference and Salience," *European Journal of Political Economy* 66 (January 2021); Alberto Alesina and Marco Tabellini, "The Political Effects of Immigration: Culture or Economics?" Working Paper, Harvard Business School, May 2022, https://www.hbs.edu/ris/Publication Files/Alesina and Tabellini_May2022_6e374744-f5f7-4ed0-9387-d0ac7cf087ff.pdf; and Christian Schnaudt and Christian Stecker, "Uncovering the Flash Potential of Immigration: Attitudes, Salience, and Far-Right Support in Europe," *International Journal of Public Opinion Research* 34, no. 4 (Winter 2022).

37. Ricourt, *The Dominican Racial Imaginary.*

38. Richard Turits, "A World Destroyed, a Nation Imposed: The 1937 Haitian Massacre in the Dominican Republic," *Hispanic American Historical Review* 82 no. 3 (August 2002).

39. Jonathan M. Katz, "What Happened When a Nation Erased Birthright Citizenship," *The Atlantic*, November 12, 2018.

40. Ricourt, *The Dominican Racial Imaginary.* On the United States, see Daniel Tichenor, *Dividing Lines: The Politics of Immigration Control in America* (Princeton, NJ: Princeton University Press, 2002).

41. For an overview of the specific measures across Latin America, see the important volume by David James Cantor, Luisa Feline Freier, and Jean-Pierre Gauci, eds., *A Liberal Tide? Immigration and Asylum Law and Policy in Latin America* (London: Institute

for Latin American Studies, University of London, 2015). In the Caribbean, migration laws were generally part of early legislation as countries obtained independence and began to write their own legal frameworks.

42. Cantor et al., *A Liberal Tide?*

43. For example, Mexico's 2011 migration law was designed to model what the Mexican government wished the U.S. government might do on immigration policy, see chapter 3.

44. On the role of diaspora organizations, see Jorge Duany, *Blurred Borders: Transnationalism Between the Hispanic Caribbean and the United States* (Charlottesville: University of North Carolina, 2011); Roger Waldinger, "Between 'Here' and 'There': Immigrant Cross-Border Activities and Loyalties," *International Migration Review* 42, no. 1 (Spring 2008). On the growth of migrant organizations in Latin America, see Luis Escala Rabadan and Xochitl Bada, "Immigrant Organizations in Latin America," in Feldmann et al., *Routledge History of Modern Latin American Migration.*

45. Diego Acosta, *The National Versus the Foreign in South America: 200 Years of Migration and Citizenship Law* (Cambridge: Cambridge University Press, 2019).

46. Acosta, *The National Versus the Foreign in South America.* It is also worth noting that there were also two regional fora for consultations on migration policy. One, founded in 1996, originally called the Puebla Process and now the Regional Conference on Migration, includes countries in Central America, Mexico, and the Dominican Republic, as well as the United States and Canada. The other one, founded in 2000, was originally called the Lima Process and is now the South American Conference on migration, and includes countries in South America.

47. See chapters 1–3 on the specific agreements and also Leiza Brumat and Diego Acosta, "Three Generations of Free Movement of Regional Migrants in Mercosur: Any Influence from the EU?" in *The Dynamics of Regional Migration Governance*, ed. Andrew Geddes, Marcia Vera Espinoza, Leila Hadj-Abdou, and Leiza Brumat (Cheltenham, UK: Edgar Elgar Publishing, 2019).

48. Valerie Lacarte, Jordi Amaral, Diego Chaves-González, Ana María Saíz, and Jeremy Harris, *Migration, Integration, and Diaspora Engagement in the Caribbean: A Policy Review* (Washington, DC: Migration Policy Institute and Inter-American Development Banks, 2021), https://www.migrationpolicy.org/sites/default/files/publications/mpi-idb-caribbean-report-2023-final.pdf.

49. Liliana Lyra Jubilut, Marcia Vera, and Gabriela Mezzanotti, *Latin America and Refugee Protection: Regimes, Logics and Challenges* (New York: Berghahn Books, 2021). The Cartagena Declaration was a response primarily to the violence in Central America at the time, which generated a displacement of hundreds of thousands of people to other countries, and was also built on the experience of displacement a decade earlier from dictatorships in South America.

50. Michael Reed-Hurtado, *The Cartagena Declaration on Refugees and People Fleeing Armed Conflict and Other Situations of Violence in Latin America*, UNHCR Legal and Protection Research Series, June 2013, https://www.refworld.org/reference/lpprs/unhcr/2013/en/97247. See also Luisa Feline Freier and Nieves Fernandez Rodriguez,

"Trends in Latin American Domestic Refugee Law," in Jubilut et al., *Latin America and Refugee Protection*.

51. On this point, see also Hollifield and Foley, *Understanding Global Migration*.

52. In dealing with displacement crises in Africa, Alexander Betts suggests that we need to understand the incentives that governments have to "stretch" the refugee regime—that is, to provide protection even when it is not legally required or always convenient for governments. While not all migration in the Americas is the result of displacement, the approach to understanding the incentives at play makes eminent sense. Betts, *Survival Migration*.

53. See, for example, Walter D. Mignolo, *The Idea of Latin America* (Blackwell Publishing, 2005); B. W. Higman, *A Concise History of the Caribbean*, 2nd ed. (Cambridge University Press, 2021).

54. Natalia Banulescu-Bogdan, "From Fear to Solidarity: The Difficulty of Shifting Public Narratives About Refugees" (Migration Policy Institute, May 2022), https://www.migrationpolicy.org/sites/default/files/publications/refugee-narratives-report-2022_final.pdf.

55. For a specific variation of this argument, on how different decision-makers in governments face distinct external pressures, see Antje Ellerman, *The Comparative Politics of Immigration: Policy Choices in Germany, Canada, Switzerland, and the United States* (Cambridge: Cambridge University Press, 2021).

56. There is an extensive bibliography on the migrant roots of Latin and Caribbean music, both the fusion of old world rhythms and styles in the new world, and the remixing of these styles by Caribbean and Latin American migrants in the United States and Europe in the twentieth century. See, for example, Ed Morales, *The Latin Beat: The Rhythms and Roots of Latin Music from Bossa Nova to Salsa and Beyond* (New York: De Capo Press, 2003).

57. Charles C. Mann, *1491: New Revelations of the Americas Before Columbus* (New York: Vintage Books, 2005).

58. Mann, *1491*, for Chile; for settlement patterns in the Caribbean, see Samuel M. Wilson, *The Archeology of the Caribbean* (Cambridge: Cambridge University Press, 2007).

59. Wilson, *The Archeology of the Caribbean*.

60. José Moya, "Migration and the Historical Formation of Latin America in a Global Perspective," *Sociologias* 20, no. 49 (2018). Moya estimates 1.6 million total European settlers to Spanish and Portuguese in Latin America. In addition, there was a small number of British, French, and Dutch settlers who moved to the Caribbean islands controlled by those countries. Note that the early 1800s marks the independence of Haiti, the first country to achieve independence. Most of the Spanish and Portuguese colonies in Latin America, except Cuba and Puerto Rico, and most English and Dutch colonies, did not become independent until the 1960s or even later.

61. Mann, *1491*; Wilson, *The Archeology of the Caribbean*.

62. World Bank Group, "Indigenous Latin America in the Twentieth Century" (Washington, DC: World Bank, 2015), https://documents1.worldbank.org/curated/en/

14589146799197454o/pdf/Indigenous-Latin-America-in-the-twenty-first-century-the
-first-decade.pdf.

63. After 1800, most of the slave trade in the Americas was to Cuba and Brazil, although some slaves were brought to other countries, especially in the Caribbean, even
after the British forbade the slave trade in 1808. For the number of African slaves, see
"Broad Regions of Disembarkation," SlaveVoyages, Transatlantic Slave Trade Database,
available at https://www.slavevoyages.org/voyage/database#tables. For the influence of
the African diaspora in Latin America and the Caribbean see, George Reid Andrew,
Afro-Latin America: 1800–2000 (Oxford: Oxford University Press, 2004); and Carrie
Gibson, *Empire's Crossroads: A History of the Caribbean from Columbus to the Present
Day* (New York: Atlantic Monthly Press, 2014).

64. Estimates from Moya, "Migration and Historical Formation in Latin America."
There is an extensive literature on European migration to the Americas, especially to
the Southern Cone countries in the second half of the nineteenth century and first three
decades of the twentieth. For representative works, see Samuel Bailey and Eduardo José
Míguez, eds., *Mass Migration to Modern Latin America* (Wilmington, DE: Scholarly
Resources, 2003); Jose C. Moya, *Cousins and Strangers: Spanish Immigrants in Buenos
Aires, 1850–1930* (Berkeley: University of California Press, 1998); and Jeffrey Lesser, *Im-
migration, Ethnicity, and National Identity in Brazil: 1808 to the Present* (New Haven,
CT: Yale University Press, 2013).

65. David FitzGerald and David Cook-Martin, *Culling the Masses: The Democratic
Origins of Racist Immigration Policies in the Americas* (Cambridge, MA: Harvard University Press, 2014).

66. Moya calculates 855,000 Asian immigrants in Spanish- and Portuguese-speaking
Latin America, mostly from China and Japan, while Roopnarine describes the arrival of
over 500,000 Indian migrants and indentured servants to the Caribbean and small migrations in the twentieth century from South Korea. Lomarsh Roopnarine, *The Indian
Caribbean: Migration and Identity in the Diaspora* (University of Mississippi Press,
2018), plus roughly 38,000 Indonesians who went to Suriname. See Rosemarijn Hoefte,
In Place of Slavery: A Social History of British Indian and Javanese Laborers in Suriname
(Gainesville: University Press of Florida, 1998). See also Moya, "Migration and Histori-
cal Formation in Latin America." See also Roberto Chao Rodriguez, *The Chinese in
Mexico, 1882–1940* (Tucson: University of Arizona Press, 2010); Evelyn Hu-DeHart and
Kathleen Lopez, "Asian Diasporas in Latin America and the Caribbean: An Historical
Overview," *Afro-Hispanic Review* 27, no. 1 (Spring 2008): 9–21; Walton Look Lai and
Chee-Beng Tan, eds. *Chinese In Latin America and the Caribbean* (Boston: Brill, 2010).

67. Moya, "Migration and Historical Formation in Latin America;" Lesser, *Immigration, Ethnicity, and National Identity in Brazil*; and Gibson, *Empire's Crossroads*. Moya
calculates 410,000 immigrants from "The Levant," in Spanish and Portuguese-speaking
Latin America, but many others arrived in the English, French, and Dutch colonies of
the Caribbean as well.

68. Lacarte et al., *Migration, Integration, and Diaspora Engagement in the Caribbean*;
Higman, *A Concise History of the Caribbean*.

69. Lara Putnam, *Caribbean Migrants and the Politics of Race in the Jazz Age* (Chapel Hill: University of North Carolina Press, 2013); Frederick Douglass Opie, *Black Labor Migration in Caribbean Guatemala, 1882–1923* (Gainesville: University Press of Florida, 2012); and Philippe I. Bourgois, *Ethnicity at Work: Divided Labor on a Central American Banana Plantation* (Baltimore: Johns Hopkins University Press, 1989).

70. As noted in chapter 1, 11 percent of people in the United States were born in Mexico while 9 percent of all Mexicans lived in the United States. Douglas S. Massey, Jorge Durand, and Nolan J. Malone, *Beyond Smoke and Mirrors: Mexican Immigration in an Era of Economic Integration* (New. York: Russell Sage Foundation, 2002). See also Jorge Durand, *Historia Mínima de Migración México-Estados Unidos* (Mexico City: El Colegio de México, 2016); Neil Foley, *Mexicans in the Making of America* (Boston: Belknap Press/Harvard University Press, 2014); Edward Telles and Christina A. Sue, *Durable Ethnicity: Mexican Americans and the Ethnic Core* (Oxford: Oxford University Press, 2019); and Katharine M. Donato, Jonathan Hiskey, Jorge Durand, and Douglas S. Massey, eds. *Continental Divides: International Migration in the Americas*, The Annals of the American Academy of Political and Social Sciences, Volume 630, August 2010.

71. Duany, *Blurred Borders*; Mike Phillips and Trevor Phillips, *Windrush: The Irresistible Rise of Multicultural Britain* (London: HarperCollins, 1999); Anke Birkenmeier, ed., *Caribbean Migrations: Legacies of Colonialism* (New Brunswick, NJ: Rutgers University Press, 2020).

72. On U.S. immigration changes, see Tichenor, *Dividing Lines*. On the United Kingdom, see Phillips and Phillips, *Windrush*.

73. Victoria Prieto-Rosas and Julieta Bengochea, "International Migration in South America" in Feldmann et al., *Routledge History of Modern Latin American Migration*.

74. Eduardo Domenech, ed., *Migración y política: El Estado interrogado. Procesos actuales en Argentina y Sudamérica* (Córdoba, Argentina: Universidad Nacional de Córdoba, 2009).

75. For good overviews of intraregional mobility before 2010, see Marcela Cerrutti and Emilio Parrado, "Migrations in South America," in *The SAGE Handbook of International Migration*, ed. C. Inglis, W. Li, and B. Khadria (London: SAGE Publications, 2020); and Victoria Prieto and Julieta Bengochea, "International Migration in South America," in Feldmann et al., *Routledge History of Modern Latin American Migration*.

76. Andrew Selee, Silvia Giorguli, Ariel G. Ruiz Soto, and Claudia Masferrer, *Investing in the Neighborhood: Changing Mexico-US Migration Patterns and Options for Sustainable Cooperation* (Washington, DC, and Mexico City: Migration Policy Institute and El Colegio de México, 2019), https://www.migrationpolicy.org/sites/default/files/publications/US-Mexico-migration-English-Final.pdf. On the origins of Central American migration, see Susanne Jonas and Nestor Rodriguez, *Guatemala-US Migration: Transforming Regions* (Austin: University of Texas Press, 2015); Cecilia Mejívar and Andrea Gómez Cervantes, "El Salvador: Civil War, Natural Disasters, and Gang Violence Drive Migration," *Migration Information Source* (Migration Policy Institute, August 29, 2018), https://www.migrationpolicy.org/article/el-salvador-civil-war-natural-disasters-and-gang-violence-drive-migration; and Sarah Bermeo and David Leblang,

"Honduras Migration: Climate Change, Violence, and Assistance," Policy Brief (Duke University, Stanford Center for International Development, March 2021), https://dcid. sanford.duke.edu/wp-content/uploads/sites/7/2021/03/Honduras-migration-Policy -Brief-Final.pdf.

77. Haas et al., *Cohesión Social*.

78. Chaves-Rodríguez and Mora, *Costa Rican Migration and Asylum Policies*.

79. Secretaria de Gobierno, "La COMAR en numeros: Noviembre 2023," December 6, 2023, https://www.gob.mx/comar/articulos/la-comar-en-numeros-353357?idiom=es.

80. Dirección General de Migración y Extranjería, "Informes Estadisticos Anuales," updated December 18, 2023, https://www.migracion.go.cr/Paginas/Centro de Documen taci%C3%B3n/Estad%C3%ADsticas.aspx.

81. Chaves-Rodríguez and Mora, *Costa Rican Migration and Asylum Policies*; Ariel G. Ruiz Soto et al., *Mexico's Immigrant Integration Policies* (unpublished manuscript in process).

82. For an overview of diaspora influence on policies in the region, see Luis Escala Rabadán and Xóchitl Bada, "Migration and Immigration Organizational Forms in Latin America," in *The Oxford Handbook of the Sociology of Latin America*, ed. Xóchitl Bada and Liliana Rivera-Sánchez (New York: Oxford University Press, 2021).

83. Lilia Rivera Sánchez, ed., *Volver a casa: Migrantes de retorno en América Latina* (Mexico City: El Colegio de México, 2020). See especially the introduction by the editor and the chapter by Claudia Masferrer and Victoria Prieto, "El perfil socio demográfico del retorno migratorio reciente. Diferencias y similitudes entre contextos de procedencia y de acogida en América Latina."

84. Sánchez, *Volver a casa*.

85. The thirty-five independent countries include eighteen that have Spanish as the official language, one that has Portuguese, one with French and Haitian Kreol, three that have Dutch and Papiamento as the official languages, and twelve where English is the official language.

86. See, for example, Edward Telles, *Pigmentocracies: Ethnicity, Race, and Color in Latin America* (University of North Carolina Press, 2014); Henry Louis Gates, Jr., *Black in Latin America* (New York: New York University Press, 2011); Mara Loveman, *National Colors: Racial Classification and the State in Latin America* (New York: Oxford University Press, 2014); Lesser, *Immigration, Ethnicity, and National Identity in Brazil*; Diego Sánchez-Ancochea, *The Costs of Inequality in Latin America* (New York: I. B. Tauris, 2020); Jeffrey G. Williamson, "Latin American Inequality: Colonial Origins, Commodity Booms, or a Missed 20th Century Leveling?," NBER Working Paper No. 20915, January 2015.

87. Philip Keefer and Carlos Scartascini, eds., *Trust in Latin America and the Caribbean* (Inter-American Development Bank, 2022). See also the dataset of the World Values Survey, available at https://www.worldvaluessurvey.org/WVSOnline.jsp.

88. On race and ethnicity in Latin America, see Telles, *Pigmentocracies*; Gates, *Black in Latin America*; Loveman, *National Colors*; and Lesser, *Immigration, Ethnicity, and National Identity in Brazil*. Many countries did, in fact, have openly racist immigration

policies in the late nineteenth and early twentieth centuries, but these were largely re-placed by more neutral criteria after World War II, making immigration policies fairly open even if integration is often more influenced by race, ethnicity, and economic strat-ification. FitzGerald and Cook-Martin, *Culling the Masses.*

89. Sánchez-Ancochea, *The Costs of Inequality in Latin America.*

90. One important study that covers several countries is Jeremy Harris, Thomas Liebig, and David Khoudour, eds., *How Do Migrants Fare in Latin America and the Caribbean?: Mapping Socio-Economic Integration* (Washington, DC: Inter-American Development Bank, Organisation for Economic Cooperation and Development, United Nations Development Programme, 2023).

91. Interview with Carolay Morales.

92. Interview with Alexander Beja, September 2024.

93. Interview with Alexander Beja.

94. Certainly compared to most Syrian refugees, for example. See Elizabeth Ferris and Kemal Kirisi, *The Consequences of Chaos: Syria's Humanitarian Crisis and the Fail-ure to Protect* (Washington, DC: Brookings Institution, 2016). On refugees in East Africa, see Alexander Betts, *The Wealth of Refugees: How Displaced People Can Create Economies* (Oxford: Oxford University Press, 2021).

95. On weak states in Latin America, see Miguel Ángel Centeno, *Blood and Debt: War and the Nation State in Latin America* (University Park: Pennsylvania State Univer-sity Press, 2003). For the Caribbean, Higman, *A Concise History of the Caribbean.*

96. A recent study on Senegalese migrants who were legalized in Argentina finds an important but uneven effect of legal status, helping with overall social mobility and sense of security, but not necessarily labor mobility. There is, as yet, no broader evidence on the actual effects of legal status on labor outcomes and other integration measures, as there is for Europe and North America. See Luisa Feline Freier and Bernarda Zubrzy-cki, "How Do Immigrant Legalization Programs Play Out in Informal Labor Markets? The Case of Senegalese Street Hawkers in Argentina," *Migration Studies*, November 25, 2019.

97. Banulescu-Bogdan, Malka, and Culbertson, *How We Talk About Migration.*

Chapter 1

1. XIV Censo de Población y Vivienda: Resultados Total Nacional de la República Bolivariana de Venezuela. 2011. Available at: http://www.ine.gob.ve/documentos/Demo grafia/CensodePoblacionyVivienda/pdf/nacional.pdf.

2. "Venezuela Manufactures a Dispute with Neighboring Colombia," *Washington Post*, September 1, 2015.

3. Colombian Ministry of Foreign Affairs, "Con 15 ferias de servicios en 13 departa-mentos del país."

4. Author interview with Juan Viloria, October 2024

5. International Monetary Fund–IMF, "Venezuelan Inflation Rates and Average Consumer Prices," October 2023, https://www.imf.org/external/datamapper/PCPIPCH @WEO/WEOWORLD/VEN.

6. *Regional Spillovers from the Venezuelan Crisis: Migration Flows and Their Impact on Latin America and the Caribbean,* prepared by Jorge Alvarez, Marco Arena, Alain Brousseau, Hamid Faruqee, Emilio Fernandez-Corugedo, Jaime Guajardo, Gerardo Peraza, and Juan Yépez Albornoz (Washington, DC: International Monetary Fund, 2022), https://www.imf.org/-/media/Files/Publications/DP/2022/English/RSVCEA.ashx.

7. On Venezuela's economic decline, see *Regional Spillovers from the Venezuelan Crisis.*

8. Diego Chaves-González and Carlos Echeverría-Estrada, *A Regional Profile of Venezuelan Refugees and Migrants in Latin America and the Caribbean* (Washington, DC: Migration Policy Institute, 2020), https://www.migrationpolicy.org/sites/default/files/publications/mpi-iom_venezuelan-profile_spanish-final.pdf.

9. Chaves-González and Echeverría-Estrada, *A Regional Profile of Venezuelan Refugees and Migrants.* For recent data, which does not disaggregate by nationality, but confirms that this trend continues, see Jeremy Harris, Thomas Liebig, and David Khoudour-Castéras, eds., *How Do Migrants Fare in Latin America and the Caribbean? Mapping Socioeconomic Integration* (Washington, DC: Inter-American Development Bank, UN Development Program, and the Organisation for Economic Cooperation and Development, 2023), https://publications.iadb.org/publications/english/document/How-Do-Migrants-Fare-in-Latin-America-and-the-Caribbean-Mapping-Socio-Economic-Integration.pdf.

10. Luciana Gandini and Andrew Selee, *Betting on Legality: Latin America and Caribbean Responses to the Venezuelan Displacement Crisis* (Washington, DC: Migration Policy Institute, May 2023).

11. Authors' interviews with Chilean Ministry of Education officials, July 2022.

12. Author interview with a teacher in La Guajira.

13. Gandini and Selee, *Betting on Legality.*

14. David Scott FitzGerald and David Cook-Martin, *Culling the Masses: The Democratic Origins of Racist Immigration Policy in the Americas* (Cambridge, MA: Harvard University Press, 2014).

15. UNHCR, "CASEN en Pandemia 2020: Caracterización de la población extranjera en Chile," 2023, 15, https://data.unhcr.org/en/documents/details/104099.

16. Luis Eduardo Thayer Correa and Maria Emilia Tijoux Merino, "Trayectorias del sujeto migrante en Chile: Elementos para un análisis del racismo y el estatus precario," *Papers* 107, no. 2, Universidad Autónoma de Barcelona, 2022. https://doi.org/10.5565/rev/papers.2998. Mercado-Órdenes, Mercedes and Ana Figueiredo, "Racismo y resistencias en migrantes Haitianos en Santiago de Chile desde una perspectiva interseccional," *Psykhe* (Santiago) 32, no. 1: 00102. https://dx.doi.org/10.7764/psykhe.2021.28333.

17. Edward Telles, *Pigmentocracies: Ethnicity, Race, and Color in Latin America* (Chapel Hill: University of North Carolina, 2014).

18. The last census of the foreign-born was done in 2020 and published in early 2021. There have been significant departures of Haitians and Venezuelans toward both Venezuela and the United States since then, but also considerable arrivals, especially of Venezuelans, so it is hard to know the exact number of each population in Chile today. See

Cristián Doña-Reveco, "Chile's Welcoming Approach Cools as Numbers Rise," *Migration Information Source*, May 18, 2022, https://www-migrationpolicy-org.translate.goog /article/chile-immigrants-rising-numbers?_x_tr_sl=en&_x_tr_tl=es&_x_tr_hl=es&_ x_tr_pto=rq#:~:text=Immigrants%20accounted%20for%20just%201,percent%20of% 20the%20country's%20population.

19. For an overview on this, see Victoria Prieto and Julia Bencochea, "International Migration in South America," in *Routledge History of Modern Latin American Migration*, ed. Andreas E. Feldmann, Xochitl Bada, Jorge Durand, and Stephanie Schultze (New York: Routledge, 2023).

20. Feldmann et al., *The Routledge Handbook on Latin American Migration*.

21. Authors' calculations based on the data in table 2.2.

22. https://www.nepo.unicamp.br/observatorio/bancointerativo/numeros-imigra cao-internacional/sincre-sismigra/.

23. Human Rights Watch, *The Venezuelan Exodus: The Need for a Regional Response to an Unprecedented Migration Crisis*, September 2018, https://www.hrw.org/report/ 2018/09/03/venezuelan-exodus/need-regional-response-unprecedented-migration -crisis.

24. There is one comparable period in the 1980s with Guatemalan and Salvadoran refugees in southern Mexico, who lived in refugee camps, but the numbers, though in the tens of thousands, were a fraction of those leaving Venezuela.

25. Lamis Elmy Abdelaaty, *Discrimination and Delegation: Explaining State Responses to Refugees* (Oxford: Oxford University Press, 2021).

26. Andrew Selee, Susan Fratzke, Samuel Davidoff-Gore, and Luisa Feline Freier, *Expanding Protection Options?: Flexible Approaches to Status for Displaced Syrians, Venezuelans, and Ukrainians* (Washington, DC: Migration Policy Institute, 2024), https://www.migrationpolicy.org/sites/default/files/publications/mpi-flexible-approa ches-protection-2024_final.pdf.

27. Interview, Roxana del Aguila, September 2024.

28. Data available in Gandini and Selee, *Betting on Legality*.

29. Based on authors' interviews with three officials from the Peruvian Migration Agency and the Foreign Ministry in November 2018 (Lima, Peru) and November 2019 (Washington, DC).

30. Gandini and Selee, *Betting on Legality*.

31. Authors' interview with Lucas Gómez, August 30, 2024.

32. "Informe de migrantes venezolanos en Colombia en mayo de 2024," Migración Ministerio de Relaciones Exteriores, https://www.migracioncolombia.gov.co/infograf ias-migracion-colombia/informe-de-migrantes-venezolanos-en-colombia-en-mayo.

33. https://www.migracioncolombia.gov.co/infografias-migracion-colombia/ informe-de-migrantes-venezolanos-en-colombia-en-mayo.

34. Gandini and Selee, *Betting on Legality*. The most recent program was launched in August 2024. "Gobierno emitió decreto para proceso extraordinario de regularización migratoria para Venezolanos," *El Universo*, August 23, 2024.

35. Interview with Alfredo López Rita, former director of Migration, Argentina,

August 30, 2024. The Argentinean government had an initial problem in implementing this measure, since many Venezuelans had entered without legal status, which would have made them ineligible for the visa. But there was an agreement among countries receiving Venezuelan migrants and refugees, known as the Quito Process, to allow entry to all Venezuelans at that point, so the migration agency was able to interpret this as allowing any entry to be considered a legal entry.

36. Liliana Lyra Jubilut and João Carlos Jarochinski Silva, "Group Recognition of Venezuelans in Brazil: An Adequate New Model?," *Forced Migrant Review* 65 (November 2020), https://www.fmreview.org/recognising-refugees/jubilut-jarochinskisilva/#: ~:text=This%20RSD%20procedure%20was%20first,with%20over%207%2C700% 20additional%20recognitions.

37. Gandini and Selee, *Betting on Legality.*

38. Interiorização, *Uma estratégia de apoio à integração socioeconómica de pessoas refugiadas e migrantes da Venezuela*, Governo Federal du Brasil, September 2023, https: //www.mds.gov.br/webarquivos/MDS/2_Acoes_e_Programas/Operacao_Acolhida/ Publicacoes/Interiorizacao_uma_estrategia_de_apoio_a_integracao_socioeconomica _de_pessoas_refugiadas_e_migrantes_da_Venezuela.pdf.

39. Official figures suggest that 54,182 Haitians were registered as arriving in Brazil 2010–2020. *Relatoria OBMigra 2020*, Ministry of Justice of Brazil, 2020, https://portalde imigracao.mj.gov.br/images/dados/relatorio-anual/2020/Resumo%20Executivo%20_ Relatório%20Anual.pdf.

40. Beatriz Eugenia Sánchez-Mojica, "No Place for Refugees? The Haitian Flow Within Latin America and the Challenge of International Protection in Disaster Situations," in Jubilut et al., *Refugee Protection in Latin America.*

41. David James Cantor, Luisa Feline Freier, and Jean-Pierre Gauci, eds., *A Liberal Tide? Immigration and Asylum Law and Policy in Latin America* (London: Institute for Latin American Studies, University of London, 2015)

42. Tricia O'Connor, "Protection for Venezuelans in the Spirit of Cartagena? Analysis of the Spirit of Cartagena and How the Protection Policies for Displaced Venezuelans in Brazil, Colombia and Peru Held Up to the Standard of the Spirit of Cartagena," School of Advanced Study, University of London, Refugee Law Initiative, RLI Working Paper No. 69, February 2024, https://sas-space.sas.ac.uk/9854/. On the Cartagena Declaration, see Jubilut et al., *Latin American Refugee Protection.*

43. In Colombia, Felipe Muñoz, who served as the first presidential advisor on migration, before Lucas Gómez, played a vital role in establishing the Temporary Stay Permits, and the three most recent Directors of Migration Colombia, Christian Krueger, Juan Francisco Espinosa, and Fernando García, were also decisive in the key decisions that were made.

44. IMF, *Regional Spillovers from the Venezuela Crisis.*

45. Andrew Selee and Jessica Bolter, *An Uneven Welcome: Latin American and Caribbean Responses to Venezuelan and Nicaraguan Migration* (Washington, DC: 2020), https://www.migrationpolicy.org/sites/default/files/publications/Venezuela-Nicaragua -Migration2020-EN-Final.pdf.

46. David Card, "Immigration and Inequality," *American Economic Review* 99, no. 2 (2009); George J. Borjas, Jeffrey Grogger, and Gordon F. Hanson, "Imperfect Substitution Between Immigrants and Natives: A Reappraisal," National Bureau of Economic Research, Working Paper No. 13887, March 2008; Giovanni Peri, "Immigrants, Productivity, and Labor Markets," *Journal of Economic Perspectives* 30, no. 4 (2016): 3–30.

47. IMF, *Regional Spillovers from the Venezuelan Crisis*.

48. For Colombia see Lukas Delgado-Prieto, "Immigration, Wages, and Employment Under Informal Markets," *Journal of Population Economics* 37, no. 54 (May 2024), https://doi.org/10.1007/s00148-024-01028-5; German Caruso, Christian Gomez Canon, and Valerie Mueller, "Spillover Effects of the Venezuelan Crisis: Migration Impacts in Colombia," *Oxford Economic Papers* 73, no. 2 (April 2021): 771–95, https://doi.org/10.1093/oep/gpz072; Leonardo Peñaloza-Pacheco, "Living with the Neighbors: The Effect of Venezuelan Forced Migration on the Labor Market in Colombia," *Journal of Labor Market Research*, 56, no. 14 (2022), https://doi.org/10.1186/s12651-022-00318-3. For Peru, see Celia Vera and Bruno Jimenez, "The Short-Term Labor Market Effect of Venezuelan Immigration in Peru," Working Paper 304, Universidad Nacional de la Plata, CEDLAS, 2022, https://www.econstor.eu/bitstream/10419/289885/1/doc_cedlas304.pdf; Fernando Morales and Martha Deinsee Pierola, "Venezuelan Migration in Peru: Short-Term Adjustments in the Labor Market," Inter-American Development Bank, Migration Unit, August 2020, https://www.econstor.eu/bitstream/10419/234715/1/IDB-WP-1146.pdf; for Brazil, see Hanbyul Ryu and Jayash Paudel, "Refugee Inflow and Labor Market Outcomes in Brazil," *Population and Development Review* 42 no. 1 (March 20220, https://doi.org/10.1111/padr.12452; Mrittika Shamsuddin, Pablo Acosta, Rovane Battaglin Schwengber, Jedediah Fix, and Nikolas Pirani, "The Labor Market Impacts of Venezuelan Refugees and Migrants in Brazil," IZA Discussion Papers, No. 15384, Institute of Labor Economics (IZA), 2022, https://www.econstor.eu/bitstream/10419/263600/1/dp15384.pdf.

49. The studies on the Roraima state in Brazil, various Colombian cities and towns, and Peru find different degrees of impact and on slightly different sectors of the workforce, but generally on some of those in the informal labor market, although these are likely short-term effects in most cases.

50. Harris et al., *How Do Migrants Fare in Latin America and the Caribbean?*.

51. Inter-American Development Bank, Laboratorio de Percepción Ciudadana y Migración, *Análisis de la percepción de la opinión pública frente a la dinámica migratoria*.

52. Balance de InSight Crime los Homicidios en 2023, InSight Crime, January 2024, https://insightcrime.org/wp-content/uploads/2023/08/Balance-de-InSight-Crime-de-los-homicidios-en-2023-Feb-2024-2.pdf.

53. Dany Bahar, Meagan Dooley, and Andrew Selee, *Venezuelan Migration, Crime, and Misperceptions: A Review of the Data from Colombia, Peru, and Chile* (Washington, DC: Brookings Institute and Migration Policy Institute, September 2020), https://www.brookings.edu/wp-content/uploads/2020/09/migration-crime-latam-eng-final.pdf. The authors and their colleague Maria Jesús Mora have since reviewed national data in these three countries as well as Ecuador, and the trends appear to remain the same

through at least 2021. Nicolás Ajzenman, Patricio Dominguez, and Raimundo Undurraga, "Immigration, Crime, and Crime (Mis)Perceptions," SSRN, October 25, 2022, https://ssrn.com/abstract=4258034 or http://dx.doi.org/10.2139/ssrn.4258034.

54. "Tren de Aragua: From Prison Gang to Transnational Criminal Enterprise," InSight Crime, October 2023, https://insightcrime.org/wp-content/uploads/2023/08/Tren-de-Aragua-From-Prison-Gang-to-Transnational-Criminal-Enterprise-InSight-Crime-Oct-2023-1.pdf.

55. See Marta Luzes, *Public Perception on Migration in Latin America and the Caribbean* (Washington, DC: Inter-American Development Bank, Public Perceptions Laboratory on Migration, 2023), https://publications.iadb.org/publications/english/document/Public-Opinion-on-migration-in-Latin-America-and-the-Caribbean.pdf. Also Oxfam, "Entre la empatía y el rechazo: Percepciones sobre la migración Venezolana en Colombia, Perú, y Ecuador," 2023, https://lac.oxfam.org/en/latest/publications/entre-la-empatia-y-el-rechazo-percepciones-sobre-la-migracion-venezolana-en; and Inter-American Development Bank, Laboratorio de Percepción Ciudadana y Migración, *Análisis de la percepción de la opinión pública frente a la dinámica migratoria.* See also "Colombianos piensan que los Venezolanos afectan economía y sociedad," *Revista Puntos*, August 31, 2023, https://revistapuntos.uniandes.edu.co/colombianos-piensan-que-venezolanos-afectan-la-economia-y-seguridad/. For a more general view of how publics form opinions about migration in displacement crises, see Natalia Banulescu-Bogdan, *From Fear to Solidarity: The Difficulty in Shifting Public Narratives on Refugees* (Washington, DC: Migration Policy Institute, May 2022), https://www.migrationpolicy.org/sites/default/files/publications/refugee-narratives-report-2022_final.pdf.

56. Luzes, *Public Perception on Migration.* On support for access to public benefits, see also Jasmin Norford, "Do Latin Americans Believe in a Social Safety Net for Immigrants?" Insight Series #149, LAPOP, Vanderbilt University, December 17, 2021, https://www.vanderbilt.edu/lapop/insights/IO949en.pdf.

57. Gandini and Selee, *Betting on Legality.*

58. UNESCO's International Institute for Higher Education in Latin America and the Caribbean (IESALC) has created a virtual space to assist students and graduates in learning about the recognition of academic degrees obtained abroad within the Latin American and Caribbean context. This initiative aims to provide information on the entities legally mandated within each jurisdiction to handle degree recognition. Colombia has taken steps to ease the process for Venezuelan professionals, endorsing initiatives that allow Venezuelan citizens to validate their bachelor's degrees without the need to apostille their documents, a decision that followed a ruling by the Constitutional Court. And Ecuador has a fast-track process for recognizing degrees from certain universities, depending on how well recognized they are internationally. Argentina allows provincial universities to recognize foreign credentials, which has, at time, allowed for some fast-tracking of the process when certain professions are in demand locally. All of these systems are imperfect given the opportunity to take advantage of foreign-born residents who could provide needed professional skills to the local economy, but they represent steps forward that can be built on. See Selee and Bolter, *An Uneven Welcome.*

59. Harris et al., *How Do Migrants Fare in Latin America and the Caribbean?*

60. Diego Chaves-González and Natalia Delgado, *A Winding Path to Integration: Venezuelan Migrants' Regularization and Labor Market Prospects* (Washington, DC: Migration Policy Institute and International Organization for Migration, October 2023).

61. Harris et al., *How Do Migrants Fare in Latin America and the Caribbean?* See also Diego Chaves-González, Jordi Amaral, and Maria Jesús Mora, *Socioeconomic Integration of Venezuelan Migrants and Refugees: The Cases of Brazil, Chile, Colombia, Ecuador, and Peru* (Washington, DC: Migration Policy Institute and International Organization for Migration, July 2021). See also Ana María Ibáñez, Andrés Moya, María Adelaida Ortega, Sandra V. Rozo, and Maria José Urbina, "Life Out of the Shadows: The Impacts of Regularization Programs on the Lives of Forced Migrants," *Journal of the European Economic Association*, September 9, 2024, https://doi.org/10.1093/jeea/jvae044; Miguel Benítez-Rueda, *The Productivity Effects of Forced Migration: Evidence from Venezuelan Migrants in Colombia*, Discussion Paper No. IDB-DP-1307, Inter-American Development Bank, December, 2023; Javier Torres, Javier Beverinotti, Gustavo Canavire-Bacarreza, *Medium and Long Run Economic Assimilation of Venezuelan Migrants to Peru*, Working Paper No. IDB-WP 1561, Inter-American Development Bank, January 2024.

62. Chaves-González et al., *Socioeconomic Integration of Venezuelan Migrants and Refugees.* Harris et al., *How Do Migrants Fare in Latin America and the Caribbean?*

63. Bowser et al., "Integrating Venezuelan Migrants into the Colombian Health System During COVID-19," *Health Systems and Reform* 8, no. 1 (2022).

64. Bowser et al., "Integrating Venezuelan Migrants,"

65. Mariángela Chávez, Juan David Forero Sánchez, José Luis Ortiz, "Migración Venezolana y su acceso a servicios de salud en Colombia: Estrategias y retos," IADB, August 18, 2023, https://blogs.iadb.org/salud/es/migracion-venezolana-y-su-acceso-a-servicios-de-salud-en-colombia-estrategias-y-retos/. Furthermore, the COVID-19 pandemic revealed tensions surrounding access to public health services, with certain citizens of host countries opposing equal access to the vaccine for migrants. For instance, while the results of the Perception Survey on Venezuelan Migration in Peru indicate that 69 percent of the surveyed individuals declared their support for Venezuelans, regardless of their migratory status, to have access to public health services, concerning access to the COVID-19 vaccine, only 43 percent of the surveyed individuals believed that the state should ensure equal access to the vaccine, while 53 percent thought that priority should be given to Peruvian citizens. See Irene Palla and Alexander Benites, "Acceso a la salud de personas migrantes Venezolanas: Apertura ciudadana y sus posibles determinantes," IDEHPUCP, June 30, 2021, https://idehpucp.pucp.edu.pe/analisis1/acceso-a-la-salud-de-personas-migrantes-venezolanas-apertura-ciudadana-y-sus-posibles-determinantes/.

66. In one country in South America, migrants who are legally present struggle to access public support for housing because the system does not yet recognize the identification numbers on the paperwork that migrants receive with their legal status. In an-

other, children can register for school, but they are ineligible for subsidized school lunches and other benefits that native-born children receive, because the social service system can only take national identification numbers. And these are only two examples of multiple cases where migrants are effectively excluded from benefits they are entitled to receive simply because systems have yet to catch up to the changing demographics of the country. Based on authors' interviews with policymakers in South American countries.

67. 407 billion Colombian pesos. Chaves-González et al., *Socioeconomic Integration of Venezuelan Migrants and Refugees.*

68. Emiliano Nicolás Gissi-Barbieri and Gonzal Ghio-Suárez, "Integración y exclusión de inmigrantes colombianos recientes en Santiago de Chile: Estrato socioeconómico y 'raza' en la geocultura del sistema-mundo," *Papeles de Población* 23, no. 93 (June/September 2017), https://www.scielo.org.mx/scielo.php?pid=S1405-742520170003 00151&script=sci_arttext; Alfonso Urzúa, Rodrigo Ferrer, Esthepany Olivares, Jeraldinne Rojas, and Romy Ramírez, "The Effect of Racial and Ethnic Discrimination on Individual and Collective Self-Esteem According to the Self-Reported Phenotype in Colombian Migrants in Chile" *Terapia Psicológica*, 37, no. 3 (2019) 225–40. https://dx.doi .org/10.4067/S0718-48082019000300225; Iskra Pavez-Soto, Juan Eduardo Ortiz-López, Priscilla Jara, Constanza Olguín, Anastassia Domaica, "Infancia haitiana migrante en Chile: Barreras y oportunidades en el proceso de escolarización," *EntreDiversidades, Revista de ciencias sociales y humanidades* 11 (Julio-Diciembre 2018): 71–97, https://www .redalyc.org/journal/4559/455959694003/455959694003.pdf; M. Rangel, "Protección social y migración: El desafío de la inclusión sin racismo ni xenofobia," serie Políticas Sociales, No. 232 (LC/TS.2019/127), Santiago, Comisión Económica para América Latina y el Caribe (CEPAL), 2019, https://repositorio.cepal.org/server/api/core/bitstreams/45116 f7a-7221-47f0-a00d-b8a06e0d21fe/content.

69. Traveling with a national ID card within South American countries is possible due to agreements like those within the Andean Community of Nations (CAN) and Mercosur. These agreements facilitate the free movement of people between member countries for tourism, transit, or residence without the need for a passport, reflecting a shared commitment to regional integration and cooperation.

70. Marcela Cerrutti and Emilio Parrado, "Intraregional Migration in South America: Trends and a Research Agenda," *Annual Review of Sociology* 41, no. 1 (2015).

71. Diego Acosta, *The National Versus the Foreigner: 200 Years of Migration and Citizenship Law* (Cambridge: Cambridge University Press, 2019).

72. Chile is currently not a full member of the Andean Community of Nations (CAN); it has been an associate member since 2006. Chile was a full member from the beginning of CAN in 1969 until it withdrew in 1976. After being an observer for several years, Chile changed its status to that of an associate member.

73. The decision to withdraw was announced by President Hugo Chávez, citing dissatisfaction with the direction of the organization, particularly in light of free trade agreements signed by Colombia and Peru with the United States, which Chávez felt were counter to the community's interests.

74. Acosta, *The National Versus the Foreigner.*

75. Diego Acosta Arcarazo, "The Expansion of Regional Free Movement Regimes. Towards a Borderless World?" in *Caught In Between Borders: Citizens, Migrants and Humans*, ed. P. Minderhoud, S. Mantu, and K. Zwaan (Wolf Legal Publishers, 2019).

76. Shuji Yamauchi and Takashi Sekiyama, "Comparing the Election Systems for Overseas Constituency Representatives in Multiple Countries" *Social Sciences* 13, no. 3 (2024): 177; Mision de Observación Electoral 2022–23, "Participación y conformación del Senado y Cámara 2022," https://www.moe.org.co/wp-content/uploads/2022/07/Con formacion-del-congreso-por-partidos-politicos-.pdf.

77. See, for example, Karsten Paerregaard, *Return to Sender: The Moral Economy of Peru's Migrant Remittances* (Washington, DC, and Berkeley, CA: Woodrow Wilson Center Press and University of California Press, 2014).

Chapter 2

1. María Eugenia D'Aubeterre Buznego, María Leticia Rivermar Pérez, and Mariana Ortega Breña. "From Amate Paper Making to Global Work: Otomí Migration from Puebla to North Carolina," *Latin American Perspectives* 41, no. 3 (2014): 118–36. Author conversations with residents of San Pablito, Pahuatitlán, Puebla, August 5, 2022.

2. There is extensive coverage on social media of these celebrations each year, but for an overview of the ceremony in 2023, see "Fiestas Patronales 2023 en honor a San Pedro y San Pablo Durham Carolina del Norte," *Revista Latina North Carolina*, July 2, 2023, https://revistalatinanc.com/2023/07/02/fiestas-patronales-2023-en-honor-a-san-pedro-y-san -pablo-durham/.

3. Over 19 percent of Mexicans identify as Indigenous, while roughly 6 percent speak an Indigenous language, according to the Mexican census. Just under 300,000 speak Otomí, while over 1.6 million speak Nahuatl, the most common Indigenous language in the country. The census figures for speakers of different Indigenous languages are available from the country's census bureau, INEGI, "Hablantes de Lengua Indígena," https:/ /cuentame.inegi.org.mx/poblacion/lindigena.aspx, while self-identification is available through "Estadísticas a propósito del Día Internacional de Pueblos Indigenas," https:// inegi.org.mx/contenidos/saladeprensa/aproposito/2022/EAP_PueblosInd22.pdf, both accessed December 29, 2023.

4. Rubén Hernández-León and Victor Zúñiga, "Mexican Immigrant Communities in the South and Social Capital: The Case of Dalton, Georgia." *Journal of Rural Social Sciences* 19, no. 1 (2003): article 2.

5. Douglas S. Massey, Rafael Alarcon, Jorge Durand, and Humberto González, *Return to Aztlan: The Social Process of International Migration from Western Mexico* (Berkeley: University of California Press, 1990).

6. Mark Weisbrot, Stephan Lefebvre, and Joseph Sammut, *Did NAFTA Help Mexico? An Assessment After 20 Years* (Washington, DC: Center for Economic and Policy Research, 2014), https://cepr.net/documents/nafta-20-years-2014-02.pdf.

7. Marie McAuliffe and Anna Tryandafillidou, eds., *World Migration Report 2022* (Geneva: International Organization for Migration, 2022), 27, https://publications.iom .int/system/files/pdf/wmr-2022_0.pdf.

8. Douglas Massey, Jorge Durand, and Nolan J. Malone, *Beyond Smoke and Mirrors: Mexican Immigration in an Era of Economic Integration* (Russell Sage Foundation, 2002).

9. Author calculations based on data from the U.S. Census Bureau's 2023 American Community Survey, "1-Year Estimates Data Profiles," accessed March 12, 2025, https://data.census.gov/table/ACSDP1Y2023.DP05?q=DP05&y=2023&moe=false; Mexico's National Institute of Statistics and Geography (INEGI), "Demograpfia y Sociedad: Poblacion," accessed March 12, 2025, https://www.inegi.org.mx/temas/estructura/.

10. Josefina Zoraida Vázquez and Lorenzo Meyer, *México frente a Estados Unidos, un ensayo histórico, 1776–2000* (Mexico City: El Fondo de Cultura Económica, 1998); William Kandel and Douglas S. Massey, "The Culture of Mexican Migration: A Theoretical and Empirical Analysis," *Social Forces* 80, no. 2 (March 2002); Patricia Arias, *Del arraigo a la Diáspora* (Miguel Ángel Porrúa, 2009); Peter H. Smith and Andrew Selee, eds., *Mexico and the United States: The Politics of Partnership* (Boulder, CO: Lynne Rienner, 2013); Sam Quinones, *Antonio's Gun and Delfino's Dream: True Stories of Mexican Migration* (Albuquerque: University of New Mexico Press, 2015).

11. Neil Foley, *Mexicans in the Making of America* (Cambridge, MA: Harvard University Belknap Press, 2017); Andrew Selee, *Vanishing Frontiers: The Forces Driving Mexico and the United States Together* (New York: Public Affairs, 2018); Juan Gonzalez, *Harvest of Empire: A History of Latinos in America, Second Revised and Updated Edition* (New York: Penguin Random House, 2022).

12. Ana Gonzalez-Barrera, "Before COVID-19, More Mexicans Came to the U.S Than Left For Mexico for the First Time in Years," Pew Research Center, July 9, 2021, https://www.pewresearch.org/short-reads/2021/07/09/before-covid-19-more-mexicans-came-to-the-u-s-than-left-for-mexico-for-the-first-time-in-years/.

13. Author calculations based on GDP data from the World Bank, see World Bank, "GDP per Capita (Constant 2015 US$)—Mexico," accessed December 20, 2023, https://data.worldbank.org/indicator/NY.GDP.PCAP.KD?end=2022&locations=MX&start=2001.

14. Randy Capps, Doris Meissner, Ariel G. Ruiz Soto, Jessica Bolter, and Sarah Pierce, *From Control to Crisis: Changing Trends and Policies Reshaping U.S.-Mexico Border Enforcement* (Washington, DC: Migration Policy Institute, 2019), https://www.migrationpolicy.org/sites/default/files/publications/BorderSecurity-ControltoCrisis-Report-Final.pdf.

15. It is worth noting that Canadian Temporary Foreign Worker Program (TFWP) visas, which are similar to the U.S. H-2A and H-2B program, also expanded in this period, from 23,245 Mexicans in 2106 to 29,798 in 2022. Statistics Canada, "Countries of Citizenship for Temporary Foreign Workers in the Agricultural Sector," accessed December 29, 2023, https://www150.statcan.gc.ca/t1/tbl1/en/tv.action?pid=3210022101&pickMembers%5B0%5D=1.1&cubeTimeFrame.startYear=2016&cubeTimeFrame.endYear=2022&referencePeriods=20160101%2C20220101.

16. Jie Zong and Jeanne Batalova, "Mexican Immigrants in the United States," *Migration Information Source*, October 9, 2014, https://www.migrationpolicy.org/article/mexican-immigrants-united-states-2013.

17. Author calculations based on data from U.S. Department of Homeland Security (DHS), see: Table 2 in Office of Homeland Security Statistics, "Yearbook of Immigration

Statistics, Persons Obtaining Lawful Permanent Resident Status by Broad Class of Admission and Region and Country of Birth," accessed December 29, 2023, https://www.dhs.gov/ohss/topics/immigration/yearbook.

18. Randy Capps, Faye Hipsman, and Doris Meissner, *Advances in U.S-Mexico Border Enforcement: A Review of the Consequence Delivery System*, MPI report on consequence delivery, https://www.migrationpolicy.org/research/advances-us-mexico-border-enforcement-review-consequence-delivery-system.

19. Muzaffar Chishti, Sarah Pierce, and Jessica Bolter, "The Obama Record on Deportations: Deporter in Chief of Not?" *Migration Information Source,* January 26, 2017, https://www.migrationpolicy.org/article/obama-record-deportations-deporter-chief-or-not.

20. Author calculations of Mexican repatriations based on data from the Interior Ministry. See SEGOB, "Boletines Estadisticos," accessed September 16, 2023, http://portales.segob.gob.mx/es/PoliticaMigratoria/Boletines_Estadisticos.

21. Most Mexican immigrants today live in California (36 percent), Texas (22 percent), Illinois (6 percent), and Arizona (5 percent), though many also reside in nontraditional destination states. Raquel Rosenbloom and Jeanne Batalova, "Mexican Immigrants in the United States," *Migration Information Source,* updated October 13, 2022, https://www.migrationpolicy.org/article/mexican-immigrants-united-states.

22. Jennifer Van Hook, Julia Gelatt, and Ariel G. Ruiz Soto, "A Turning Point for the Unauthorized Immigrant Population in the United States," Migration Policy Institute, September 2023, https://www.migrationpolicy.org/news/turning-point-us-unauthorized-immigrant-population.

23. U.S. Citizenship and Immigration Services, "Count of Active DACA Recipients By Country of Birth as of June 30, 2024," updated August 29, 2024, https://www.uscis.gov/sites/default/files/document/data/active_daca_recipients_fy2024_q3.xlsx.

24. Visits by the authors to the hospital in San Pedro Necta and surrounding communities in July 2021, July 2022, and July 2023. See also Andrew Selee, "To Solve the Border Crisis, Look Beyond the Border," *Foreign Policy,* November 8, 2021, https://foreignpolicy.com/2021/11/08/border-crisis-guatemala-migration-honduras-central-latin-america/.

25. Andrew Selee, Luis Argueta, and Juan José Hurtado Paz y Paz, *Migration from Huehuetenango in Guatemala's Western Highlands: Policy and Development Responses* (Washington, DC, and Guatemala City: Migration Policy institute and Asociación Pop No'j, March 2022), https://www.migrationpolicy.org/sites/default/files/publications/mpi-huehuetenango-report-eng_final.pdf.

26. Susanne Jonas and Nestor Rodriguez, *Guatemala-US Migration: Transforming Regions* (Austin: University of Texas, 2014); Cecilia Menjívar and Andrea Gómez Cervantes, "El Salvador: Civil War, Natural Disasters, and Gang Violence Drive Migration," *Migration Information Source,* July 2018; Nicole Ward and Jeanne Batalova, "Central American Immigrants in the United States," *Migration Information Source,* May 10, 2023.

27. Michael Clemens, "Violence, Development, and Migration Waves: Evidence from Child Migrant Apprehensions," Working Paper 459, Center for Global Development, July 21, 2017, https://www.cgdev.org/publication/violence-development-and-migration-waves-evidence-central-american-child-migrant.

28. Andrew Selee and Ariel Ruiz Soto, *Building a New Regional Migration System: Redefining U.S Cooperation with Mexico and Central America* (Washington, DC: Migration Policy Institute, 2020), 1–27, https://www.migrationpolicy.org/research/new-region al-migration-system-us-mexico-central-america.

29. The murder rate has dropped by 92 percent from 2015 to 2023, as the incarceration rate has risen to over 1 percent of the population. See Kejal Vyas and Santiago Perez, "Country with the Highest Murder Rate Now Has the Highest Incarceration Rate," *Wall Street Journal*, July 10, 2023.

30. Selee et al., *Migration from Huehuetenango in Guatemala's Western Highlands*; Ariel G. Ruiz Soto, Rosella Bottone, Jarret Waters, Sarah Williams, Ashley Louie, and Yuehan Wang, *Charting a New Regional Course of Action: The Complex Motivations and Costs of Central American Migration* (Washington, DC, and Panama City: Migration Policy Institute, World Food Programme, and MIT Civic Design Data Lab, Inter-American Development Bank, and Organization of American States, November 2021), https://www.migrationpolicy.org/sites/default/files/publications/mpi-wfp-mit_migration -motivations-costs_final.pdf.

31. Sarah Bermeo and David Leblang, "Climate, Violence, and Honduran Migration to the United States," Brookings Institution, April 1, 2021, https://www.brookings.edu/ articles/climate-violence-and-honduran-migration-to-the-united-states/; Daniel H. Simon and Fernando Riosmena, "Environmental Migration in Latin America," in *International Handbook of Population and Environment*, ed. L. M. Hunter, C. Gray, and J. Véron, International Handbooks of Population, vol. 10 (Cham: Springer, 2022).

32. Ruiz Soto et al., *Charting a New Regional Course of Action*

33. Luciana Gandini, Aletia Fernández de la Reguera, and Juan Carlos Narváez Gutiérrez, *Caravanas* (Mexico City: UNAM, 2020), http://www.libros.unam.mx/caravanas -9786073032087-ebook.html.

34. Ruiz Soto et al., *Charting a New Regional Course of Action*; Selee et al., *Migration from Huehuetenango*.

35. Andrew Selee and Ariel G. Ruiz Soto, "The Real Migration Crisis is in Central America," *Foreign Affairs*, April 13, 2021, https://www.foreignaffairs.com/articles/cen tral-america-caribbean/2021-04-13/real-migration-crisis-central-america.

36. MPI calculations of migrant expulsion data from CBP, "Southwest Land Border Encounters," updated December 23, 2023, https://www.cbp.gov/newsroom/stats/south west-land-border-encounters.

37. Statistics Canada, "Countries of Citizenship for Temporary Foreign Workers in the Agricultural Sector," updated April 13, 2023, https://www150.statcan.gc.ca/t1/tbl1/en/tv .action?pid=3210022101&pickMembers%5B0%5D=1.1&cubeTimeFrame.startYear=2016& cubeTimeFrame.endYear=2022&referencePeriods=20160101%2C20220101.

38. Ariel G. Ruiz Soto and Andrew Selee, *U.S. Legal Pathways for Mexican and Central American Immigrants, by the Numbers* (Washington, DC: Migration Policy Institute, August 2024), https://www.migrationpolicy.org/research/us-legal-pathways-mexicans -central-americans.

39. Fernando Landini, Arnold Brodbeck, María Vera, Úrsula Torres Parejo, Isabel González Enriquez, and Miguel Ángel García, *Impact of Regular Temporary Migration*

to Canada and the United States on the Living Conditions and Migration Intentions of Families and Communities in Guatemala (Guatemala City: Action Against Hunger), May 2023, https://accioncontraelhambre.org.gt/wp-content/uploads/2023/09/Impact-of -regular-temporary-migration-to-Canada-and-the-U.S.-FINAL-INFORM-2023.pdf; Cristobal Ramón, Ariel G. Ruiz Soto, María Jesús Mora, and Ana Martín Gil, *Temporary Worker Programs in Canada, Mexico, and Costa Rica: Promising Pathways for Managing Central American Migration?* (Washington, DC: Migration Policy Institute, June 2022), https://www.migrationpolicy.org/research/temporary-worker-programs-canada -mexico-costa-rica; Cristobal Ramón, *Investing in Alternatives to Irregular Migration from Central America: Options to Expand U.S. Employment Pathways* (Washington, DC: Migration Policy Institute, November 2021), https://www.migrationpolicy.org/sites /default/files/publications/labor-pathways-central-america_eng_final.pdf.

40. Sistema de Integración Centroamericana, "El Convenio Centroamericano de Libre Movilidad (CA-4)," accessed December 12, 2023, https://www.sica.int/ocam/ca4.

41. María Jesús Mora, Ariel G. Ruiz Soto, and Andrew Selee, *Building on Regular Pathways to Address Migration Pressures in the Americas* (Washington, DC: Migration Policy Institute, June 2024), https://www.migrationpolicy.org/research/regular-path ways-americas.

42. On the debate on whether Belize is a Caribbean or Central American nation—or both—see also Godfrey Smith, *George Price: A Life Revealed* (Kingston, Jamaica: Ian Randle Publishers, 2011). George Price, Belize's first prime minister, who was of African and Latin descent (including a grandmother who was Yucatecan Maya) maintained that Belize should be considered as part of both subregions.

43. Sonia Parella Rubio, "Los flujos de mujeres centroamericanas hacia España como exponente de migración forzada: Causas, datos y algunas reflexiones," in *La inserción laboral y social de los inmigrantes en España*, ed. Joaquín Arango Vila-Bella (Madrid: Cajamar, 2022).

44. San Pablito and San Pedro Necta are also both largely Indigenous communities, with most of San Pedro Necta's residents speaking Mayan Mam and most of San Pablito's speaking Otomí, although the rest of the municipality of Pahuatlán is dominated by a mixture of Nahua and Spanish speakers.

45. Dilip Ratha et al., *Remittances Remain Resilient but Are Slowing* (Washington DC: KNOMAD-World Bank, 2023), https://knomad.org/publication/migration-and-de velopment-brief-38.

46. Author analyses of data from the World Bank, "Personal Remittances, Received (Current US$)," accessed September 5, 2024, https://data.worldbank.org/indicator/BX .TRF.PWKR.CD.DT?end=2023&locations=GT-SV-HN-MX&name_desc=false&start= 2012&view=chart.

47. Juan José Li Ng, "México: Remesas acumulan 10 años consecutivos al alza y rompen récord," BBVA Research, updated February 2, 2024, https://www.bbvaresearch .com/publicaciones/mexico-remesas-acumulan-10-anos-consecutivos-al-alza-y-rom pen-record-63313-md-en-2023/.

48. Andrew Selee, Ariel G. Ruiz Soto, Andrea Tanco, Luis Argueta, and Jessica

Bolter, *Laying the Foundation for Regional Cooperation: Migration Policy and Institutional Capacity in Mexico and Central America* (Washington DC: Migration Policy Institute, 2021), https://www.migrationpolicy.org/research/regional-cooperation-migration-capacity-mexico-central-america.

49. Mexican Foreign Ministry, "El consulado53 de México en EE.UU. está listo para recibir a nuestra comunidad de más de 230 mil paisanos en Nueva Jersey," updated September 24, 2023, https://www.gob.mx/sre/videos/el-consulado-53-de-mexico-en-ee-uu-esta-listo-para-recibir-a-nuestra-comunidad-de-mas-de-230-mil-paisanos-en-nueva-jersey.

50. For a good summary of the literature on migration and development, see Jason DeParle, *A Good Provider Is One Who Leaves* (New York: Viking, 2019); Kathleen Newland, *What We Know About Migration and Development* (Washington, DC: Migration Policy Institute, September 2013), https://www.migrationpolicy.org/sites/default/files/publications/Migration-Development-WhatWeKnow.pdf.

51. Interview with author, August 5, 2022.

52. Selee, *Vanishing Frontiers*, chapter 7.

53. Ariel G. Ruiz Soto, Rodrigo Dominguez-Villegas, Luis Argueta, and Randy Capps, *Sustainable Reintegration: Strategies to Support Migrants Returning to Mexico and Central America* (Washington, DC: Migration Policy Institute, January 2019), https://www.migrationpolicy.org/research/sustainable-reintegration-migrants-mexico-central-america.

54. Claudia Masferrer, *Atlas of Return Migration from the United States to Mexico* (Mexico City: El Colegio de México, 2021).

55. Carolina Quinteros, Jeannette Aguilar, Natalia Rivera Bajaña, *Generación de Conocimiento y Evidencia para la Reintegración Económica-Laboral de Migrantes Retornados en los Países del Norte de Centroamérica (PNCA)* (Washington, DC: Fundación Panamericana para el Desarrollo, September 2020), https://padf.org/wp-content/uploads/2020/09/PADF_Generacion-de-Conocimientos.pdf.

56. Jacqueline Hagan, Ruben Hernandez-Leon, and Jean-Luc Demonsant, *Skills of the "Unskilled": Work and Mobility Among Mexican Migrants* (Berkeley: University of California Press, 2015).

57. Asociación de Investigación y Estudios Sociales (ASIES), *El retorno de población migrante en el norte de Centroamérica en el marco de la pandemia de COVID-19* (Guatemala City: ASIES, 2022), http://asies.org.gt/pdf/el_retorno_de_poblacion_migrante_en_el_norte_de_centroamerica_en_el_marco_de_la_pandemia_de_covid_19.pdf.

58. IOM, "IOM's Policy on the Full Spectrum of Return Readmission and Reintegration," accessed September 6, 2024, https://www.iom.int/return-and-reintegration.

59. Ruiz Soto et al., *Sustainable Reintegration*.

60. Ariel G. Ruiz Soto, Maria Jesus Mora, and Andrea Tanco, "Inmigrantes estadounidenses y familias de estatus mixto en México," in *El Sueño Mexicano: Estudios sobre la migración estadounidense* (Mexico: Secretaría de Relaciones Exteriores e Instituto Nacional de Estadística y Geografía, 2022); and U.S. Department of State, "U.S. Relations with Mexico," updated September 13, 2023, https://www.state.gov/u-s-relations-with-mexico/.

61. Victor Zuñiga and Silvia Giorguli, *The 0.5 Generation: Children Moving from the United States to Mexico* (Berkeley: University of California Press, 2024).

62. Alexandra Délano, "From Limited to Active Engagement: Mexico's Emigration Policies from a Foreign Policy Perspective (2000–2006)," *International Migration Review* 43, no. 4 (Winter 2009); Rafael Fernández de Castro, "Perspectivas teóricas en los estudios de la relación México-Estados Unidos: El caso de la cooperación intergubernamental," in *La política exterior de México: Enfoques para su análisis*, ed. C. Toro and O. Pellicer (México: El Colegio de México), 45–67.

63. Manuel García y Griego and Mónica Verea Campos, "Colaboración sin concordancia: La migración en la nueva agenda bilateral México-Estados Unidos," in *Nueva agenda bilateral en la relación México-Estados Unidos*, comp. Mónica Verea Campos, Rafael Fernández de Castro, and Sidney Weintraub (México: ITAM/UNAM/CISAN/FCE, 1998), 107–34; Ana Covarrubias Velasco and Blanca Torres Ramírez, *Cambio de siglo: La política exterior de la apertura económica y política* (El Colegio de México, 2010), https://muse.jhu.edu/pub/320/oa_monograph/chapter/2584708.

64. Clare Ribando Seelke, "Mexico: Evolution of the Mérida Initiative, 2007–2019," Congressional Research Service, updated March 11, 2019, https://crsreports.congress.gov/product/pdf/IF/IF10578/12.

65. Julie Hirschfield Davis and Michael D. Shear, *Border Wars: Inside Trump's Assault on Immigration* (New York: Simon and Schuster, 2019).

66. Mexican visa requirements vary by country of origin and some include exemptions for migrants with valid visas or a legal status in the United States. See Muzzafar Chishti and Jessica Bolter, "Controversial U.S. Title 42 Expulsions Policy Is Coming to an End, Bringing New Border Challenges," *Migration Information Source,* March 31, 2022, https://www.migrationpolicy.org/article/title-42-expulsions-policy; Mexican Embassy in Peru, "Visas: Información Importante," accessed September 11, 2024, https://embamex.sre.gob.mx/peru/index.php/sconsulares/visas.

67. U.S. Department of State, "Secretary Antony J. Blinken and Secretary of Homeland Security Alejandro Mayorkas at a Joint Press Availability," updated April 27, 2023. https://www.state.gov/secretary-antony-j-blinken-and-secretary-of-homeland-security-alejandro-mayorkas-at-a-joint-press-availability/

68. MPI analyses of migrant encounters data from U.S. Customs and Border Protection (CBP), "Southwest Land Border Encounters," updated August 28, 2024, https://www.cbp.gov/newsroom/stats/southwest-land-border-encounters.

69. Xóchitl Bada and Andreas E. Feldmann, "How Insecurity Is Transforming Migration Patterns in the North American Corridor: Lessons from Michoacán," in *New Migration Patterns in the Americas: Challenges for the Twenty-First Century*, ed. Andreas E. Feldmann, Xóchitl Bada, and Stephanie Schultz (London: Palgrave Macmillan, 2019).

70. Forbes, "La percepción de inseguridad en México sube 62.3% en el segundo trimestre de 2023," *Forbes Mexico,* July 19, 2023, https://www.forbes.com.mx/la-percepcion-de-inseguridad-en-mexico-sube-a-62-3-en-el-segundo-trimestre-de-2023/.

71. Mexican Interior Ministry (SEGOB), "Decreto por el que se reforman diversos

artículos de la Ley de Migración y de la Ley sobre Refugiados, Protección Complementaria y Asilo Político, en materia de Infancia Migrante," Diario Oficial de la Federación, November 11, 2020, https://www.dof.gob.mx/nota_detalle.php?codigo=5604705&fecha=11/11/2020#gsc.tab=0.

72. Sergio Ortiz Borbolla, "Niños, niñas y adolescentes migrantes corren peligro ante falta de protección de los gobiernos de México y Estados Unidos," Washington Office on Latin America, updated April 13, 2023, https://www.wola.org/es/analisis/ninos-ninas-adolescentes-migrantes-peligro-proteccion-mexico-estados-unidos/.

73. Mexican National Insitute of Migration, "INM informa de trabajos de transformación en estaciones migratorias para no repetición de hecho como el de Cd. Juárez el 27 de marzo de 2023," press release, March 25, 2024, https://www.gob.mx/inm/prensa/inm-informa-de-trabajos-de-transformacion-en-estaciones-migratorias-para-no-repeticion-de-hechos-como-el-de-cd-juarez-el-27-de-marzo-2023.

74. CNN Español, "¿Qué pasó en el incendio en un centro de migrantes de Ciudad Juárez?," CNN Español, March 29, 2023, https://cnnespanol.cnn.com/2023/03/29/que-paso-incendio-migrantes-ciudad-juarez-orix/.

75. Mexican National Institute of Migration, "Suspende INM temporalmente Estancias Provisionales en el país," press release, May 10, 2023, https://www.gob.mx/inm/prensa/suspende-inm-temporalmente-estancias-provisionales-en-el-pais.

76. Arturo Rojas, "INM mantiene servicio en 17 estancias migratorias, con capacidad para 4,786 personas," El Economista, May 15, 2023, https://www.eleconomista.com.mx/politica/INM-mantiene-servicio-en-17-estancias-migratorias-con-capacidad-para-4786-personas-20230515-0111.html; Mexican National Institute of Migration, "INM informa de trabajos de transformación en estaciones migratorias para no repetición de hecho como el de Cd. Juárez el 27 de marzo de 2023," press release, March 25, 2024, https://www.eleconomista.com.mx/politica/INM-mantiene-servicio-en-17-estancias-migratorias-con-capacidad-para-4786-personas-20230515-0111.html.

77. MPI calculations based on data from the Mexican Ministry of Interior (SEGOB). See SEGOB, "Boletín Mensuales de Estadísticas Migratorias," accessed September 10, 2024, http://portales.segob.gob.mx/es/PoliticaMigratoria/Boletines_Estadisticos; Instituto para las Mujeres en la Migración, "Factsheet: Removal and Return of Non-Mexican Nationals from the United States to Mexico," June 2024, https://imumi.org/attachments/2024/Removal_an_Return_of_Non_Mexican_Nationals_from_the_US_to_Mx.pdf.

78. Ariel G Ruiz Soto, María Jesús Mora, and Andrea Tanco, "Inmigrantes estadounidenses y familias de estatus mixto en México: Características demográficas que influyen en su vida e integración," in El Sueño Mexicano: Estudios sobre la Migración Estadounidense (Mexico City: Mexican Foreign Ministry, 2022), https://www.gob.mx/cms/uploads/attachment/file/766771/Libro_INEGI-2022-web.pdf.

79. Under the 1951 Refugee Convention, a person is recognized as a refugee is they are unable or unwilling to return to their country of origin due to fear of being persecuted for their race, religion, nationality, membership of a particular group, or political opinion. See UNCHR, Convention and Protocol Relating to the Status of Refugees, accessed

September 14, 2023, https://www.unhcr.org/sites/default/files/legacy-pdf/3b66c2aa10.pdf.

80. Andrew Selee, Valerie Lacarte, Ariel G. Ruiz Soto, Diego Chaves-González, María Jesús Mora, and Andrea Tanco, "In a Dramatic Shift, the Americas Have Become a Leading Migration Destination," *Migration Information Source,* April 11, 2023, https://www.migrationpolicy.org/article/latin-america-caribbean-immigration-shift.

81. Edgar H. Clemente, "Mexico on Track to Break Asylum Application Record," Associated Press, September 14, 2023, https://apnews.com/article/mexico-migration-asylum-guatemala-6dcbe91b2fd53b91e06e3a022b2e2f8a?emci=3477959c-d553-ee11-9937-00224832e811&emdi=8a044f00-d853-ee11-9937-00224832e811&ceid=4606001&utm_source=substack&utm_medium=email.

82. SEGOB, "La COMAR en numeros, Cierre de diciembre 2024," January 3, 2025, https://www.gob.mx/comar/es/articulos/la-comar-en-numeros-387226?idiom=es.

83. Elizabeth Ferris and Katharine M. Donato, *Refugee Relocation in Mexico: Findings from the UNHCR Local Integration Program* (UNHCR, 2023), https://drive.google.com/file/d/1iUY2f1inetrRLFQG9qrMil6lM8RjBG83/view.

84. The White House, "Los Angeles Declaration on Migration and Protection," June 10, 2022, https://www.whitehouse.gov/briefing-room/statements-releases/2022/06/10/los-angeles-declaration-on-migration-and-protection/.

85. Secretaria de Relaciones Exteriores, "Interministerial Commission for Comprehensive Migration Management adopts the Mexican Model of Human Mobility," May 16, 2024, https://www.gob.mx/sre/prensa/interministerial-commission-for-comprehensive-migration-management-ciaimm-adopts-the-mexican-model-of-human-mobility?idiom=en#:~:text=The%20Mexican%20Model%20of%20Human%20Mobility%20addresses%20migration%20from%20a,South%20America%20to%20Central%20America.

86. Los Angeles Declaration on Migration and Protection, "Promoting Regular Pathways for Migration and International Protection," accessed September 11, 2024, https://losangelesdeclaration.com/implementation-los-angeles-declaration/promoting-regular-pathways-migration-and-international; Los Angeles Declaration on Migration and Protection, "Fact Sheet: Third Ministerial Meeting on the Los Angeles Declaration on Migration and Protection in Guatemala," updated May 7, 2024, https://www.whitehouse.gov/briefing-room/statements-releases/2024/05/07/fact-sheet-third-ministerial-meeting-on-the-los-angeles-declarationon-migration-and-protection-in-guatemala/.

87. United Nations Development Programme, "Sembrando vida y jóvenes construyendo el futureo en Centroamérica y el Caribe," accessed September 11, 2024, https://www.undp.org/es/mexico/proyectos/sembrando-vida-y-jovenes-construyendo-el-futuro-en-centroamerica-y-el-caribe; Mexican Agency for International Cooperation, "Sembrando vida y jóvenes construyendo el futuro en Centroamérica y el Caribe," updated August 21, 2024, https://www.youtube.com/watch?v=ZwE970fBvTo.

88. "518,000 migrantes, 42.7% Venezolanos, han cruzado Honduras," *La Prensa,* December 15, 2023, https://www.laprensa.hn/honduras/estadisticas-migracion-2023-sueno-americano-estados-unidos-crisis-social-CC16634789.

89. Authors' conversations with residents in La Carpio, September 22, 2022. For a

history of La Carpio, see Cindy Regidor, "La Carpio, hogar de miles de nicaragüenses en Costa Rica," *El Confidencial*, September 19, 2021. For information on SIFAIS, see Katherine Estrada Tellez, "SIFAIS, un espacio de transformación social para Nicarguenses en la Carpio," *El Confidencial*, October 15, 2022, https://confidencial.digital/migrantes/ reportajes/sifais-un-espacio-de-transformacion-social-para-nicaraguenses-en-la -carpio/. For a history of La Carpio in its early years, see Carlos García Sandoval, "La Carpio: La experiencia de segregación urbana y estigmatización social," February 2005, unpublished manuscript available online from the Universidad de Costa Rica, https:// ccp.ucr.ac.cr/noticias/migraif/pdf/sandoval.pdf.

90. The World Bank, "GDP Per Capita (PPP, Current International $), Latin America and the Caribbean," accessed September 11, 2024, https://data.worldbank.org/indicator /NY.GDP.PCAP.PP.CD?locations=NI-HN-GT-SV-MX-CR.

91. Andrew Selee, Ariel G. Ruiz Soto, Andrea Tanco, Luis Argueta, and Jessica Bolter, *Laying the Foundation for Regional Cooperation Migration Policy and Institutional Capacity in Mexico and Central America* (Washington, DC: Migration Policy Institute, 2021), https://www.migrationpolicy.org/sites/default/files/publications/mpi-latam_ foundation-regional-cooperation_eng-final.pdf; Costa Rican Directorate General of Migration and Foreign Affairs (DGME) and Directorate of Integration and Human Development, *Plan Nacional de Integración: Costa Rica 2023–2027* (San Jose, Costa Rica: DGME), https://www.migracion.go.cr/Documentos compartidos/Politicas/Plan Nacional 2023-2027.pdf.

92. Diego Chaves-González and Maria Jesus Mora, *The State of Costa Rican Migration and Immigrant Integration Policy* (Washington, DC: Migration Policy Institute, November 2021), https://www.migrationpolicy.org/research/costa-rican-migration-im migrant-integration-policy.

93. Dirección General de Migración y Extranjería, "Informes Estadísticos Anuales— Solicitudes y aprobaciones y denegatorias de Refugio Año 2022," accessed December 21, 2023; Dirección General de Migración y Extranjería, "Informes Estadísticos Anuales— Solicitudes y aprobaciones y denegatorias de Refugio a noviembre 2023," accessed December 21, 2023, https://migracion.go.cr/SitePages/Inicio.aspx.

94. Authors' calculations based on data from Costa Rica's General Directorate of Migration and Foreign Affairs, "Informes Estadísticos Anuales," updated September 25, 2024, https://migracion.go.cr/SitePages/Inicio.aspx.

95. Chaves-González and Mora, *The State of Costa Rican Migration and Immigrant Integration Policies*.

96. MPI analyses of data from the Government of Costa Rica, Dirección General de Migración y Extranjería, *Estadísticas*.

97. For example, there were over 22,000 temporary visas and over 19,000 permanent visas issued to Venezuelans in Costa Rica after 2016, while only a little over 19,000 Venezuelans applied for asylum. It is likely that the same people who got temporary visas later transitioned to permanent residence, and that many of those who applied for asylum later obtained other visas before their cases were resolved, based on the data. See Gandini and Selee, *Betting on Legality*.

98. Chaves-González and Mora, *The State of Costa Rican Migration and Immigrant Integration Policies.*

99. Kate Hooper and Meghan Benton, *The Future of Remote Work: Digital Nomads and the Implications for Immigration Systems* (Washington DC: Migration Policy Institute, 2022), 1–33, https://www.migrationpolicy.org/research/remote-work-immigration.

100. Mora et al., *Building on Regular Pathways to Address Migration Pressures in the Americas.*

101. Natalia Odio González, "Pueblos Indígenas podrán acceder a su derecho de la nacionalidad Costarricense," Universidad de Costa Rica, March 16, 2019, https://accionsocial.ucr.ac.cr/noticias/pueblos-indigenas-podran-acceder-su-derecho-la-nacionalidad-costarricense.

102. Chaves-González and Mora, *The State of Costa Rican Migration and Immigrant Integration Policies.*

103. Selee et al., *Laying the Foundation for Regional Cooperation*, chapter 4.

104. Selee et al., *Laying the Foundation for Regional Cooperation*, chapter 4.

105. Selee et al., *Laying the Foundation for Regional Cooperation*, chapter 4.

106. From January 2010 through December 2023. The first regularization was program known as "Crisol de Razas" ("Melting Pot of the Races," 2010–14), while after 2015, there were two programs, known by the decrees that created them, Decree 167 for the general population of foreign-born and Decree 168 for Chinese nationals. Information and data available at Government of Panama, Migración, "Estadísticas," accessed December 30, 2023, https://www.migracion.gob.pa/estadisticas/.

107. Interviews with one current and two former Panamanian officials and one representative of an international organization, July and August 2020.

108. See the discussion on this in Selee et al., *Laying the Foundations for Regional Cooperation*, 48.

109. Selee et al., *Laying the Foundation for Regional Cooperation*, 48–49.

110. On the history of race and ethnicity in Costa Rica, see Carlos Gradín, "Race, Ethnicity, Immigration, and Living Conditions in Costa Rica," *Review of Income and Wealth* 62, Special Issue 1 (August 2016). See also Philippe I. Bourgois, *Ethnicity at Work: Divided Labor on a Central American Banana Plantation* (Baltimore, MD: Johns Hopkins University Press, 1989).

111. Maria Jesús Mora, "Costa Rica Has Welcoming Policies for Migrants, but Nicaraguans Face Subtle Barriers," *Migration Information Source*, November 5, 2021, https://www.migrationpolicy.org/article/costa-rica-nicaragua-migrants-subtle-barriers.

112. Edward Telles and Tianna Paschel, "Who Is Black, White, or Mixed Race? How Skin Color, Status, and Nation Shape Racial Classification in Latin America," *American Journal of Sociology* 12, no. 3 (November 2014). See also Marcus Johnson, "The Historical Intersection of Race and Citizenship in Panama," Black Perspectives, May 20, 2023, https://www.aaihs.org/the-historical-intersection-of-race-and-citizenship-in-panama/. For a more detailed analysis of how understandings of race among Panamanian migrants abroad and Panamanians of African descent in Panama interacted throughout history to reshape notions of blackness and racial identity among Panamanians, see Kaysha Corinealdi, *Panama in Black* (Durham, NC: Duke University Press, 2022).

113. Caitlyn Yates and Juan Pappier, "How the Treacherous Darien Gap Became a Migrations Crossroads of the Americas," *Migration Information Source*, September 20, 2023, https://www.migrationpolicy.org/article/darien-gap-migration-crossroads.

114. Caitlyn Yates and Jessica Bolter, *African Migration Through the Americas: Drivers, Routes, and Policy Responses* (Washington, DC: Migration Policy Institute, October 2021), https://www.migrationpolicy.org/sites/default/files/publications/mpi-african-migration-americas-eng_final.pdf.

115. Government of Panama, Migración, Estadísticas, "Tránsito irregular por el Darien," https://www.migracion.gob.pa/wp-content/uploads/IRREGULARES-X-DARIEN-2023.pdf

116. IOM, "Number of Migrants Who Embarked on the Dangerous Darien Gap Route Nearly Doubled in 2022," updated January 17, 2023, https://www.iom.int/news/number-migrants-who-embarked-dangerous-darien-gap-route-nearly-doubled-2022; United Nations, "Protect Those on the Move Using Deadly Darién Crossing," updated December 7, 2023, https://news.un.org/en/story/2023/12/1144502; Daniel F. Runde and Thomas Bryja, *Mind the Darién Gap, Migration Bottleneck of the Americas* (Washington, DC: Center for Strategic and International Studies, May 2024), https://csis-website-prod.s3.amazonaws.com/s3fs-public/2024-05/240516_Runde_Darien_Gap.pdf?VersionId=XONWYsj9xeB6dpoEvpETGwaSZ4S18QzL.

117. Santiago Pérez, "Migrant Wave Disrupts Life in Panama's Darien Gap," *Wall Street Journal*, July 8, 2023. See also *Bottleneck of the Americas: Crime and Migration in the Darien Gap* (Brussels: International Crisis Group, 2023), https://icg-prod.s3.amazonaws.com/s3fs-public/2023-11/102-darien-gap %281%29.pdf.

118. Luke Taylor, "'We're Flooded with Trash': Pollution Crisis as 500,000 Migrants a Year Attempt Perilous Darién Gap Crossing," *The Guardian*, September 10, 2024.

119. U.S. Department of Homeland Security, "United Sates Signs Arrangement with Panama to Implement Removal Flight Program," Press Release, July 1, 2024, https://www.dhs.gov/news/2024/07/01/united-states-signs-arrangement-panama-implement-removal-flight-program; AFP, "Panama Deports 130 Indian Migrants Who Crossed Darién Jungle," September 6, 2024, https://ticotimes.net/2024/09/06/panama-deports-130-indian-migrants-who-crossed-darien-jungle.

Chapter 3

1. The Estimates of Migrant Stock, as reported by the Population Division of the U.N. Department for Economic and Social Affairs (UNDESA), is derived primarily from census data which are updated in each country with a relatively low frequency. Also, the definition of a migrant under this methodology varies somewhat across countries as foreign-born residents who have been naturalized may not be considered migrants in some cases, while in other cases children born to migrants are considered citizens, and therefore are not considered migrants. Furthermore, the period of residency to be considered a migrant (as opposed to a temporary visitor) can be as long as one year. As such, the estimates provided here may differ notably from counts of migrants available from other sources, especially where recent rapid migrant flows have been observed, and the methodology does not capture such flows immediately. Nonetheless, these data from

the UN are the most common reference for migration levels in the world, as they are derived from the best and most comparable information available in the countries. For 2020, the population of immigrants from Venezuela is taken from the R4V platform, as these estimates are considered more current than the UN estimates.

2. Valerie Lacarte, "Assessing the Next Displacement Crisis in the Making in the Americas," Commentary, Migration Policy Institute, October 2023, https://www. migrationpolicy.org/news/haiti-next-displacement-crisis-americas.

3. For purposes of this chapter, "U.S.-born citizens" refers to people born in the fifty states or Washington, DC. Other U.S. citizens born in the U.S. territories are designated according to their territory of birth, i.e., people born in Puerto Ricans and U.S. Virgin Islands.

4. "Why Do Americans Get Caribbean Citizenship in 2022?," *Immigrant Invest,* August 31, 2022, https://immigrantinvest.com/insider/americans-relocating-to-caribbe an-en/.

5. Some of this increase may be due to better counting of Venezuelan migrants by governments and UN agencies rather than a sudden spike in Venezuelan arrivals. R4V, "Refugiados y Migrantes Venezolanos en la Región—Agosto 2023" (fact sheet, September 2023), https://www.r4v.info/node/90974.

6. Sheila I. Velez Martinez, "Desde Quisqueya Hacia Borinquen: Experiences and Visibility of Immigrant Dominican Women in Puerto Rico: Violence, Lucha and Hope in Their Own Voices," *ILSA Journal of International & Comparative Law* 18, no. 3 (2012): 683–706.

7. Danielle Verbrigghe, "Dominican Immigrants Risk Death at Sea, Only to Find Hardship on a New Shore," Walter Cronkite School of Journalism and Mass Communication at Arizona State University, October 29, 2012, https://cronkite.asu.edu/projects/buffett/puertorico/yola.html.

8. Minority Rights Group, "Dominicans in Puerto Rico," https://minorityrights.org/communities/dominicans/.

9. Author interview with Ambassador Zulfikar Ally, November 8, 2023, Embassy of Guyana in Washington, DC.

10. International Organization for Migration (IOM), *Planning for Prosperity: Labour Migration and Guyana's Emerging Economy Summary Report* (San José: Costa Rica: IOM, 2021), https://programamesoamerica.iom.int/sites/default/files/summary_of_re port._planning_for_prosperity._labour_migration_and_guyanas_economy._nl.pdf.

11. Net migration rate: –24,678 in 2019; 802 in 2020; –4,316 in 2021. MPI analysis of World Development Indicators data downloaded from World Bank, "Guyana," accessed January 8, 2024, https://databank.worldbank.org/reports.aspx?source=2&country=ARE.

12. Valerie Lacarte, Jordi Amaral, Diego Chaves-González, Ana María Saíz, and Jeremy Harris, *Migration, Integration, and Diaspora Engagement in the Caribbean: A Policy Review* (Washington, DC: Migration Policy Institute and Inter-American Development Bank, October 2022), https://www.migrationpolicy.org/news/haiti-next-dis placement-crisis-americas.

13. A 2012 report from the Cuban Foreign Ministry indicates that between 1961 and

2012, more than 400,000 Cubans had participated in government-led external cooperation programs implemented in 157 countries. The programs in education, "Yo Si Puedo,"
and medical and health services, "Operacion Milagto," were among the most important
initiatives. From Milagros Martinez Reinosa "Cuba's Cooperation with CARICOM
from Grant Aid to Compensated Development Cooperation," in *Pan-Caribbean
Integration—Beyond CARICOM*, ed. Patsy Lewis, Terri-Ann Gilbert-Roberts, and Jessica Byron (London: Routledge, 2018).

14. Lewis et al., *Pan-Caribbean Integration*. Through its international public Latin
American School of Medicine (Escuela Latinoamericana de Medicina, ELAM) based in
Havana, the Cuban government provides high-quality medical training at a low cost to
students coming from underserved communities, with the objective that they return to
their own or other underserved communities after graduation. Many Caribbean states
have benefited from the education and full scholarship opportunities provided by
ELAM, including many women.

15. In addition to Haiti, these countries are Antigua and Barbuda, Dominica, St.
Lucia, and St. Vincent and the Grenadines.

16. According to this June 2020 statement from CARICOM, at least 473 Cuban medical personnel were providing medical support in eight countries at the time: Antigua
and Barbuda, Barbados, Dominica, Grenada, Jamaica, St. Kitts and Nevis, Saint Lucia,
and St. Vincent and the Grenadines, https://today.caricom.org/2020/06/23/statement-by
-the-organisation-of-eastern-caribbean-states-on-cuban-medical-brigades/.

17. International Organization for Migration (IOM), *Migration in the Caribbean:
Current Trends, Opportunities and Challenges* (San José, Costa Rica: IOM, 2017), 8,
https://www.migrationpolicy.org/news/haiti-next-displacement-crisis-americas.

18. Lacarte et al., *Migration, Integration, and Diaspora Engagement in the Caribbean*,
1–59.

19. OAS Permanent Council, Intervention by Alejo Campos, Crimestoppers, November 9, 2023, https://www.youtube.com/watch?v=RY41CAdEJs0.

20. W. Lozano, "Proletariado agricola extranjero y migraciones estacionales: Traba-
jadores haitianos en la agricultura dominicana," *Población y Desarrollo* (1992), 38–67,
https://pubmed.ncbi.nlm.nih.gov/12178311/.

21. Kendall Medford, "In the Dominican Republic, Language Barriers Complicate
Life for Haitian Migrants," NACLA, November 17, 2022, https://nacla.org/dominican-re
public-language-barriers-complicate-life-haitian-migrants#:~:text=While%2520it%25
20is%2520nearly%2520impossible,500%252C000%2520to%2520nearly%25202%
2520million.

22. Lozano, "Proletariado agricola extranjero y migraciones estacionales."

23. Diego Acosta and Jeremy Harris, *Migration Policy Regimes in Latin America and
the Caribbean: Immigration, Regional Free Movement, Refuge, and Nationality* (Inter-
American Development Bank, 2022), 6–293, https://publications.iadb.org/en/migration
-policy-regimes-latin-america-and-caribbean-immigration-regional-free-movement
-refuge-and.

24. Extraordinary regularization processes are temporary and are usually issued

through administrative measures. See Acosta and Harris, *Migration Policy Regimes in Latin America and the Caribbean.*

25. Louis A. Woods et al., "The Composition and Distribution of Ethnic Groups in Belize: Immigration and Emigration Patterns, 1980–1991," *Latin American Research Review* 32, no. 3 (1997): 63–88.

26. Woods, "The Composition and Distribution of Ethnic Groups in Belize."

27. Interviews with Gilroy Middleton, vice minister and CEO, Migration, Foreign Ministry, August 19, 2021; Diane Locke, representative of the IOM in Belize, August 17, 2021; and Melanie Smith-Santiago, professor, University of Belize, August 23, 2021.

28. See IOM, "Regional Study: Migratory Regularization Programmes and Processes" (San José, Costa Rica: IOM, 2021), 22–26, https://programamesocaribe.iom.int/sites/default/files/regional_study._migratory_regularization_programmes_and_pro cesses._web_version.pdf.

29. This Special Regularization Plan was for "migrants who entered the country legally and who require Visitors Permit extensions to remain in Belize and who have not been able to maintain a regular status between April 2020 and September 2021." Government of Belize, "Regularization of Foreign Nationals" (press release, September 28, 2021), https://www.pressoffice.gov.bz/regularization-of-foreign-nationals/.

30. Remarks by Gilroy Middleton, chief executive officer, Ministry of Foreign Affairs, Foreign Trade and Immigration (Government of Belize) during the event "Retos y oportunidades de una agenda migratoria en América Latina," organized by Fundación Carolina and the Migration Policy Institute, April 13, 2023, Madrid, https://www.youtube.com/watch?v=HRbnekvJM_k.

31. Aaron Humes, "Government Says Vetting for 12,765 Migrants in Amnesty P Will Continue Until March 2024," *Breaking Belize News*, November 8, 2023, https://www.breakingbelizenews.com/2023/11/08/government-says-vetting-for-12765-migrants-in-amnesty-program-will-continue-until-march-2024/?utm_source=substack&utm_medium=email.

32. Trevor Phillips and Michael Phillips, *Windrush: The Irresistible Rise of Multiracial Britain* (London and New York: HarperCollins, 1999).

33. "On this day 60 years ago, the first Commonwealth Immigrants Act came into effect," Free Movement, July 1, 2022, https://freemovement.org.uk/on-this-day-sixty-years-ago-the-first-commonwealth-immigrants-act-came-into-effect/.

34. Jia Lynn Yang, *One Mighty and Irresistible Tide: The Epic Struggle over American Immigration, 1924–1965* (New York: Norton, 2021).

35. Gerald E. Dirks, "Immigration Policy in Canada," *The Canadian Encyclopedia*, February 7, 2006, https://www.thecanadianencyclopedia.ca/en/article/immigration-policy.

36. Lacarte et al., *Migration, Integration, and Diaspora Engagement in the Caribbean.*

37. Lacarte et al., *Migration, Integration, and Diaspora Engagement in the Caribbean.*

38. Marla E. Salmon, Jean Yan, Hermi Hewitt, and Victoria Guisinger, "Managed Migration: The Caribbean Approach to Addressing Nursing Services Capacity," *Health Services Research* 42, no. 3 pt. 2 (2007): 1354–72.

39. Dillon DeShong, "Caricom Leaders Agreed to Deal for Free Movement of People by 2024," LOOP Caribbean News, July 26, 2023.

40. CARICOM, "Treaty Establishing the Caribbean Community," July 4, 1973, http://www.sice.oas.org/Trade/CCME/Chaguaramastreaty_e.pdf.

41. CARICOM, "Revised Treaty of Chaguaramas Establishing the Caribbean Community, Including the CARICOM Single Market and Economy," July 5, 2001, Article 45, https://caricom.org/treaties/revised-treaty-of-chaguaramas-establishing-the-caricom-including-csme/.

42. Although the government of Haiti was represented by Prime Minister Ariel Henry at the time of the CARICOM announcement, his legitimacy as head of state was questioned after he took office in the midst of a governance crisis, heightened by the assassination of President Jovenel Moise in July 2021. As a full member state of CARICOM, it is expected that Haiti will still participate in the process and vote in any regional decisions made in the implementation of the full free mobility regime. Once country conditions are normalized, it will have access to the expanded mobility regime.

43. The categories of skills are Graduates, Media Persons, Artists, Musicians, Sportspersons, Nurses, Teachers, Artisans with a Caribbean Vocational Qualification (CVQ), Holders of Associate Degrees, Domestic Workers, Agricultural Workers, and Private Security Officers.

44. The visa-free stay may be restricted if a CARICOM national is deemed a "charge on the public funds" or for national security concerns. CARICOM, *Single Market and Economy: Free Movement—Travel and Work*, 3rd ed. (Georgetown, Guyana: CARICOM, 2017), https://csme.caricom.org/documents/booklets/65-free-movement-travel-and-work-3rd-edition/file.

45. The Bahamas and Montserrat have committed to maintain the 1973 status quo via the agreement to enable entry into force of the Revised Treaty of Chaguaramas, and Agreements between the Community and The Bahamas and Montserrat.

46. Estela Aragón and Briana Mawby, *Free Movement of Persons in the Caribbean: Economic and Security Dimensions* (San José, Costa Rica: IOM, 2020), 52. As affirmed by the Caribbean Court of Justice in the case of Shanique Myrie versus Barbados.

47. For a country-by-country breakdown, see Aragón and Mawby, *Free Movement of Persons in the Caribbean*, 48–49.

48. CARICOM, "Revised Treaty of Chaguaramas."

49. Wanya Illes, "Labour Migration in the Caribbean: Mechanisms, Challenges, and Good Practices" (remarks by a representative of the CARICOM Secretariat, CSME Unit, during public event, IOM, September 1, 2021).

50. Aragón and Mawby, *Free Movement of Persons in the Caribbean*, 29.

51. Interview with Clarence Henry, Organisation of Eastern Caribbean States Commission, November 2023.

52. Interview Wanya Illes, CARICOM Secretariat, October 2023.

53. World Bank, "Data for Haiti, Jamaica," https://data.worldbank.org/?locations=HT-JM.

54. Interview, Leo Preville CARICOM Secretariat, October 2023.

55. Janise Elie, "'It Feels Like Dominica Is Finished': Life amid the Ruins Left by Hurricane Maria," *The Guardian*, November 1, 2017, https://www.theguardian.com/global-development/2017/nov/01/it-feels-like-dominica-is-finished-life-amid-the-ruins-left-by-hurricane-maria.

56. "Dominica's Journey to Become the World's First Climate Resilient Country," The World Bank, September 26, 2023, https://www.worldbank.org/en/news/feature/2023/09/26/dominica-s-journey-to-become-the-world-s-first-climate-resilient-country.

57. Ama Francis, "Free-Movement Agreements and Climate-Induced Migration: A Caribbean Case Study," Sabin Center for Climate Change Law, Columbia Law School, September 2019, https://scholarship.law.columbia.edu/sabin_climate_change/62.

58. Travel to Suriname opened up to Haitians in 2015, which often serves as a stop-over to French Guiana, where Cubans will fly to Suriname's capital on temporary visas and often cross the Maroni River with smugglers.

59. The New Humanitarian. "In a French Outpost in South America, no Secret EU Gateway for Fleeing Cubans." February 3, 2021, https://www.thenewhumanitarian.org/photo-feature/2021/2/3/french-guiana-cuba-migrants-EU-asylum-life-in-limbo.

60. Luciana Gandini and Andrew Selee, *Betting on Legality: Latin America and Caribbean Responses to the Venezuelan Displacement Crisis* (Washington, DC: Migration Policy Institute, May 2023).

61. Gandini and Selee, *Betting on Legality*.

62. United Nations Trinidad and Tobago, "Media Release: UN in T&T Welcomes Decision to Include Migrant and Refugee Children in National Education," news release, July 14, 2023, https://trinidadandtobago.un.org/en/239598-media-release-un-tt-welcomes-decision-include-migrant-and-refugee-children-national.

63. Gandini and Selee, *Betting on Legality*, and author interview with Bridget Wooding, Caribbean Migration and Displacement Observatory (OBMICA).

64. Gandini and Selee, *Betting on Legality*.

65. Interview with Bridget Wooding, OBMICA.

66. United Nations Human Rights Office of the High Commissioner, "Dominican Republic: UN Experts Condemn Detention and Deportation of Pregnant and Postpartum Hatian Women," news release, September 12, 2023, https://www.ohchr.org/en/press-releases/2023/09/dominican-republic-un-experts-condemn-detention-and-deportation-pregnant-and; Caitlin Hu and Etant Dupain, "Exclusive: Dominican Republic Expelled Hundreds of Children to Haiti Without Their Families This Year," CNN, November 22, 2022, https://edition.cnn.com/2022/11/21/americas/dominican-republic-expels-haiti-children-intl-latam/index.html.

67. Victoria Latham, "What to Know About Loss and Damage Going Into COP28," DT Global, December 6, 2023., https://dt-global.com/featured/loss-and-damage/.

68. National reports on Migration Governance Indicators are available on the IOM Publications Platform, https://publications.iom.int/.

Conclusion

1. Charles C. Mann, *1491: New Revelations of the Americas Before Columbus* (New York: Vintage Books, 2005).

2. It was likely many fewer before 2010, but so few that no one was tracking the numbers before then. Caitlyn Yates, "How the Treacherous Darien Gap Became a Migration Crossroads of the Americas," *Migration Information Source*, September 20, 2023, https://www.migrationpolicy.org/article/darien-gap-migration-crossroads.

3. Caitlyn Yates and Jessica Bolter, *African Migration Through the Americas: Drivers, Routes, and Policy Responses* (Washington, DC: Migration Policy Institute, October 2021), https://www.migrationpolicy.org/sites/default/files/publications/mpi-african-migration-americas-eng_final.pdf; Yates, "How the Treacherous Darien Gap Became a Migration Crossroads." On African and Asian migration to Latin America, including the passage through the Darien Gap, see also the collection of journalistic reports in Maria Teresa Ronderos, ed., *Migrantes de Otro Mundo* (Bogota: Penguin Random House, 2021).

4. There were roughly 83,000 Haitian citizens plus 17,000 Chilean and Brazilian citizens, who are believed to be mostly children of Haitians born in those countries. There were also over 18,000 Cubans and another 15,000 or so migrants from other countries. For the full statistics, see Gobierno de Panama, Migracion, Estadística, "Tránsito Irregular por el Darien 2021," https://www.migracion.gob.pa/images/img2023/pdf/IRREGULARES_POR_DARIEN_DICIEMBRE_2021.pdf.

5. In September 2021, when around 15,000 Haitians arrived in Del Rio, Texas, over a few days, the Biden administration began deporting Haitians to their country of origin, generating a massive backlash from advocates and international organizations who raised concerns about sending migrants to a country in crisis. After that, the number of Haitians crossing through the Darien Gap dropped significantly. Nick Miroff, "Most of the Migrants in Del Rio, Texas Camp Have Been Sent Back to Haiti or Returned to Mexico, DHS Figures Show," *Washington Post*, October 1, 2021.

6. Gobierno de Panama, Migracion, Estadística, "Transito Irregular por el Darien 2023," with updated figures as of November 2023, https://www.migracion.gob.pa/images/img2023/pdf/TRÁNSITO_IRREGULAR_POR_DARIÉN.pdf.

7. Colleen Putzel-Kavanaugh and Ariel G. Ruiz Soto, "Shifting Patterns and Policies Reshape Migration to the U.S.-Mexico Border in Major Ways in 2023," Commentary, Migration Policy Institute, October 2023, https://www.migrationpolicy.org/news/border-numbers-fy2023.

8. "The Three Routes of Migrants That Are Victims of the Coyote State in Nicaragua" (Connectas, 2024), https://www.connectas.org/especiales/rutas-de-los-migrantes-victimas-del-estado-nicaragua-coyote/index-en.html.

9. There were 45,748 asylum applications in 2022 by Venezuelans, 36,012 from Colombians, 8,937 by Peruvians, 3,017 by Hondurans, 2,118 by Nicaraguans, 1,501 by Salvadorans, and 1,392 by Cubans. Mas Que Cifras, "Asilo en España," accessed January 7, 2024, https://www.masquecifras.org/. Many other citizens from Latin America and the Caribbean arrive without seeking asylum.

10. Kate Hooper, *Spain's Labor Migration Policies in the Aftermath of Economic Crisis*

(Migration Policy Europe, 2019), https://www.migrationpolicy.org/sites/default/files/publications/MPIE-SpainMigrationPathways-Final.pdf.

11. Dany Bahar, "The Often Overlooked 'Pull' Factor: Border Crossings and Labor Market Tightness in the US," Working Paper 695, Center for Global Development, May 2024, https://www.cgdev.org/sites/default/files/Bahar_Border_Crossings_and_Labor_Markets_Working_Paper_Final.pdf. See also Andrew Selee, "Why Immigration and Labor Shortages Aren't Two Separate Problems," *Wall Street Journal*, December 17, 2023, https://www.wsj.com/us-news/immigration-labor-shortages-2024-c363bf8a.

12. On Spain, in particular, see Joaquin Leguina Herran and Alejandro Maccarrón Larumbe, *La inmigración en el mercado laboral español* (Madrid: CEU Ediciones, 2023), https://www.uspceu.com/Portals/0/docs/observatorio-demografico/informes/Observatorio_Demografico_n12_AF.pdf.

13. In the case of Ecuador, a rapidly rising crime rate, tied to the sophistication of gangs that became part of international drug trafficking, appears to have become another reason to migrate. See Juan Diego Posada and Lara Loaiza, "Four Reasons Why Ecuador Is in a Security Crisis," Insight Crime, August 10, 2023, https://insightcrime.org/news/4-reasons-why-ecuador-is-in-a-security-crisis/.

14. Fernando Riosmena, "Environmental Change, Its Social Impacts, and Migration Responses Within and Out of Latin America: A Theoretical Inquiry," in *Routledge History of Modern Latin American Migration*, ed. Andreas E. Feldmann, Xóchitl Bada, Jorge Durand, and Stephanie Schütz (New York: Routledge, 2024).

15. There are exceptions, particularly among Guatemalans, Salvadorans, and some Hondurans, who appear to hire smugglers in their hometowns, even if those smugglers often transport them through a complex network of affiliated smugglers. See Ariel G. Ruiz Soto, Rosella Bottone, Jarret Waters, Sarah Williams, Ashley Louie, and Yuehan Wang, *Charting a New Regional Course of Action: The Complex Motivations and Costs of Central American Migration* (Washington, DC, and Panama City: Migration Policy Institute, World Food Programme, and MIT Civic Design Data Lab, Inter-American Development Bank, and Organization of American States, November 2021), https://www.migrationpolicy.org/sites/default/files/publications/mpi-wfp-mit_migration-motivations-costs_final.pdf and Andrew Selee, Luis Argueta, and Juan José Hurtado Paz y Paz, *Migration from Huehuetenango in Guatemala's Western Highlands: Policy and Development Responses* (Washington, DC, and Guatemala City: Migration Policy institute and Asociación Pop No'j, March 2022), https://www.migrationpolicy.org/sites/default/files/publications/mpi-huehuetenango-report-eng_final.pdf. Julie Turkewitz, "Live from the Jungle: Migrants Become Influencers on Social Media," *New York Times*, December 20, 2023. For an analysis of this trend broadly, see also Michelle F. Ferris-Dobles, "New Communication Technologies and People's Movement," in Feldmann et al., *Routledge History of Modern Latin American Migration*; and Rianne Dekker and Godfried Engbersen, "How Social Media Transform Migrant Networks and Facilitate Migration," Work Paper 644, International Migration Institute, University of Oxford, November 2012. See, for example, Julie Turkewitz, "A Ticket to Disney? Politicians Charge Millions to Send Migrants to the U.S.," *New York Times*, September 14, 2023.

16. Ariel G. Ruiz Soto, Colleen Putzel-Kavanaugh, and Doris Meissner, *U.S.-Mexico Border: Immigration Enforcement and Control in a Fast-Evolving Landscape* (Washington, DC: Migration Policy Institute, January 2023).

17. Maribeth Sheridan, "Immigrants Caught in Mexico's Merry-Go-Round," *Washington Post*, September 14, 2024.

18. Authors' calculations based on Customs and Border Protection, "National Encounters," https://www.cbp.gov/newsroom/stats/nationwide-encounters.

19. On the broader strategy, see Katie Tobin, *The Los Angeles Declaration Continues to Shape the Regional and Global Migration Response* (Carnegie Endowment, September 14, 2024), https://carnegieendowment.org/research/2024/09/americas-migration-los-angeles-declaration-north-south?lang=en. On Safe Mobility Offices, see *The Influence of Safe Mobility Offices on Migration in Latin America* (Mixed Migration Center, 2024), https://mixedmigration.org/wp-content/uploads/2024/09/344_The-Influence-of-Safe-Mobility-Offices-on-Mixed-migration-in-Latin-America_12092024.pdf.

20. Maria Jesus Mora, Ariel G. Ruiz-Soto, and Andrew Selee, *Building on Regular Pathways to Address Migration Pressures in the Americas* (Migration Policy Institute and International Organization for Migration, January 2024), https://www.migrationpolicy.org/sites/default/files/publications/mpi-iom_regular-pathways-americas-2024-final.pdf.

21. For the most extensive analysis of how the declaration came together, see Tobin, *The Los Angeles Declaration Continues to Shape the Regional and Global Migration Response*. For the full text, see The White House, "Los Angeles Declaration on Migration and Protection," June 10, 2022, https://www.whitehouse.gov/briefing-room/statements-releases/2022/06/10/los-angeles-declaration-on-migration-and-protection/.

22. Tobin, *The Los Angeles Declaration*, confirmed by the authors' background conversations with policymakers in several of these countries.

23. Interview with the authors on November 1, 2024.

24. Valerie Lacarte, "Addressing the Next Displacement Crisis in the Making in the Americas," Commentary, Migration Policy Institute, October 2023, https://www.migrationpolicy.org/news/haiti-next-displacement-crisis-americas.

25. Liliana Lyra Jubilut, Marcia Vera Espinoza, and Gabriela Mezzanotti, "Introduction," in *Latin America and Refugee Protection: Regimes, Logics, and Challenges*, ed. Liliana Lyra Jubilut, Marcia Vera Espinoza, and Gabriela Mezzanotti (New York: Berghahn, 2021). Citation from the full text of the *Cartagena Declaration on Refugees*, https://www.oas.org/dil/1984_cartagena_declaration_on_refugees.pdf.

26. Luisa Feline Freier and Nieves Fernandez Rodriguez, "Trends in Latin American Domestic Refugee Law," in Jubilut et al., *Latin America and Refugee Protection*. See also Luciana Gandini and Andrew Selee, *Betting on Legality: Latin America and Caribbean Responses to the Venezuelan Displacement Crisis* (Washington, DC: Migration Policy Institute, May 2023).

27. For a comparative analysis in Africa, which has a similar declaration that is meant to expand the refugee definition, see Alexander Betts, *Survival Migration: Failed Governance and the Crisis of Displacement* (Ithaca, NY: Cornell University Press, 2013),

which tries to understand the incentives that sometimes lead states to use the broader definition and sometimes do not.

28. Andrew Selee, Ariel G. Ruiz Soto, Andrea Tanco, Luis Argueta, and Jessica Bolter, *Laying the Foundation for Regional Cooperation Migration Policy and Institutional Capacity in Mexico and Central America* (Washington, DC: Migration Policy Institute, 2021), https://www.migrationpolicy.org/sites/default/files/publications/mpi-latam_foundation-regional-cooperation_eng-final.pdf. See also chapter 3 in this book.

29. Lamis Elmy Abdelaaty, *Discrimination and Delegation: Explaining State Responses to Refugees* (Oxford: Oxford University Press, 2021).

30. Abdelaaty, *Discrimination and Delegation*.

31. On the role of international support for these efforts, see Luciana Gandini, Diego Gonzales-Chavez, and Maria Jesus Mora, *Financing for Displacement: Where Does International Support for the Venezuelan Displacement Crisis Go?* (Washington, DC: Migration Policy Institute, forthcoming).

32. Acosta and Harris, *Migration Policy Regimes in Latin and the Caribbean*; Maria Jesús Mora, Ariel G. Ruiz-Soto, and Andrew Selee, *Building on Regular Pathways to Address Migration in the Americas; Mapeo y análisis de los programas y esquemas de migración laboral temporal en las Américas: buenas prácticas, prioridades y retos* (San José: Oficina Internacional del Trabajo, 2024).

33. Luisa Feline Freier, Isabel Berganza, and Cécile, "The Cartagena Refugee Definition and Venezuelan Displacement in Latin America," *International Migration,* December 22, 2020, https://doi.org/10.1111/imig.12791. See also João Carlos Jarochinski Silva, Alexandra Castro Franco, and Cyntia Sampaio, "How the Venezuelan Exodus Challenges a Regional Protection Response 'Creative' Solutions to an Unprecedented Phenomenon in Colombia and Brazil," in Jubilut et al., *Latin America and Refugee Protection*.

34. Gandini and Selee, *Betting on Legality*.

35. Gandini and Selee, *Betting on Legality*.

36. Many of these efforts have been highlighted at city-focused conferences organized by the municipality of Barranquilla, Colombia (December 12, 2023) and the U.S. State Department in Denver, Colorado (April 24–30, 2023), attended by the authors.

37. Acosta and Harris, *Migration Policy Regimes in Latin America and the Caribbean*.

38. Ruiz Soto et al., *Changing Migration Narratives in Northern Central America*. For Mexico, see "Perspectivas sobre las personas migrantes," Universidad del Valle de Mexico, Centro de Opinion Publica, April 17, 2024.

39. Michael Rios, "Panamá to Launch Deportation Flights to China and India," CNN, August 22, 2024.

40. Marta Luzes and Lucina Rodríguez Guillén, *Public Opinion on Migration in Latin America and the Caribbean*, Inter-American Development Bank, 2023, https://publications.iadb.org/publications/english/document/Public-Opinion-on-migration-in-Latin-America-and-the-Caribbean.pdf; Ruiz Soto et al., *Changing Migration Narratives in Central America*.

41. James F. Hollifield and Neil Foley, eds., *Understanding Global Migration* (Stanford, CA: Stanford University Press, 2022); James F. Hollifield, *Immigrants, Markets,*

and States: The Political Economy of Postwar Europe (Cambridge, MA: Harvard University Press, 1992). See also Daniel Tichenor, *Dividing Lines: The Politics of Immigration Control in America* (Princeton, NJ: Princeton University Press, 2002); Aristide Zolberg, *A Nation by Design: Immigration Policy in the Fashioning of America* (Harvard University Press, 2008); James Hampshire, *The Politics of Immigration: Contradictions of the Liberal State* (Polity, 2013); and Sarah Song, *Immigration and Democracy* (Oxford University Press, 2019).

42. Milagros Ricourt, *The Dominican Racial Imaginary* (New Brunswick, NJ: Rutgers University Press, 2016).

43. Luis Eduardo Thayer Correa and Maria Emilia Tijoux Merino, "Trayectorias del sujeto migrante en Chile: Elementos para un análisis del racismo y el estatus precario," *Papers* 107, no. 2, Universidad Autónoma de Barcelona, 2022. https://doi.org/10.5565/rev/papers.2998" Marcela Cerrutti and Emilio Parrado, "Intraregional Migration in South America: Trends and a Research Agenda," *Annual Review of Sociology* 41, no. 1 (2015).

44. Edward Telles, *Pigmentocracies: Ethnicity, Race, and Color in Latin America* (Chapel Hill: University of North Carolina, 2014).; Peter Wade, *Race and Ethnicity in Latin America* (Pluto Press, 2010); Henry Louis Gates, *Black in Latin America* (New York University Press, 2011).

45. Lukas Delgado-Prieto, "Immigration, Wages, and Employment Under Informal Markets," *Journal of Population Economics* 37, no. 54 (May 2024), https://doi.org/10.1007/s00148-024-01028-5; Leonardo Peñaloza-Pacheco, "Living with the Neighbors: The Effect of Venezuelan Forced Migration on the Labor Market in Colombia," *Journal for Labor Market Research* 56, article 14, 2022; Celia Vera and Bruno Jimenez, "The Short-Term Labor Market Effect of Venezuelan Immigration in Peru," Working Paper 304, Universidad Nacional de la Plata, CEDLAS, 2022, https://www.econstor.eu/bitstream/10419/289885/1/doc_cedlas304.pdf; Fernando Morales and Martha Deinsee Pierola, "Venezuelan Migration in Peru: Short-Term Adjustments in the Labor Market," Inter-American Development Bank, Migration Unit, August 2020, https://www.econstor.eu/bitstream/10419/234715/1/IDB-WP-1146.pdf; Hanbyul Ryu and Jayash Paudel, "Refugee Inflow and Labor Market Outcomes in Brazil," *Population and Development Review* 42, no. 1 (March 20220, https://doi.org/10.1111/padr.12452.

46. "Regional Spillovers from the Venezuelan Crisis : Migration Flows and Their Impact on Latin America and the Caribbean," prepared by Jorge Alvarez, Marco Arena, Alain Brousseau, Hamid Faruqee, Emilio Fernandez-Corugedo, Jaime Guajardo, Gerardo Peraza, and Juan Yépez Albornoz (Washington, DC: International Monetary Fund, 2022), https://www.imf.org/-/media/Files/Publications/DP/2022/English/RSVCEA.ashx.

47. Luzes and Guillen, *Public Opinion on Migration in Latin America and the Caribbean.*

48. Dany Bahar, Meagan Dooley, and Andrew Selee, *Venezuelan Migration, Crime, and Misperceptions: A Review of the Data from Colombia, Peru, and Chile* (Washington, DC: Brookings Institute and Migration Policy Institute, September 2020).

49. Luzes and Guillen, *Public Opinion on Migration in Latin America and the Caribbean.*

50. Tren de Aragua: From Prison Gang to Transnational Criminal Enterprise, In-Sight Crime, October 2023, https://insightcrime.org/wp-content/uploads/2023/08/Tren-de-Aragua-From-Prison-Gang-to-Transnational-Criminal-Enterprise-InSight-Crime-Oct-2023-1.pdf.

51. Jeffrey D. Pugh, Luis F. Jiménez, and Bettina Latuff, "Welcome Wears Thin for Colombians in Ecuador as Venezuelans Become More Visible," *Migration Information Source*, January 9, 2020, https://www.migrationpolicy.org/article/welcome-wears-thin-for-colombians-ecuador.

52. Ariel G. Ruiz Soto, Doris Meissner, and Andrew Selee, *Managing Migration Regionally* (Migration Policy Institute, forthcoming).

53. These incentives matter less in Latin America and the Caribbean than some other parts of the world, such as the countries in Africa analyzed in Betts, *Survival Migration*. But they are still a vital contribution that may sometimes alter the equation for policy decision-making.

54. Silvia E. Giorguli-Saucedo, Victor M. García-Guerrero, and Claudia Masferrer, "Demographic Environment and Migration Perspectives in Latin America and the Caribbean," in Feldmann et al., *Routledge History of Modern Latin American Migration*.

Index

The letter *f* following a page number denotes a figure; the letter *t* denotes a table.

U.S. State Department, 77
U.S. Virgin Islands, 98, 100

Veneactiva, 59
Venezuela: Andean Community and, 57; asylum and, 9t, 41t, 47–50, 85–86, 114–15, 125; Beja and, 1–3, 26; Census of, 32; Chávez and, 32, 34; children and, 44–45; Chile and, 2, 23, 34–42, 49, 53–56, 59, 133–34, 140; Colombia and, 1–3, 10, 21, 23, 26, 31–43, 46–49, 52–58, 79, 86–87, 91, 97t, 98, 132–33, 137, 140; economic issues and, 10, 23, 31, 33–34, 49, 60, 87, 89; education and, 36, 38, 53, 115–16; healthcare and, 38, 54–55, 59, 115–16; housing and, 38, 44, 59; immigrant demographics and, 2, 32; income and, 39; inflation and, 32–34; International Organization for Migration (IOM) and, 38–39, 43, 47, 115; labor market and, 49–50, 54; legal migration and, 79; Los Angeles Declaration and, 126; Maduro and, 32–34; music and, 91; oil and, 23, 31–32, 34, 46; passports and, 3, 45, 47; PTP and, 44–45; public opinion and, 46; R4V and, 50–51; refugees and, 9t, 38, 41t, 42–51, 59, 114–15, 126, 128; regularization and, 2, 44–45, 48, 50, 59, 114–16; residency and, 48, 57; slavery and, 21; Spain and, 87; Special Stay Permit (PEP) and, 46–47; Summit of the Americas and, 126; trade and, 48; travel preregistration and, 79; United Nations High Commissioner for Refugees (UNHCR) and, 43–44, 50, 115, 128; Viloria and, 31–35, 38, 42; visas and, 38, 45–48, 54, 116
Viloria, Juan Carlos, 31–35, 38, 42
violence: Central America and, 69–70; displacement and, 31, 34, 53, 58; historical perspective on, 12, 16, 20; massacres, 14; Mexico and, 80–81
visas: agricultural, 125; Border Worker, 71; Brazil and, 49; Caribbean and, 93, 105, 116; Chile and, 37, 51t; Colombia and, 51t; Costa Rica and, 86; Dominican Republic and, 116; Ecuador and, 51t, 58; Guatemala and, 71–72; H-2, 66, 72, 125; Haiti and, 38, 54, 116, 118; historical perspective on, 6, 11, 15, 26; Mercosur and, 48, 51t, 131; Mexico and, 66, 71, 79; Panama and, 87; Peru and, 46, 51t, 57, 59; PTP, 45; remote work, 86; Uruguay and, 51t; Venezuela and, 38, 45–48, 54, 116

women: discrimination and, 55; domestic labor and, 99; exploitation of, 102, 118; National System of Integral Development for the Family (DIF) and, 80–81; pregnant, 38, 116; recruitment of, 108; sexual harassment and, 89, 99, 118; Veneactiva and, 59
World Bank, 130

Zapotec, 20

The authorized representative in the EU for product safety and compliance is:
Mare Nostrum Group
B.V Doelen 72
4831 GR Breda
The Netherlands

www.ingramcontent.com/pod-product-compliance
Lightning Source LLC
Chambersburg PA
CBHW030833270326
41928CB00007B/1024